Spirituality and Social Care

Contributing to Personal and Community Well-Being

Edited by Mary Nash and Bruce Stewart

Jessica Kingsley Publishers
London and Philadelphia

First published in the United Kingdom in 2002
by Jessica Kingsley Publishers Ltd
116 Pentonville Road
London N1 9JB, England
and
325 Chestnut Street
Philadelphia, PA 19106, USA
www.jkp.com

Copyright © Jessica Kingsley Publishers 2002

Library of Congress Cataloging in Publication Data
Spirituality and social care : contributing to personal and community well-being / edited by Mary Nash and Bruce Stewart.
    p. cm.
  Includes bibliographical references and index.
  ISBN 1-84310-024-X (pbk. : alk. Paper)
    1. Religion and sociology. 2. Spirituality--Social aspects. I. Nash, Mary. II. Stewart, Bruce, 1951-
BL60 .S664 2002
291.1'7832--dc21

                                                              2002021528

British Library Cataloguing in Publication Data
A CIP catalogue record for this book is available from the British Library

ISBN 1 84310 024 X
Printed and Bound in Great Britain by
Athenaeum Press, Gateshead, Tyne and Wear

Spirituality and Social Care

of related interest

Spirituality in Health Care Contexts
Edited by Helen Orchard
ISBN 1 85302 969 6

Spiritual Dimensions of Pastoral Care
Practical Theology in a Multidisciplinary Context
Edited by David Willows and John Swinton
ISBN 1 85302 892 4

Spirituality in Mental Health Care
John Swinton
ISBN 1 85302 804 5

Spirituality, Healing and Medicine
Return to the Silence
David Aldridge
ISBN 1 85302 554 2

Spirituality and the Autism Spectrum
Of Falling Sparrows
Abe Isanon
ISBN 1 84310 026 6

The Spiritual Dimension of Ageing
Elizabeth Mackinlay
ISBN 1 84310 008 8

Contents

To my mother and father, with thanks for giving me,
each in their own way, a sensitivity to spirituality;
and to my granddaughter, Miriam,
that we may share this gift together.

Mary Nash

To my mother for her unwavering support,
and to my wife Marie, son Don and daughter Annalise
who have added depth to my spiritual understanding.
Bruce Stewart

Acknowledgements

This book has taken three years to complete and was conceived on the final days before Bruce left New Zealand in March 1999. We would like to acknowledge the support of our families and friends in sustaining, challenging and encouraging us in the preparation of this publication. We also want to thank the contributors who earnestly engaged in completing their parts of the book. It has been a privilege to edit their chapters. Our thanks to Massey University, School of Sociology, Social Policy and Social Work for its support with this project.

Mary acknowledges the inspiration she received at the 2001 Symposium, 'Spiritual Resources for the Social Work of Reconciliation and the Development of Peaceable Community', at the School of Social Work Theory and Practice in the Inter-University Centre, Dubrovnik Graduate Centre. Massey University facilitated her attendance there. Mary thanks her colleagues for their support.

Bruce thanks Stanton Yellowknife Regional Hospital and staff at the Mental Health Clinic in the Northwest Territories of Canada for their moral support. Thanks also to the School of Sociology, Social Policy and Social Work, Massey University, and Celia Briar, Gwen Ellis and John Bradley (deceased), for guiding him through his postgraduate studies, which led to his embarking upon this book.

Introduction

Bruce Stewart and Mary Nash

How can spirituality contribute to well-being and to the helping relationship? We consider that there are many ways of working with spiritual awareness in relation to personal, interpersonal and societal caring, some of which are explored in this book. In our view spirituality opens the door to integrity and genuineness in our relations with others who may be limited by personal difficulties, situational circumstances, or oppression. Our contributors define spirituality in a variety of ways and most of them make a distinction between spirituality and religion, in which the former can be more broadly defined than the latter. They reflect on spirituality's relevance to culture; self-determination; transformation; the helping relationship; and social-political activism.

We have adopted a broad definition of the term 'social care', using it as an umbrella term including social work, counseling, psychotherapy, community development and social change activities. Many of our contributors will make more specific reference to their use of the term 'social care' as they present different positions in relation to spirituality and social care. This provides the reader with a number of viewpoints from which to reflect upon the richness and evolving nature of this dimension of the helping professions. As co-editors we do not emphasize any particular approach as preferable to another. However, both editors recognize that we have been influenced by the living traditions of the indigenous people in our respective countries of Canada and New Zealand.

We all face challenges to helping in Western society. In this introduction we argue that spirituality supports all aspects of human development by providing meaning and purpose in life, creating harmony and balance in relationships, deepening the therapeutic effect of professional helping, and integrating the pursuit of personal need with resolving social and political inequity. Particularly interesting is the challenge of putting one's spiritual wisdom (the knowledge of the heart) into practice. In order to do this professionally, it is important to be fully aware of spirituality's contribution to well-being. Aspects of all three of these challenges are covered in the chapters that follow and this introduction briefly considers each one in turn. We conclude with an overview of the chapters.

Challenges to helping in Western society

Western society is frequently depicted as a postmodern, postindustrial global village. With its economic and technological complexity, rapid demographic shifts, and heightened individualism, consensus is giving way to a multitude of views and lifestyles.

Alienation and consensus in a postmodern world

The trend to affirm a variety of lifestyles has further minimized consensus and commonality between various segments and cultural groups in society. Postmodern theorists have turned away from the possibility that a universal objective and dynamic conditions shaping all people exist. Yet it can still be argued that one's environment, although fluid, does create commonly held perceptions. The recognition of these shared dynamic conditions may well be essential if we are to comprehend and activate more global efforts to resolve matters of ethics and justice.

In the Western world many groups feel a loss of culture or power due to inequities and divisions between people. These distinctions can be enriching for some but can leave others feeling subjugated due to a perception of hostility and marginalization in their communities. For the latter a tendency to individualize responsibility and accountability for hardship further devalues individuals who are genuinely oppressed by conditions beyond their control. This adds to the potential for further self-blame, social limitation and disenfranchisement.

On a global level, tremendous upheavals are taking place. Oppressive social conditions reduce cooperation amongst people and devalue their dignity, and this erodes their fundamental sense of purpose and self-determination. This upheaval seems to be fueled by what has been described as the disease of modern times where profound value loss results in hopelessness, alienation, and cynicism (Witmer and Sweeney 1992).

Spiritual trends in modern societies

Many are becoming aware that they lack a sense of spiritual direction. People feel pain and have a sense of spiritual emptiness that runs deep (Cowley and Derezotes 1994). Despite this loss or perhaps in response to it, research reveals that the American public still considers religion and spirituality to be important and that participation in conventional religious institutions or various types of spiritual gatherings is strong (Canda 1988a, 1988b).

Today people still report that they personally believe in God or some spiritual force. Many report having had a mystical experience and that they pray or engage in some spiritual practice. A spiritual renewal in alternative and traditional sources is discernible. It is a movement reflecting a deep-seated hunger for something more or something lost. These sources include 12 step recovery groups and mystical, esoteric, shamanic, and pagan traditions. Some of this renewal includes participation in sweat lodges, goddess circles and rituals of many small spiritual schools and new age groups. Still others describe unusual experiences such as UFO abductions, paranormal and out-of-body experiences and often indicate that they are experienced as meaningful, transformational, and spiritual (Lukoff, Lu and Turner 1998). All of this supports the notion that organized religion persists but also that a sizable group of people is seeking new ways to understand and express themselves spiritually.

Spiritual perspectives

Pellebon and Anderson (1999) argue that spirituality is a significant part of a person's belief system be they helping practitioner or a client. The central function of religion/spirituality is considered integrative, and this is particularly evident in cultures that do not separate religious and spiritual beliefs from psychological well-being. The Maori, for example

> understands the physical realm as being immersed in and integrated with the spiritual realm. Every act, natural phenomena and other influences were considered to have both physical and spiritual implications. All these are associated with the belief that supernatural forces govern and influence the way people interact with each other and relate to the environment. (Henare 1988, p.15)

We are only too aware, since the events of 11 September 2001, that the personal and intense nature of the major worldviews provides the potential not only to help but also to create harmful conditions. Individual and group moral development can be stunted when teachings become rigid and unquestioning acceptance is demanded. Rigid and authoritarian religious beliefs can foster conditions of faith that are toxic and induce mental processing that is likened to cult brainwashing and here the preparation of suicide bombers comes to mind. Church regulations can exclude those deemed threatening or unacceptable or place them in a tenuous position when receiving help from others. Examples here are the divisions within some of the Christian denominations over homosexuality, women priests or abortion.

Despite the shattering of any possible complacency regarding the place of religious belief in human affairs, we would argue that there is potential for a spiritual worldview to encourage tolerance between cultures and to support and enhance respect for the others' rules, laws, and ethical codes. This can bring together a diverse group of people if difference is uplifting or if commonality in fundamental values and beliefs is recognized.

It becomes clear that a spiritual worldview is a central influence affecting all of our relationships. Conflicts are likely to arise between groups when a particular worldview becomes charged with ethnocentricity or intolerance toward difference.

Challenges to spirituality in practice

Recently, one of the editors of this book was contacted by a doctoral student, who was distressed by what she perceived to be negativity towards her research on the part of clinical social workers and faculty. Her topic was an exploration of the place of spirituality in social work. There are certainly challenges to accepting that the spiritual dimension should be acknowledged within the helping processes used by social care professionals. These challenges are connected to two particular matters. There is a lack of clarity about the distinction between religion and spirituality. There is insufficient information about how to achieve practitioner competence when drawing upon the spiritual dimension in the helping relationship. The practitioner who wishes to gain such competence needs to confront and understand the value of surrendering to a higher power. At the same time, excessive client preoccupation with spiritual matters needs careful handling.

Distinguishing spirituality from religion

Although some may equate spirituality with religion, it can be and often is regarded as broader in scope than religion. Some recognize that religion may hold negative connotations and seek to avoid the risk of any contamination between it and spirituality. Spirituality is a term with many meanings, and in her excellent review of the literature Carroll (1998) distinguishes the two:

> Spirituality refers to one's basic nature and the process of finding meaning and purpose whereas religion involves a set of organized, institutionalized beliefs and social functions as a means of spiritual expression and experience. (Carroll 1998, p.2)

Here it is worth recalling Siporin's particularly lucid account of the spiritual dimension in human beings, cited by Sermabeikian (1994):

> The spiritual element of the person is the aspect of an individual's psyche, consciousness and unconsciousness, that is also called the human soul. It is in terms of the spiritual dimension that a person strives for transcendental values, meanings, experience and development; for knowledge of an ultimate reality; for belonging and relatedness with the moral universe and community; and for union with the immanent, supernatural powers

> that guide people and the universe for good and evil. The spiritual aspect of the person is not subsumed or dealt with in psychoanalytic ego theory or in cognitive theory, though it has a place in Jungian and existentialist therapies. (Siporin 1985, pp.210–211)

Siporin was reflecting on the human condition, in which spirituality is part of human nature. He argued that people will seek self-awareness, transpersonal development and the fulfillment of their potential and this may be regarded as spiritual work.

Drawing on Canda's research findings (1990) Carroll argues that one can usefully distinguish two aspects of spirituality. It is part of the human condition, the wholeness of humanity and an essential part of each human being's make up and in this sense she refers to it as 'spirituality-in-essence'. At the same time, as each person seeks to make sense of life and its purpose for him or herself, it can be termed 'spirituality-as-one-dimension' (Carroll 1998, p.3). A little reflection on this distinction and Siporin's account above suggests a helpful similarity and common understanding on the breadth and depth of what we refer to as spirituality and its distinction from religion.

Preparation and safety issues

Social work educators and professionals agree that the practitioner must know his or her limits and strengths in the helping relationship and set their boundaries accordingly. To do this they need to be able to harness their beliefs and values for therapeutic advantage without abusing their power and the client's vulnerability (Bergin 1991). This is also an essential condition for practitioner competence and personal awareness where the spiritual dimension is concerned.

Normal training experience for each field of practice applies here but research also suggests that a practitioner's own spiritual development is necessary. One's spiritual development contributes in a special way to competence and awareness in this area more than pure clinical training in psychotherapy and religion alone (Genia 1994). If the spiritual perspectives between practitioner and client are compatible, spiritual discussions regarding difficulties are likely to be easier. If however they differ and the issues are beyond the practitioner's expertise, s/he may need to refer the client to an appropriate spiritual figure or resource person.

Preoccupation with religious or spiritual problems can precipitate a number of psychological difficulties, which have been recognized as a new diagnostic category in the 1994 Diagnostic and Statistical Manual of Mental Disorders (Chandler, Holden and Kolander 1992; Lukoff *et al.* 1998). Attention needs to be paid to whether a client's spiritual orientation facilitates healing encounters, self-acceptance and reconciliation with others or with a higher power or whether it masks and disconnects the client from relevant thoughts and feelings. Working in the spiritual dimension may therapeutically challenge unhealthy beliefs or practices that appear to restrict client development.

The symbols and rituals used in spiritual and/or religious gatherings can foster hope, sacred knowledge and forgiveness, as several of the authors in this volume point out. They can also contribute to passivity, avoidance or a mechanical response in engaging in one's problems if they become poorly differentiated from reality (Noble 1987). The importance of good supervision in this area cannot be overemphasized.

Spirituality's contribution to well-being

Individuals have a tendency to search for meaning and purpose in their lives and if they are in touch with their spirituality there is potential for growth and transformation. Awareness of the sacred and connection to something more within and beyond the searcher (Hoare 1991) may occur. If spiritual awareness is simply repressed this can lead to the pain of disillusionment while excessive preoccupation with spirituality can for some be psychologically overwhelming. Therefore these forces of expression need to be balanced for spiritual development to achieve harmony within them (Chandler *et al.* 1992).

Spirituality's potential to transform comes through the development of deep insights into the meaning and significance of one's life and the integration of all aspects of one's being (Joseph 1987; Noble 1987). This can produce a sense of wholeness free from inner conflict. The search for fulfillment can be an inward and/or outward journey. Self-transcendence, which is an important aspect of spiritual development, heightens a sense that the ordinary physical and socially defined limits of the self are incomplete. Transpersonal theory suggests that personal development can go beyond fulfillment of ego-based identity needs and strengths (Strohl 1998). The theory provides an explanation of trans-egoic capacities for intuition, creativity, holism and states of consciousness in which self and the world are experienced in interrelationship and unity (Cody 1994). These connecting qualities reduce the separation between inner spiritual development and responsibility to society (Cowley 1993).

Transpersonal theory suggests that people grow toward interdependence and unification with others. Consciousness is transformed into an awareness of oneness and the inseparability of the individual from the material world (Stewart 1999). Unified connection invariably links one's wellness to others (Westgate 1996; Witmer and Sweeney 1992). Transformation beyond the individual may mean that health through personal emancipation cannot be separated from community liberation and justice (Myers and Speight 1994).

A significant part of wellness is based on enhancing determination of self and others. People have a need for self-determination. There is a connection between the freedom to determine one's own goals, morals and spiritual perspectives and a responsibility to support the same for other people. Recognition of the importance of personal freedom is linked to ensuring this for others and this in turn heightens a rationale of mutuality (Bulhan 1988).

Spirituality, pain and healing

Enlightenment arising from spiritual experience assists in healing by helping us to re-evaluate the role of suffering and alienation (Moore 1992). Our search for meaning and a search for relationships that contribute to this meaning often drive this process (Dyson, Cobb and Forman 1997). For example there is evidence that illness, suffering and death can be perceived as spiritual encounters that activate a search within or beyond self for personal meaning. If meaning can be found an individual can find peace and healing (Coward and Reed 1996). If not, all domains of life may be affected and spiritual distress experienced (Dyson *et al.* 1997; Ross 1995).

Relieving pain is in part associated with healing of self and others (Wendler 1996). The healing phenomena associated with spirituality are contentious within the helping field. Yet in the literature spirituality is commonly associated with healing and healing experiences are often regarded as spiritual experiences. Aponte (1998) argues that unconditional love, which he perceives as rooted in spirituality, opens the doors to conciliation to self and others and forms the basis for spiritual acts of forgiveness.

Spirituality's capacity to heal can come from deepening our sense of meaning in pain by carrying us closer to who we are and encouraging us to live up to all of our potentials including the disowned aspects of our humanity. Its influence can challenge us to live with and learn from our limitations/imperfections rather than suffering from them (Carroll 1998). We can also find that our suffering, disappointment, hurt and rejection are not exclusive to us but are universal conditions (Canda 1988a).

Spiritually sensitive practice

Each individual holds a particular perspective that can be shaped by a religious or philosophical belief system (Canda 1988b). Similar influences shape spirituality and helping. Practitioners who are self-aware are more likely to recognize these influences on their worldview. This adds to the awareness of culture's impact on people's views and the potential influence of spirituality as part of culture. The re-emergence of spirituality in practice also corresponds to the growing recognition that it is inseparable from the helping relationship. Spirituality is a dimension of cultural diversity, which highlights that it must be included in order to achieve competence in cross-cultural work. The principles underpinning the helping relationship can also serve as a model to further support spirituality's capacity to heal, transform pain and address both individual growth and social justice (Morell 1996).

Spiritually sensitive practice supports the inherent dignity and worth of the client, regardless of beliefs, values and actions, and tends to emphasize nonhierarchical relatedness (Mack 1994). In a spiritually sensitive practice the relationship is typified by a greater sense of connection between oneself and the other. Buber talked of this when he said there are two types of relationship: the 'I/It relationship', in which one treats the other as different from oneself, as something of an object; and the 'I/Thou relationship', in which the other is treated as oneself. Within an I/Thou relationship, an energized merger between the two people becomes possible. In such a meeting, according to Buber, God is to be found (West 1997). The I/Thou relationship is developed through dialog and mutual discovery between worker and client while respecting the client as expert in his or her own life (Friedman 1988). Spiritually sensitive practice suggests opportunities for deepened meaning, empathy and enhanced intuition in the spiritual merger between client and helper.

Introducing the chapters

There are many ways in which social care practitioners may understand and apply the spiritual dimension to their work with people. This book is designed with two main parts. Part One, 'Mapping the Territory', offers some theoretical views on spirituality and social care. Part Two, 'Walking the Talk', is subdivided into two sections: the first looks at spirituality and social care with an emphasis on the personal stance of the practitioner, the second provides instances of the application of theory to practice and introduces different intervention styles. It contains work that draws on both research and personal experience.

Contributors have been selected because of their knowledge and expertise in particular areas. Our intention has been to cover a variety of approaches, both theoretical and practical, and to give work with indigenous people a conscious emphasis. There are many areas which could have been covered, but the selection does not imply that they are in any way less important than those included.

Part One, 'Mapping the Territory', begins with Jim Consedine's challenge to the reader to recognize the connection between spirituality and social justice in the social care spectrum. 'Spirituality and Social Justice' discusses the need for a sustained personal spirituality for those engaged in long-term struggle for justice. It examines the spiritual side of social change, the 'dark' side of some social structures, and the relationship between an individualistic culture and one based on the values of the common good. Consedine reflects on a holistic spirituality based on seeking the common good, honoring wisdom and practicing sustainability.

Bruce Stewart's discussion of spirituality and well-being follows, bringing with it the micro approach that is appropriate for the counseling dimension. In 'Spirituality and Culture' Stewart has provided an overview of spirituality, counseling and social work. He defines spirituality as reaching beyond religion and addresses the importance of culture; self-determination; personal and social political change; growth and trans-formation; and the implications of spirituality for the helping relationship. Stewart argues that spirituality raises awareness about diversity and con-nection; encourages integration of the personal and the social-political; supports human development; provides meaning and purpose in life; and can transform suffering and alienation in the counseling process into opportunities for personal development. These two chapters, the one looking at spirituality and structural analysis, the other reflecting on spiri-tuality and personal analysis, set the stage for the practice articles which follow in the second part of this book.

In the second part, 'Walking the Talk', we begin with practitioner per-spectives and then move into the application of spiritual awareness in practice. Mary Eastham has drawn on both her academic and experiential knowledge to write on the subject of vocation and spirituality and her deeply reflective chapter, 'Vocation and Social Care', covers key areas about which the social care worker needs insight. The purpose of this chapter is to articulate one dimension of the spirituality of the practitioner. If practitioners view their work as a vocation, they can draw on spiritual and psychological concepts that have significant therapeutic value. This chapter discusses the concept of vocation from both a religious and secular perspective. It then focuses on vocational aspects of social care which ame-liorate suffering and empower people in need to transform their lives. The chapter develops the thesis that practitioners can facilitate the healing journey of others to the extent that they have already begun this journey in their own lives. It explores the spiritual development of the 'secular healer' and proposes strategies to nurture the nurturer in times of professional crisis.

This discussion leads the way for Mary Woods to look at the particular issues surrounding spirituality and the involvement of volunteers in spiritual care in her chapter, 'Spirituality and Volunteers: The Leaven in the Dough'. Volunteers as board members promote an organization's vision and as caregivers, they complement the work of professionals. Volunteers' motivations arise from a wide range of sources including spirituality. Energy from spiritual sources enables some volunteers to work with people in very hard situations. Managers need to be aware of the spiritual content of volunteers' motivations in order to make appropriate placements and to create a climate that encourages their continued effective involvement. The final section of this chapter provides some practical examples of spirituality in action with volunteers.

Professionals as well as volunteers are involved in drawing on spirituality in their social care work. As with volunteers they need to be educated and learn to work to the highest standards possible. Ksenija Napan is passionately interested in continuous improvement of teaching/learning processes by shaping them to fit students' cultural, social, spiritual, physical and learning needs. In her chapter, 'Being, Loving and Contributing', she argues that every teaching is an opportunity for learning and that every giving is an opportunity for receiving. She believes that the purpose of teaching/learning is to bring forth the world and improve quality of life on this planet. As the world we live in rapidly changes, we need to modify our teaching practices too.

Spiritual components of teaching and practicing have too long been neglected, and this chapter is an opportunity to bridge the existing gaps. Using story, narrative and autobiography, Napan involves the reader in her ideas about the importance of getting the teaching relationship right. Patronizing relationships between teachers and students as well as helpers and clients are exposed, explored and critically analyzed while ideas for alternative approaches are suggested. The practical, vocational and spiritual choices that are made by social practitioners, students and clients in order to improve the quality of their lives are examined. Napan reflects on the light these choices shed on the process of finding a place where physical, psychological, social and spiritual can live at peace when we practice social care.

In the next chapter, 'Spirituality and Social Work in a Culturally Appropriate Curriculum', Mary Nash contextualizes the teaching of spirituality for social work students in New Zealand, briefly looking at recent literature including that exploring faculty practices and student receptiveness. The cultural imperative for including this topic in the writer's own Bachelor of Social Work degree is discussed and the curriculum described. Issues to do with introducing students to indigenous spirituality are explored with reference to the writer's experience. The discussion focuses on curriculum issues, cultural issues and implications in the classroom setting.

Moving into the application of spirituality to social care, there are two significant chapters on cross-cultural work with First Nation people in the North West Territory of Canada. These have been jointly authored by Romeo Beatch and Bruce Stewart, 'Integrating Western and Aboriginal Healing Practices', and Bruce Stewart and Ross Wheeler, 'Talk Story'. We believe these chapters go well together, the first providing some concepts and ideas reflected upon in the second.

Aboriginal communities in North America often display significant problems related to depression, suicide, addiction, family violence and incarceration. Beatch and Stewart argue that Western-trained counseling practitioners, have attempted to assist Aboriginal people to reduce levels of maladjustment but this cultural group has not easily endorsed a Western rehabilitative process. Those in the helping field, particularly counseling practitioners, are likely to be challenged in dealing with possible causal links to distressed behavior given the appearance of widespread community malaise and impoverishment within Aboriginal communities. Frustration on the part of cross-cultural practitioners in finding effective treatment is likely to raise a question about what kind of perspective and treatment is needed to reduce a sense of deep-seated alienation and suffering.

The reader stays with these ideas as Stewart interviews Ross Wheeler in their chapter, 'Talk Story'. This chapter considers addiction work in cross-cultural settings by exploring practice in remote communities and in a small urban community situated in the high Arctic. The approach blends philosophy and practice from Western '12 Step' programs, Catholicism and First Nation (Dene) beliefs. The practitioner's focus is helping Dene and European peoples recover from alcohol and drug addiction by problem identification, acceptance, social involvement and fellowship. Spiritual gatherings and individual counseling sessions provide healing and relief from suffering and alienation. It involves activating and developing a relationship with God/Creator, as it is understood, connection to the land, adherence to elder teaching and promoting individual and collective well-being by affirming sacredness.

Three chapters complete the volume, and they cover children's spirituality, the spirituality of working with people with intellectual disabilities and issues of spirituality in ageing. Judith Morris writes about children's expression of spirituality through play therapy in 'Heroes' Journeys'. She discusses her understanding of what is meant by spirituality and spiritual healing and illustrates this from her work with children, informed by Jung's concept of 'Self' and the 'transcendent' function. Morris looks at the need for spiritual healing from trauma – the need for a force, more powerful than the individual and outside the individual (Jung offers this as part of the concept of Self). Case studies of work with children provide practical illustration of the author's theoretical insights.

A very different chapter follows, one in which Patrick Favaro writes about his experience of spirituality and the L'Arche community, 'Spirituality and People with Disabilities'. He believes that people who choose professions or lifestyles in which they support others are often moved to do so by life experiences, belief systems, dissatisfaction with other paths, or by some unexplainable force within themselves. Such choices are a manifestation of our spirituality. Favaro reflects on the spirituality of L'Arche, the need for its members to have a sense of belonging and communion, to participate in authentic and 'known' relationships. His writing draws out similar themes to those of Mary Woods, particularly evident when he reflects on the spiritual inspiration which motivates and sustains volunteers, and the use of ritual and celebration in this kind of work.

Finally, Randolph Herman reflects on 'End of Life Planning with the Aged', a chapter informed by the author's practical experience and theoretical knowledge. In it he teases out some of the major issues facing end of life planning for frail elderly and how social caring must include the spiritual dimension. Herman argues that assistance in the completion of an advance health care directive can take on the best characteristics of a ritual, thus facilitating and maximiszing self-determination at a time when the client often feels the most powerless.

In each chapter we have encouraged the authors to define key terms and to provide a balance between theoretical concepts and their practical application. We believe readers will be able to recognize how successful contributors have been in following this suggestion and that as a result each chapter has thought-provoking material as well as useful, practical ideas. We have deliberately included a generous range of references in some chapters, based on our recognition that for some areas what published work there is available is not necessarily easy to locate. Readers who wish to pursue a topic further will have the resources to enable them to do so.

References

Aponte, H.J. (1998) 'Love, the Spiritual Wellspring of Forgiveness: An Example of Spirituality in Therapy.' *Journal of Family Therapy 20*, 1, 37–58.

Bergin, A. (1991) 'Values and Religious Issues and Psychotherapy and Mental Health.' *American Psychologist 46*, 4, 394–403.

Bulhan, H.A. (1988) *Frantz Fanon and the Psychology of Oppression.* New York: Plenum Press.

Canda, E.R. (1988a) 'Conceptualizing Spirituality for Social Work: Insights from Diverse Perspectives.' *Social Thought*, Winter, 30–46.

Canda, E.R. (1988b) 'Spirituality, Religious Diversity, and Social Work Practice.' *Social Casework: The Journal of Contemporary Social Work 69*, 4, 238–247.

Canda, E.R. (1990) 'Afterworld: Sprituality re-examined.' *Spirituality and Social Work Communicator 1*, 1, 13–14.

Carroll, M. (1998) 'Social Work's Conceptualization of Spirituality.' *Social Thought: Journal of Religion in the Social Services 18*, 2, 1–14.

Chandler, C.K., Holden, J.M. and Kolander, C.A. (1992) 'Counseling for Spiritual Wellness: Theory and Practice.' *Journal of Counseling & Development 71*, 2, 168–175.

Cody, W.K. (1994) 'Meaning and Mystery in Nursing Practice.' *Nursing Science Quarterly 7*, 2, 48–51.

Coward, D.D. and Reed, P.G. (1996) 'Self-Transcendence: A Resource for Healing at the End of Life.' *Issues in Mental Health Nursing 17*, 3, 275–288.

Cowley, Au-Deane, S. (1993) 'Transpersonal Social Work: A Theory for the 1990's.' *Social Work 38*, 5, 527–534.

Cowley, Au-Deane, S. and Derezotes, D. (1994) 'Transpersonal Psychology and Social Work Education.' *Journal of Social Work Education 30*, 1, 32–41.

Dyson, J., Cobb, M. and Forman, D. (1997) 'The Meaning of Spirituality: A Literature Review.' *Journal of Advanced Nursing 26*, 6, 1183–1188.

Friedman, M. (1998) 'The Healing Dialogue in Psychotherapy.' *Journal of Humanistic Psychology 28*, 4, 19–41.

Genia, V. (1994) 'Secular Psychotherapists and Religious Clients: Professional Considerations and Recommendations'. *Journal of Counseling & Development 72*, 395–398.

Henare, M. (1988) 'Standards and Foundations of Maori Society.' In Royal Commission on Social Policy. *Vol III, Part One: Future Directions*. Wellington: Government Print.

Hoare, C.H. (1991) 'Psychosocial Identity Development and Cultural Others.' *Journal of Counseling & Development 70*, 1, 45–53.

Joseph, M.V. (1987) 'The Religious and Spiritual Aspects of Clinical Practice: A Neglected Dimension of Social Work.' *Social Thought 13*, 1, 12–23.

Lukoff, D., Lu, F. and Turner, R. (1998) 'From spiritual emergency to spiritual problem: the transpersonal roots of the new DSM-IV category'. *Journal of Humanistic Psychology 38*, 2, 21–50.

Mack, M.L. (1994) 'Understanding Spirituality in Counseling Psychology: Considerations for Research, Training and Practice.' *Counseling and Values 39*, 15–31.

Moore, T. (1992) *Care of the Soul: A Guide for Cultivating Depth and Sacredness in Everyday Life*. New York: HarperCollins Publishers.

Morell, C. (1996) 'Radicalizing Recovery: Addiction, Spirituality, and Politics.' *Social Work 41*, 3, 306–312.

Myers, L.J. and Speight, S.L. (1994) 'Optimal Theory and the Psychology of Human Diversity.' In E.J. Trickett, R.J. Watts and D. Birman (eds) *Human Diversity: Perspectives on People in Context*. San Francisco: Jossey-Bass.

Noble, K.D. (1987) 'Psychological Health and the Experience of Transcendence.' *The Counseling Psychologist 15*, 4, 601–604.

Pellebon, D.A. and Anderson, S.C. (1999) 'Understanding the Life Issues of Spiritually-Based Clients.' *Families in Society: The Journal of Contemporary Human Services*, May–June, 229–238.

Ross, L. (1995) 'The Spiritual Dimension: Its Importance to Patients' Health, Well-Being and Quality of Life and its Implications for Nursing Practice.' *International Journal of Nursing Studies 32*, 5, 457–468.

Sermabeikian, P. (1994) 'Our Clients, Ourselves: The Spiritual Perspective and Social Work Practice.' *Social Work 39*, 2, 178–183.

Siporin, M. (1985) 'Current Social Work Perspectives on Clinical Practice.' *Clinical Social Work Journal 13*, 198–217.

Stewart, B. (1999) 'Spirituality in Counseling: Assisting counselors and the depressed.' Unpublished Master's thesis, Massey University, New Zealand.

Strohl, J.E. (1998) 'Transpersonalism: Ego Meets Soul.' *Journal of Counseling & Development 79*, 397–403.

Wendler, M.C. (1996) 'Understanding Healing: a Conceptual Analysis.' *Journal of Advanced Nursing 24*, 4, 836–842.

West, W. (1997) 'Integrating Counseling, Psychotherapy and Healing: An Inquiry into counselors and Psychotherapists Whose Work Includes Healing'. *British Journal of Guidance & counseling 25*, 3, 291–311.

Westgate, C.E. (1996) 'Spiritual Wellness and Depression.' *Journal of Counseling & Development 75*, 1, 26–35.

Witmer, J.M. and Sweeney, T.J. (1992) 'A Holistic Model for Wellness and Prevention over the Life Span.' *Journal of Counseling & Development 71*, 2, 140–148.

PART ONE

Mapping the Territory

Chapter One

Spirituality and Social Justice

Jim Consedine

Linking spirituality to social justice is an integral part of any truly human movement for social change. Many people who see injustice seek to bring about an end to it. Caught up in either the revolutionary fervor and idealism of youth or the more measured approach of mature adulthood, they often throw all their emotional and physical energy into the campaign for change. Too often, while their social analysis can be accurate and their strategy for political change on target, they can forget the personal cost of becoming involved in a movement which makes huge demands on them. This can drain their inner or spiritual resources leaving them feeling exhausted and washed up. Often they give up because they no longer have the inner energy for the struggle.

What we know about social change in our Western society is that the masses rarely, if ever, rise up demanding it. Usually it is a small, dedicated group which can effect even widespread and radical change. What is required of them to stay the distance, achieve their aims, and grow in the process, is a constant nurturing of their own inner selves, their own spirits, their souls. There are too many soured, even bitter, former revolutionaries stuck in movements that have long since ground to a halt, victims of the very struggle to which they once felt so committed. Emma Goldman's famous dictum 'If I can't dance, I don't want to be part of your revolution' is as true now as it was in her time. Dancing means spirit. It means joy. It means celebration. It means life. It means hope. It means spirituality.

A complex world

I recently listened to a news item from the Silicon Valley where a 28-year-old man, who had founded a dot.com computer company, had gone bust. A multi-millionaire, he had been working just five years and was casting a wary eye at his future prospects. He spoke with gay abandon of the great adventure it had all been. He had no comment about his employees who had been dumped, or his product which had been shown to be largely a mirage. He had been hailed a star for five years. What was now worrying him was that he was now being shunned by the industry. At 28, he felt his shelf life to be largely over.

My thought was, how insane is all this? First, that he had got so rich with such little effort, and second, that he couldn't see a way forward at such a young age. Who is telling him such things? Who makes these judgment calls? The answer is probably other people like himself. I couldn't help but wonder as to whether we have really reached such a level of insanity.

The dot.com image of the brave new world is little more than an advertising slogan without solid roots or foundation. It is one of those gimmicky images that leaves the impression that without the latest computer technology life is hardly worth living. That may well be the case for the bankrupt ex-tycoon mentioned above but for more than 90 percent of the world's peoples, it's a thought that never crosses their minds. Their chances of owning a computer are as remote as owning a villa in the south of France. Staying alive is the dominant need they have. Seeking food, shelter, employment, family stability and income is their focus. To them the world of dot.com is fantasy.

Living as we do in a culture where 15-second sound bites are the norm, I think it is important to cast a jaundiced eye upon new slogans that crop up and are pushed with velocity in the media by public and corporate officials. In a way our world is dominated by slogans. Advertisers love them. Thatcherism, the New Right, Rogernomics and New Age are just four that illustrate movements of magnitude. The latest appears to be 'the knowledge economy'. Like many modern concepts, it is being presented as a new way to salvation. But fundamental to any acceptance of such a slogan are such questions as, who is presenting it? For whom is it being presented?

Who will benefit? Does better knowledge for all mean a better life for all? Does information equate with knowledge? Who is drawing a distinction between new information and new knowledge? Information is one thing, but knowledge implies truth based on wisdom. We have an incredible amount of information to hand. But do we have the wisdom to handle our new information? What use is all this information? Who is asking about the values upon which it is built and used? Is 'the marketplace', where the bottom line is the profit margin, the place to decide such matters? These are all important questions.

We are running huge risks in presuming to build the future without wider public debate about what values we want that future to be built on and how we are going to live in that future. These are questions of philosophy, theology and spirituality which I do not see being addressed adequately anywhere, least of all in corporate media. They are not new questions. But they are important questions that are generally shut out of mainstream discussions by a dominant consumer culture which has found no place for such questions to be asked, much less answered. We are paying a huge price for such ignorance in our time.

A spiritual side to life

Mainstream Western culture has generally lost its rootedness in a spiritual dimension and the values that encompass that. The result has been massive social alienation and a growing dysfunction. Throw into that social milieu an ideology founded on self-advancement, individualism, competition and the acquisition of material goods and money as its primary litmus test of success, and you have the pot pourri that constitutes modern society.

The question is, when are we going to recognize this spiritual bankruptcy, and place it alongside unemployment, institutionalized racism and poverty as being a principal cause of crime and alienation and a primary need to be addressed? Our society worships technological advance, the acquisition of power and wealth, and fiercely protects its class structure of 'them and us'. Why, for example, aren't Christians saying more often that a solid foundation for building a fair and just society requires the pursuit of the common good, rather than elite interests? After all, this has been a part of traditional Christian teaching for more than 1000 years.

In recent years, I have spent a lot of time asking questions, reflecting and studying what has happened in Croatia, Serbia and Bosnia in the 1990s. I've been wondering what type of spirit was behind apartheid and drove the Nazi machine. What was it that was unleashed in Rwanda? Why were so many mindless atrocities committed by educated and seemingly reasonable people? Why did so many, even many good religious people, go bad and rape, torture, pillage and murder their country's best citizens? Was it a power unleashed? If so, does that power last forever? Is it redeemable?

It's an important question to ask in the light of the 11 September 2001 attacks on the twin towers of the World Trade center in Manhattan and the Pentagon in Washington DC. These hugely symbolic targets crumbled in a way that has left us marked forever. What power of evil unleashed these attacks? Who is the power behind such carnage? Is it merely some small group of Arab dissidents as the US government claimed? Or is there a spiritual power which has enveloped such a group? Is it merely a political strategy by bad or mad people? Or is there a malevolent spiritual power behind it?

What was the US response to the attacks? The decision was to launch a war and to begin days and weeks of murderous bombing raids over Afghanistan with death and destruction as a primary aim. Was that a purely military and political decision or was there a spiritual power behind such action? Is such a power good or malevolent? Was the aim merely to rid the world of terrorists (who gets to define terrorism?) or was it also the consolidation of transnational business interests and the position of the US as the dominant political and economic empire? After all, the spin-offs include enormous profits for the corporate media, the arms manufacturers and oil companies (all of whom helped propel President Bush into office), huge popularity for the US leader, and the development of a strong platform for his bid for a second term. History shows these issues, although rarely discussed publicly, all form part of the war equation.

What was missing from the debate about terrorism was a serious attempt to answer the question of why so many Muslims would want to become martyrs before their time. What is it that encourages people to such martyrdom? Why, for example, have so many Palestinians become suicide bombers? This is not their heritage. Christians know something of martyrdom. It is usually inflicted, not sought. One short answer could be desperation. Whatever else these attacks mean, these people were desperate. We need urgently to hear what these masses are saying about their plight if we are ever to have an adequate understanding of these attacks.

'Terrorists' do not act within a vacuum. These actions, terrible as they are, have emerged as a new tactic of resistance and political strategy from the real life desperation of millions of disenfranchised people, many of them Muslim, some Christian. They are reacting to the dominance in every sphere of their lives of Western cultural values and the US military. They reject Western values, and the exploitation associated with the culture of globalization and the power that enforces it. Groups such as Hammas and Fatah in Palestine and the al-Qaeda network in Afghanistan represent a sizeable portion in their respective countries of those suffering from abject poverty, preventable disease, land displacement and injustice. These are conditions which affect so much of the Third World.

The official teaching of the Catholic Church recognizes the existence of finite, created powers of a personal kind. In reflecting on this, Karl Rahner noted that very little additional teaching has been developed since the time of St Thomas Aquinas and the Scholastics. It seems to be an important and seemingly somewhat neglected area of theology. On the other hand, Protestant theologians like Walter Wink (1984, 1986, 1992, 1998) have developed substantial teaching in this area.

Violence – the dark side of spirit

Does an evil power exist that is bigger and more powerful than us? I have a developing belief that such a power of evil does exist and it is larger than the individual component parts of any social system. With Walter Wink, I have come to understand that each social unit has a spirit of either good or evil within and unless the presence of such a spirit is addressed then positive social change will be thwarted. In essence, each social grouping has its own spirit, distinct from its component parts.

Many call this the culture of the institution or the movement. I have watched good people enter the police, parliament, the military, various government institutions, the prison service, some corporations, even some religious institutions, and encounter a spirit, a culture, that is negative and life destroying. They have found themselves under a type of negative power that is corrupting and eventually all pervasive, one that has left its corrosive mark clearly on them. And they have changed – for the worse. Similarly I have seen many enter positive and fair-minded organizations and movements and they have been enhanced and grown through the process of involvement with them. Further, I have seen good people combine to turn the negative spirit of an institution or a movement around to something positive.

It seems these evil spiritual powers are redeemable. They have a beginning and an end. They need not last forever. But they have to be tackled with all the power, skills, prayer, commitment and courage one can muster. In South Africa, in a thousand and one different ways, people united to confront both the powers behind and the social structures of apartheid. For millions it was a spiritual journey as much as a social and political one. On another continent, Martin Luther King spearheaded a social revolution against racial prejudice that was built on an understanding that racism was not just a social manifestation of discrimination but had an evil power underpinning it.

Many now understand the evil power that exists behind the prison-industrial complex in the US which has ballooned to five times its size in just 20 years, despite falling crime rates. Greedy people are making huge money from it and thousands are finding employment in it. There are enormous vested interests involved in expanding it. Some socially conscious New Zealanders, including prison chaplains, recognize the power that keeps our own prison system growing, when crime rates in most areas has been declining for nearly ten years.

The same applies to the military-industrial complex in the USA, which has for the past 15 years had no obvious enemies yet now spends three times the budget on defense as it did at the height of the Cold War. How does this come about? Is there a malevolent power underpinning the arms race that keeps it expanding at an ever-increasing rate, regardless of the threat? None understand this power better than the Plowshares movement (Wilcox 2001) in their efforts to confront the evil of nuclear weapons. In their approach, they clearly recognize and confront the power behind the missiles through prayer, fasting, symbolic action and non-violent resistance. My belief is that unless the presence of the spiritual side to an organization is acknowledged and, if necessary, confronted, then positive social change will be short lived.

Four cornerstones – a spirituality for today

There is an alternative vision of how life can be but for many it will require some fundamental changes. Our consumer culture is virtually the antithesis of it. This vision is built on much of the old combined with some of the best of the new. I believe that it has at least four major interrelated parts that need to be addressed: the common good, sustainability, wisdom and an holistic spirituality. Only with these four cornerstones will we be able to develop a just, more inclusive and spiritually sound future for all.

The common good

We need to start by looking at how we promote collective values that develop the common good and not individualistic self-interest. New knowledge needs to be assessed by the value system underpinning the common good. The common good can be defined as

> the whole network of social conditions which enable human individuals and groups to flourish and live a fully genuine human life. Far from each being primarily for him or herself, all are responsible for all. (Catholic Bishops of England and Wales 1996)

There are four conditions required to make this happen:

1. *The principle of subsidiarity* supports a dispersal of authority as close to the grass roots as good government allows. It prefers local to central decision-making. It has everyone working at the level of his or her capacity.

2. *The principle of solidarity* implies the interconnectedness of all human beings, one with the other, regardless of race, gender,

culture, age or religion. We form one family. Solidarity teaches us to stand with one another, particularly when either of the final two principles are threatened - that of human rights or an option for the poor. It recognizes the humanity of all people regardless of culture, race or class.

3. *The protection of human rights,* our understanding of which has been accelerating this past century, is the third subsidiary principle. No longer are we able to dehumanize various groupings of people because of their differences to us. Each person now has certain legislated protection under charters from the United Nations, which help protect the fabric of the common good.

4. *The fourth subsidiary principle of the common good is that of an option for the poor.* By that is meant that the most vulnerable, the poorest economically and the most handicapped must be protected and respected if the common good is to be achieved.

All four principles have to be applied to achieve the common good of all (Catholic Bishops of England and Wales 1996). Two or three are not enough. It is like letting a racehorse run on two or three legs when running requires all four. In order to pursue social equity ordinary people have to really care about one another. They have to want to see justice practiced and everybody get a fair deal. To make and sustain such a choice is a function of the spirit. Everything we do in relation to one another be it good or bad is a function of the spirit.

Why aren't we saying more often that a solid foundation for building a fair and just society requires the pursuit of the common good, not elite interests? Why aren't we proposing practical structures which incorporate these essential elements and values? For too long we have had to put up with an ideology which would have us compete at every level creating a wasteland of losers and a shrinking elite of powerful winners.

The biggest issue we face these days is the relentless march towards corporate globalization. Some degree of globalization is inevitable and already with us but economic and cultural globalization is a disaster waiting to happen. Once the genie is fully out of the bottle there will be no turning back. The huge demonstrations against the World Trade organization and APEC in Seattle, Melbourne, Gothenburg, Barcelona, Salzburg and Genoa during the first years of the new millennium show how many ordinary people think.

Imposing the will of the most powerful corporate and governmental interests simply divides the world up among the most powerful, not unlike the way Africa was carved up by the colonizing powers at the 1886 Brussels conference. What a disaster that proved to be. Built as it is on a materialist philosophy, globalization makes a god of profit. It represents the new golden calf, the new idolatry. The new colonizers are the transnational corporations. They are accountable to virtually no one but their major shareholders, an already rich and powerful elite. We are handing our democratic processes over to these corporate moguls. Their ultimate demand will be for a huge portion of our souls.

To enforce their ways with violence compounds their sinfulness, yet that in essence is what this global system now allows. For example, this is what initiated the war on Iraq and has kept the sanctions in place. Iraq threatened access to oil therefore Iraq had to be tamed. And so the sanctions remain, killing thousands of children each month. What clearly is lacking here is not new knowledge but wisdom and justice and a concern for the common good.

On the world stage we can see how the absence of this principle of the common good has a huge impact. At the G8 meeting of the world's eight richest nations in Genoa in July 2001, debate about relief of world debt, about the whole question of climate change, about a perceived pending economic recession and about the issue of tariffs and protectionism left poorer countries feeling further marginalized and angry at their exclusion from consideration. One week later in Zanzibar at the summit of the 49 poorest countries, the focus was different. They were appealing in graphic language for life itself and for the future existence of their countries in the face of mounting debt, disease spread through poverty and low prices for their primary products. If the principles of the common good, especially those of solidarity and protection of the poor, had been sought at the G8 meeting by the wealthy nations, there might have been no need for the poorer nations to meet a week later.

But when there is no recognition in the dominant culture of the need to sustain, nurture and develop such spiritual dimensions to our lives, is it any wonder that a crippling of the spirit occurs? Where in the public arena does this discussion ever take place? When was the last time we saw television seriously explore the spiritual dimension of life and people? We never do. Why are we so shy of acknowledging spiritual matters when 90 percent of the world's peoples have religious traditions involving meditation, prayer, contemplation, quiet times, retreats and reflection?

Some are now recognizing this spiritual dimension again. For example, many know of restorative justice practices in New Zealand, especially among juvenile offenders and their victims through Family Group conferences. One of the aims of this creative focus is to help change people's hearts, to bring about genuine apology, a desire to make reparation where possible and begin a healing process. In essence this is a spiritual journey, though not all may see it like that. In the restorative conference to get participants focused and respectful of what is about to happen, we encourage 'karakia', or prayer, or a quiet time of reflection, or a meditative reading. In such a setting, real change can occur.

I would argue that the recognition and acceptance of the principle of the common good is the most urgent task of our time. This is an absolute principle for fair and just social living, as essential to the commonweal as oxygen is for individual people.

Sustainability

At the heart of our future lies the recognition that we cannot keep gobbling up the resources of this fragile planet and expect to provide an adequate future for coming generations. The notion of a continuing expansion of economic development and GNP without recognition of contracting resources and a fairer distribution of them is sinful. It offends the very nature of God and the dignity of humanity, and provides the second cornerstone.

The planet is in crisis. Because of human decisions, things get worse year by year. More than 1.3 billion people (over one-fifth of the world's population) live beneath the international poverty line of US$1 per day. A further 1.6 billion people survive on between one and two dollars. In 1960 the combined incomes of the richest fifth of the world's population were 30 times greater than the world's poorest fifth. By 1991 it was over 60 times and in 1998, 78 times as high. In 1997, external debt payments made up 92.3 percent of the GDP of countries of low development (United Nations Development program 1999). This largely means an out-flowing from the world's poorest countries to banks in the world's richest countries. This is sinfulness of epic proportions.

Forty-eight sub-Saharan countries are drowning in debt, paying US$13.5 billion in interest every year. Most of those nations have crumbling health systems, poor education, and are being ravaged by AIDS. In Zambia, for example, the average life expectancy has plummeted to 37 years. One in five adults is infected with HIV (United Nations Development program 1999). And still, Western creditors insist, the debt must be paid. There has been partial recognition of the problem. The International Monetary Fund (IMF) and World Bank have agreed to cancel a large part of the debt of 22 countries under the Higher Indebted Poor Countries (HIPC) initiative. But with this debt relief comes a bewildering array of conditions. It is difficult to see how any of them can survive without radical change in Western thinking.

In 1997, the under-five mortality rate in industrialized countries was eight per 100,000 live births. In 1997, the under-five mortality rate in developing countries was 169 per 100,000. That same year, 41 percent of the total Third World population had no access to safe water, and 57 percent had no access to sanitation (United Nations Development program 1999). On the other hand, the 20 percent of the world's people who live in the highest-income countries (which include the US, Canada, Australia, New Zealand and the United Kingdom) consume 86 percent of the world's resources. The bottom 20 percent in the lowest-income countries consume less than 10 percent (United Nations Development program 1999).

Sinful too is what we are doing to climate change. The impact of global warming is unrelenting and sustained yet some major industrialized countries are treating it as little less than a blip on a TV monitor. How else can one understand the impasse reached over the Kyoto agreement and the wishy-washy version we now have? Back in 1997 when it was formulated it was watered down by US Vice-President Al Gore to better suit US business interests. Not content with that, now his conqueror at the polls, George W. Bush, has walked away from even that lukewarm version. The power of big money is almost omnipotent. Anything that interferes with the wishes of major transnational corporations is seen as unwelcome interference in their pursuit of profits.

Yet the threat of rising seas due to global warming is undeniable. Foley notes how, in January 1999, Peter Barrett, a geologist at Victoria University in Wellington, warned an international conference that the entire West Antarctic sheet, which is grounded below sea level, was becoming unstable and could soon break away. Massive chunks of ice, covering thousands of square kilometers, are already breaking off and melting as they drift northwards into warmer waters. In addition, in the mid-1990s the Larsen A ice-shelf toppled and broke away. It was some 8000 square kilometers in surface area. Both these were dwarfs compared to Larsen B, which in early 1998 showed signs of following suit. It has a surface area nearly twice the size of Norfolk Island and would be the single largest iceberg spawned over the past fifty years (Foley 1999). Barrett's warning has fallen on deaf ears even though a number of Pacific nations now face being swamped if the trend continues.

There is a whole range of other issues of justice, which sit at the heart of who we are as a world community and where we are heading. Take for example the continued arms proliferation, the use of nuclear-armed ships and aircraft, the devastation of communities through deforestation and mining, the preventable deaths caused by diseases including AIDS. The list could go on and on. Many of these injustices are preventable and curable. What is required is a change in mindset and the adoption of community values which promote the common good. We need to enhance and protect our fragile planet and place human good and life itself in all its forms at the center of every social equation.

Wisdom

The third cornerstone is wisdom. The deliberate marginalization of wisdom and the wise people of our communities is a cause of major concern. This ignorant attitude, so prevalent in the market, withers any deepening of spirituality at its very source and allows for a very shallow corporate culture to develop. Intellectual knowledge, per se, is only one component of life and may not even be the most important. This is in no way to negate the huge benefit that the knowledge we have in medical, scientific and social fields has been to the human family. But 'new knowledge' that ignores old wisdom is inherently flawed. This issue sits at the heart of the alienation so prevalent in society today.

To use any knowledge in a social context is to employ value judgments as to its use. To what purpose is current new knowledge being put and who is benefitting? This is where wisdom plays an important part. Wisdom is the accrued insights garnered through experience and knowledge and retained for the benefit of the common good. It includes astuteness, discernment, judgment, foresight, sagacity, common sense and understanding. It is a gift much praised in sacred writings from all traditions. It is given high praise in the Hebrew scriptures. Yet we have become the first generation in history to sneer at wisdom and ignore it. Modern market culture does not want to know a history, does not want to learn from the past. Generally anyone with experience is quickly made redundant, particularly if they have the temerity to question any new dogma that appears on the scene.

The past 20 years have seen the development of rampant individualism, self-advancement, free market competition and the acquisition of material goods and money as measuring stones for the new litmus test of success. This type of ideology sits at the heart of globalization. The result is that mainstream Western culture has generally lost its rootedness in a tradition of wisdom and the spiritual dimension and the values that encompass that. The new perceived wisdom is often not more than five years old! The result has been massive social alienation and a growing dysfunction.

We have had a generation growing up with little accrued wisdom regarding such basic questions as the meaning of life and death, ways of coping with sickness, weakness and disappointment. Even things like how to grow vegetables and the centrality of good work in their lives and the life of their communities remain foreign to many. It seems we have also largely abandoned old rituals without replacing them with meaningful modern ones. Rites of passage, of marriage, of the welcoming of new life and the farewelling of the old, have fallen into disuse. We have reserved very little space for the elderly except in their own exclusive retirement zones. Today a large proportion of young folk can grow up without knowing both parents, without close contact with elders, without ever seeing a death or funeral. They can grow up without officially passing from childhood to adolescence into adulthood, without making a lifelong commitment to anyone or anything as jobs and partners come and go.

There has been a knowledge explosion already in the past 40 years (aren't 96% of the scientists who ever lived still alive?) and we are paying dearly for its lack of integration with other important facets of life. In the market place, wisdom is neither sought nor honored. Information is the new god. But information without sound roots in spirituality, wisdom and genuine community can be yet another tool of enslavement.

An holistic spirituality

Social action demands the nurturing of an holistic spirituality in order to live well. It is an area long ignored and we are paying a huge price for that neglect. In New Zealand, which has the most secular culture in the developed world, we wonder why our suicide rates are so high compared to economically poorer countries. We wonder why so many people drink and take drugs to excess. We wonder at the wanton violence so prevalent and the destructiveness of so much behavior. Many economically poorer countries seem to have a much more enlivened spiritual presence than our country because they respect their spiritual traditions and the wisdom accrued over centuries. I believe that people drink and drug to excess in New Zealand to deaden the pain of living in a society that is so spiritually bankrupt in its communal culture. I believe that much violence flows from a sense of hopelessness that feeds on the lack of fulfillment resulting from our materialist culture. The simple divide now is between those who are succeeding and those who are not. This is spiritually barren territory. It is characterized by burnout, social dysfunction, elitism and a range of neuroses.

We need to rediscover pathways that reconnect us to our spiritual roots. We need to revisit the best of the spiritual and religious traditions that have bound societies together for centuries and look again at the essentials. Of course it will mean that different people and groupings will continue to see things in slightly different ways. We need to reconnect with the land we live on, the air we breathe, the water we drink, the food we eat, the mountains and hills we climb. To reconnect results in spiritual awareness. We need to find the spirit of life that exists outside ourselves. And we need to tap into the goodness of that spirit as a means of nourishment for our individual souls. In addition, our social groupings need to rediscover the importance of the spiritual side of their existence and nurture it.

Not all cultures have lost their spiritual dimension and many, including the diaspora Celts and Polynesians, to name but two, are looking again at some of the deep-rooted dimensions of their spiritual traditions so that their better aspects can be integrated into a more meaningful life in this 21st century. Everything our grandparents taught us wasn't necessarily old hat! But we need to know that much of their knowledge, their wisdom, will not fit the computer programs of the modern age because it is knowledge of the spirit, of the soul. It can only be measured by people with soul.

This is where indigenous peoples including Maori and other Polynesian cultures have a real gift to offer the wider community. We, in Aotearoa New Zealand, are so lucky to have them among us. They have so much to teach the rest of us. The recognition of the integration of spirituality and life which is, for example, found in Maori 'kaupapa' programs is a good model. This integration is also found in Samoan, Niuean, Tongan and other Pacific cultures prevalent in New Zealand. It is not generally found in the dominant culture.

What this means is that all different cultures need to develop models whereby the spiritual dimension of life is integrated into daily life. We need to acknowledge that something bigger than ourselves – the 'Spirit of Life', 'Io', a 'Higher Power', 'God', the 'Cosmic Christ' – exists without and within and needs to be recognized and be acknowledged as part of what we know, our collective knowledge. What makes for a holistic spirituality is the recognition that we are all interdependent, that we need to see the divine spark in one another and respect that, and that we need to specifically protect the most vulnerable, the poorest and the most powerless.

The struggle for justice is at the heart of such a truly authentic holistic spirituality. For those who walk guided by the spirit of God, the alleviation of poverty, hunger and disease is our problem and calls us to respond. That response is an essential part of our pilgrimage and requires certain spiritual components if we are to be sustained for the long haul.

Spiritual people who take their walk with God and one another seriously need to witness in their lives to what they advocate for others. For many, this change will mean living a simpler lifestyle, actively working to expose injustice and building fairer and more sustainable roads to the future. It means consuming less, sharing more, seeking the good of our poorer neighbor ahead of our own needs. If we truly do believe and trust in God, then the crass materialism, which sits at the heart of Western thinking and acting, has to go. This change will mean the rediscovery of community in one form or another.

Developing such spirituality is a process that requires good analysis, a certain passion, much dedication and discipline, consistent prayer and the support of community. St Benedict got it right in the 5th century, as did St Francis of Assisi 700 years later. The great prophets of the 20th century including Mohandas Gandhi (Kytle 1969/1982), Mother Jones (Gorn, 1951), E.F. Schumacher (1973), Joan Chittister (1995), the Berrigan brothers (Berrigan 1987; Berrigan and McAlister 1989), Martin Luther King (1997), Dorothy Day (1998), Cesar Chavez (Matthiessen 1969), Suzanne Aubert (Munro 1996) and Desmond Tutu (1994) have also taught us about spirituality. They have taught us to practice social justice by taking a preferential option for the poor and living what we preach. They have also taught us a lot about the centrality of prayer and worship within community. None of them were lone rangers. They have taught us that spiritual discipline and commitment is required as a basis for radical social change.

Now as we enter a new century we need to learn from these great teachers from the past and also heed the voices of those who cry for liberation now. A chorus of voices continues to call from the Third World for debt relief, for freedom from economic and cultural exploitation, and for their right to live lives worthy of human beings. We need to hear the cry of others who seek to save the very planet upon which we live; those who seek to keep an ecological balance so as to preserve its life and that of the various species, which call it home.

Conclusion

The linking of the struggle for justice to an ongoing spirituality is important. Burnout among social justice activists is a perennial problem. Many never fully recover the spirit that led them initially to make a commitment to improve the lot of others and remove injustice. A good, strong, accurate analysis is essential but not enough. The development of a process that nurtures the spirit of the individual and the justice movement is required for any sustained commitment. My point is that just as a garden needs watering, so our individual and collective spirits need nurturing with positive life affirming food. In order to do that we need to recognize how necessary this is and build its development into our everyday lives. At this moment, our dominant culture does not recognize this as a need.

We need to acknowledge that we can do little on our own and need to work closely with others. Such work for social change leads us often to cooperate with other ideological voices and be part of wider movements. But we need to stand tall in our own spirituality and in no way be apologetic for it. The power behind that tradition goes back to the dawn of creation. We should be proud to recognize and stand in such a tradition. When receiving his Nobel Prize for Chemistry in Stockholm in 2000, Alan MacDiarmid, a New Zealander, reminded us that 'in becoming who we are, we stand on the shoulders of giants'. How right he was. Would that the world heeded his voice.

Making lasting social change demands such spiritual awareness. It helps keep us humble, committed, focused and conscious of one another. It helps keep us refreshed and energized for the long haul. Without it we face early burnout; with it we can go on forever.

References

Berrigan, D. (1987) *To Dwell in Peace*. San Francisco, CA: Harper and Row.

Berrigan, P. and McAlister, E. (1989) *The Time's Discipline*. Baltimore, MD: Fortcamp.

Catholic Bishops of England and Wales (1996) *The Common Good and the Catholic Church's Social Teachings*. Westminster, London: The Catholic Bishops of England and Wales.

Chittister, J. (1995) *The Fire in These Ashes*. Kansas City, MO: Sheed and Ward.

Day, D. (1998) *Selected Writings.* Edited by R. Ellsberg. Maryknoll, NY: Orbis Books.

Foley, G. (1999) 'The Threat of Rising Seas.' *The Ecologist 29,* 2, 76.

Gorn, E.J. (1951) *Mother Jones: The Most Dangerous Woman in America.* New York: Hill and Wang.

King, M.L. (1997) *I Have a Dream.* New York: Scholastic Press.

Kytle, C. (1969/1982) *Gandhi: Soldier of Non-Violence.* Cabin John, MD: Seven Locks Press.

Matthiessen, P. (1969) *Sal Si Puedes: Cesar Chavez and the New American Revolution.* New York: Dell.

Munro, J. (1996) *The Story of Suzanne Auberto.* Auckland, New Zealand: Auckland University Press and Brigid Williams Books.

Schumacher, E.F. (1973) *Small is Beautiful.* London: Blond and Briggs.

Tutu, D. (1994) *The Rainbow People of God: South Africa's Victory over Apartheid.* London: Doubleday.

United Nations Development Programme (1999) *Human Development Report 1999.* New York and Geneva: International Labour Office.

Wilcox, F. (2001) *Disciples and Dissidents, Prison Writings of the Prince of Peace Plowshares.* Athol, MA: Haley's.

Wink, W. (1984) *Naming the Powers: The Language of Power in the New Testament.* Philadelphia: Fortress Press.

Wink, W. (1986) *Unmasking the Powers: The Invisible Forces that Determine Human Existence.* Philadelphia: Fortress Press.

Wink, W. (1992) *Engaging the Powers: Discernment and Resistance in a World of Domination.* Philadelphia: Fortress Press.

Wink, W. (1998) *The Powers that Be: Theology for a New Millennium.* New York: Doubleday.

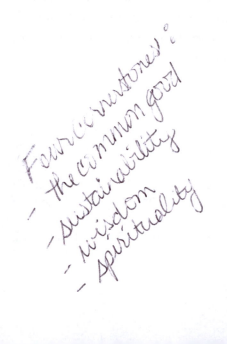

Chapter Two

Spirituality and Culture
Challenges for Competent Practice in Social Care

Bruce Stewart

This chapter describes the re-emergence of academic and clinical interest in spirituality as a key element in promoting wellness and community cooperation. Fields such as social work and counseling have historically been active in community wellness but spirituality's capacity for inclusiveness and connection is now encouraging a range of people including self-help organizations, therapeutic fields and social policy analysts to join together sharing their common goals. Within this broad spectrum of people there is a renewed dedication to social justice, ecological harmony, the realigning of economic and political inequities and support for cultural empowerment of disenfranchised individuals and groups (Mindell 1996; Morell 1996). Many who identify with these goals understand their practice must contend with a multitude of interrelated dimensions. They accept that wellness springs from holistic, ecological and systemic processes. The resulting multidimensional approach sets the stage for grappling with the inclusion of spirituality into the area of social care in the context of our complex postmodern society.

A perspective on competent practice: finding consensus in a relative world

Constructionism and postmodernism have significantly influenced theories about how we perceive reality and this has in turn affected the helping process. We are now sensitive about the capacity of every discipline to construct its perspective on reality (Flaskas 1994). From this vantage, family problems can be represented as a single narrative in a multitude of possibilities. In the same vein the treatment for these problems is often considered as a social construction of alternative narratives (Saleebey 1994). Therapy by way of narrative represents one example of a larger philosophy that accepts multiple realities and places truth in relative rather than absolute terms. The strength of relativism is its tolerance and potential for understanding diverse religious, spiritual and cultural expression. One of the dangers however is that if reality is socially constructed then clients and therapist alike may lose their moral compass.

While research indicates that practices are neither totally objective nor value-free, bias can be minimized by practitioners' concerted self-reflection (Bergin 1991; Carter 1991) and shared discernment through supervision. This includes acknowledging that their work has been influenced by a scientific education oriented to the concepts of objectivity and neutrality, which reinforces tentativeness or reluctance towards forming firm conclusions. Accordingly the views of clients are more likely endorsed as contextually valid. At the same time this type of endorsement may lack the strength of conviction that is often essential to the change process. Many in the helping field are now caught in a bind, needing guideposts for competent behavior while embracing a constructive, multiple epistemological perspective.

The nature of the dilemma created by searching for competence in the midst of relativism can be partially alleviated by asserting the fundamental importance of beliefs and values in their work and finding reliable common ground regarding principles of practice (O'Hara 1997). Research reveals a consensus of ethical views for many helpers in the form of common beliefs and a cherished value base. Bergin's (1991) study of therapists found a strong consensus about what constitutes good mental health in terms of values and morality. The consensus highlights much of the ethical basis for practice, which guides these practitioners in orienting client choices and goals. Consensus of this kind can offer direction to practitioners about the kind of values and principles affecting people's disturbance or improvement. They provide a framework in which to anchor intervention with a sense of educated conviction.

A spiritual perspective adds to a moral frame of reference by guiding individual and communal virtues and potentially offering inclusive healing through value-oriented therapy (Bergin 1991; Sims 1994). An example of this is with the 'Golden Rule' that gives importance to caring and forgiveness for all clients (Witmer and Sweeney 1992, p.141). Spiritual perspectives can also play an important role in fostering a constructive framework and are fundamental to the helping field. Aponte (1998) has boldly argued that every school of therapy and every training institute can be traced to a spiritual platform upon which the values and worldview of its therapy are based. Given this, it may be that in the age of uncertainty, spiritual orientations may provide an untapped resource for therapeutic guidance.

Overall establishing an assured yet flexible approach in one's work is a challenge in the postmodern world (Flaskas 1994). It requires being critical of self and society and adopting a balanced and open approach to client differences (Paterson and Trathen 1994). An example of this approach will be illustrated later in Chapter Eight: 'Talk Story'. As Bergin (1991) points out, a working consensus provides the strength of conviction within the field but needs to be counterbalanced by avoiding coercive practices and missionary attitudes in regard to beliefs and values. In this context being both reflective and critical also helps in distinguishing what constitutes better practice and healthier constructions of reality.

Overcoming barriers to spirituality

The place of spirituality is often not acknowledged in Western helping relationships (May 1991). Western beliefs such as those typically arising from modern science, materialism, secularism and individualism persuasively shape the helping field and are deemed by some writers as inhibiting spiritual development (Durie 1989; Moore 1996). To begin with, Western therapy situated within a larger landscape naturally emphasizes individualism and secularism. Individualism is an orientation focused on improving worth and functioning through therapy by suggesting that the individual is responsible for learning to accept and adjust to misfortune in their lives (Bulhan 1988). It is a view that discounts well-being based on connection to external social and environmental elements in one's world (Morell 1996; Weinrach and Thomas 1998). Secularism further separates the individual from their world by separating the relationship between the physical and spiritual realms. This undermines any awareness that the nonphysical dimensions of values and ideas can actually affect or reflect the physical world. Understandably in this view, phenomena such as dreams, prayers or otherworldly experiences cannot be credibly linked to creating change in the physical realm (Ingersoll 1994; Van de Castle 1994).

Materialism is a view that authenticates physically based reality. It asserts that only matter is real, and that everything including human consciousness is subsumed under it (Stewart 1999). In a material-oriented world, worth and value are measured by physical appearances and a person's material possessions. It validates such things as monetary wealth, formal education levels and specific physical appearances (Myers *et al.* 1991).

Modern Western science further supports the importance of a physically based reality. It purports that through positivism, reductionism and Cartesian dualism a more accurate view of the world can be obtained (Durie 1995; Merchant and Dupuy 1996). The scientific method focuses primary attention on externally observed and quantified data in isolation from their broader context and without reference to any nonphysical elements. It upholds this perception by attempting to understand complex phenomena through investigating elemental events in a process argued as value-free (Harman 1998; O'Hara 1995; Park 1996).

Despite the above influences there is a shift away from human isolation, the dominance of quantitative science and mind–matter separations. It is clear that culture significantly shapes our views and precludes the possibility of complete objectivity through positivism (Hoare 1991). It is also more commonly argued that post-positivist validity is possible by holistic, integrative processes involving a dynamic of subjectivity with the external world (Merchant and Dupuy 1996).

Western science is also extending itself through new developments. These developments tend to reaffirm more ancient cosmic perceptions of the sage, indigenous healer and psychic. They are supported by current research in modern physics, neuroscience and natural sciences (Adams 1995; Stewart 1999; Strohl 1998). The 'new science', as it is termed, suggests the possibility of an expanded synchronous pattern where something that happens in one place can create similar activities in another area and may even encode its influence simultaneously to all places (Park 1996, p.322). It is described in biological terms as occurring when a member of a particular species learns a new pattern, which activates a 'causative field' that alters a fundamental behavioral blueprint. If the new behavior is repeated enough, a 'morphic resonance' is established that will affect every member of the species (Luoma 1998, p.35; Mindell 1996, p.74). The impetus behind these scientific theories is in response to observed evidence of seemingly exceptional capacities of clairvoyance, remote sensing, psychic knowledge and healing powers within some people (Barasch Nov–Dec 2000).

The new science perspective, says Willis Harman (1998), is creating an evolution of thinking that is leading to a global transformation of consciousness. It is in stark contrast to the limits on time and place that the modern science's linear cause and effect model suggests. Yet there remain those who would argue against statements of a human capacity for extrasensory abilities. One example comes from Persinger, a brain neuroscientist who states that many of the subjective accounts of experiences beyond one's immediate space and time are merely the result of small bursts of energy in the brain. He says these energy bursts can create micro-seizures that induce the kind of reports described as mystical and paranormal. At the same time, Persinger notes the possibility of greater connection when he speculates that the human brain may be in sync with the earth's electromagnetic fields and is sensitive to disturbances in the earth's crust (Regush July/August 1995).

Overall dominant cultural beliefs influence thinking in the helping field and appear to discourage practitioners from evaluating spirituality's potential usefulness (Prest and Keller 1993). As spirituality invites the metaphysical realm it does not easily represent what is observed in the material world. It therefore can be ignored or denied as a force in materialist and industrialized cultures (Cornett 1992; Merchant and Dupuy 1996). Despite new developments in Western science practitioners are still likely to be discomforted by the enmeshment of value and subjectivism in client accounts of psychic energy, spiritual power and personal transcendence (Prest and Keller 1993). In addition secular, individualistic and materialistic aspects of society will continue to encourage them to discount a spiritual reality of interconnection and responsiveness to a holistic collective reality (Durie 1995; Patterson 1998). Unfortunately an individual who does not feel a sense of belonging and responsibility to something larger than themselves is apt to experience spiritual alienation from oneself and others. In order to deal with this loss an individual may need to confront their particular barriers to spirituality while searching within Western and non-Western culture for core beliefs and values that genuinely connect them to something larger.

Placing spirituality in culture

Religious and spiritual dimensions of culture are among the most important factors that structure human experience, beliefs, values, behavior and illness patterns. There is a growing sensitivity to religious and spiritual issues as an important part of helpers' competence in working in culturally diverse environments (Durie 1995; Lukoff, Lu and Turner 1998). The variety of spiritual perspectives within and amongst cultural groups places more pressure on those in the helping field to comprehend a multitude of beliefs and values. In this regard there are some fundamental concepts that can usefully guide practitioners seeking to develop a deeper understanding of spiritual diversity within culture.

The Judeo-Christian tradition is a foundation of Western society. It comprises Jewish and Christian faith traditions, which have been a pivotal influence in social work and the helping field (Byrd and Byrd 1993; Prest and Keller 1993; Ritter and O'Neil 1989). For some followers of this tradition the divine is understood in terms of a personal relationship with a transcendent patriarchal and hierarchical 'God' whose existence is in a separate world beyond the earth (Heliotrope 1997). Within this group, the divine may be considered separate to the material world while others may endorse the concept of an otherworld 'God' whose image is contained within all things on earth (Kilpatrick and Holland 1990). In this latter view 'God' is simultaneously transcendent or beyond and immanent or within all aspects of an earthly world (Fox 1981).

Some spiritual views challenge biblical thinking with feminine symbols of divinity and alternatives to the perceived superiority of masculine psychology (Campbell and Moyers 1988). Ecological feminists in particular have outlined an alternative to the Judeo-Christian perspective. They view sacredness as arising from a preference for natural ecology and/or feminine gender. Their divinity is earth-bound and perhaps conceptualized as a nurturing 'Goddess'. Likened to a 'Mother Earth', the Goddess represents the earth as a living organism constituted by all human and non-human form within a complete and evolving whole (Stewart 1999). Their earthly sacredness is ancient and holistic, positing that everything in a living world participates in an intricate web of life through interconnection and interdependence (Christ 1989). Many of these global earth-based spiritualities are represented in female forms such as the 'Black Madonna, Kwan Yin, Kali, Amatersu, Tonantzin, Sedi, White Buffalo, Woman and others' (Donaldson 1996, pp.201–202).

The literature provides a number of definitions and descriptions of spirituality. Carroll (1998) writes about 'spirituality-as-essence' and 'spirituality-as-one-dimension'. The former refers to a primary spirit-energy common to all humanity and having a capacity for interconnectedness with all things (Witmer and Sweeney 1992). Spirituality-as-one-dimension is more a specific transcendent dimension, which clarifies the extent and quality of our connection with self, others and the unknown (Elkins *et al.* 1988). These two definitions (which are not exclusive) approximate spirituality as a pervasive earthly presence known as immanence as well as a higher other worldly transcendent divinity (Benland 1988). Combining both definitions can extend the notion of divinity and sacredness. It may include the metaphysical forces behind concepts of love, spirit, life-force and principle (Aponte 1998; Morell 1996). Equally the transcendent can become an awareness of a dimension of unseen order containing magic, mystery and higher power. This dimension can also include a sense of mystical creatures and/or divine being(s) such as 'God', 'Goddess' and 'Great Spirit' (Stewart 1999, pp.37–39).

Overall the literature indicates that various spiritual beliefs and values produce a number of interpretations and potentially overlapping meanings. Practitioners' awareness about the potential diversity in client spiritual views can assist them in achieving openness about different interpretations of meaning and avoid institutionalizing or domesticating spirituality (Reed 1992).

Identifying culture's relevance to spirituality

As indicated spirituality can be situated in culture and can highlight significant aspects of that culture's viewpoint. In return culture is a fundamental influence in forming a person's beliefs and values and is a basis for each person's sense of meaning and direction in life (Carter 1991; May 1975; Saleebey 1994). One's culture provides a personal framework in which to receive, organize, rationalize and understand our experiences in the world. Spirituality is considered by some as embedded in all aspects of one's culture and is nurtured and fundamentally shaped by a person's worldview (Aponte 1998). Western-style helping has been criticized as culturally encapsulated and inherently less open to non-Western perspectives (Fukuyama 1990; Hoare 1991; Pedersen 1996). Therefore understanding spirituality may mean comprehending that Western culture can create its own bias and parochial tendencies particularly with its emphasis on individualism and the work ethic.

Being aware of the multicultural debate

Developing a multicultural perspective has become important in the helping field. The literature indicates many definitions and dimensions of culture influencing practice. One inclusive definition by Fukuyama (1990, p.7) says culture can include sex, age, sexual orientation, religious beliefs, ethnicity, race, and socioeconomic status. The advantage of perceiving culture broadly is that it becomes a stepping stone for attending to differences amongst people and facilitates a generic therapeutic approach (Pate and Bondi 1992; Pedersen 1991).

Some literature in the multicultural field challenges the viability of a generic view to helping. The literature here suggests that a universalistic helping approach is insufficient in attending to the specific cultural needs and issues prevalent in people's lives. They argue that a culture-specific knowledge is more viable for problems and conditions related to economic and political marginalization, racism, oppression, and stereotyping and majority/minority status. Still other literature contends that a transcultural approach, which involves a comprehensive knowledge across cultures, is able to respond to both specific and universal cultural need for each individual case (Stewart 1999).

The debate about the viability of generalized or culture-specific approaches is partly a function of differences in defining culture and the capacity of any definition to deal with differences and commonalities. Patterson (1996) says that a broad view of multiculturalism is preferred for its comprehensiveness and complements a general momentum towards a more unified worldview due to an ever-increasing global communications network and cross-cultural exchanges. He adds that contemporary societal changes encourage the helping field to activate its past focus on empowerment and support for healthy relationships in order to be relevant to all cultural groups.

Spiritual themes are also evident in the debate (Bishop and Glynn 1992). Myers *et al.* (1991) offer a holistic perspective about spirituality and the individual. They suggest at our core we possess an identity/spiritual essence that is universally connected and interdependent with all things. For them our spiritual essence evolves over time and creates unique individual and cultural pathways. This ongoing evolution becomes the basis for our ever-changing commonality and differences with all humanity. Therefore at any time all people have elements of commonality and difference with one another through their uniqueness, cultural identities and their association to a collective spiritual essence. It has also been argued that perceiving our spiritual link to all beings by sharing a universal core helps to identify with everyone, which in turn heightens the potential to commit oneself to universal peace, justice and humanness (Bennett 1996).

Development of a spiritual practice

Spirituality is a significant part of cultural beliefs and values despite the lack of references to this in conventional literature (Adams 1995; Genia 1994). The spiritual dimension has also been neglected or excluded in treatment by therapists. However, research indicates that the general population has a much higher rate of belief in a supreme power, considers spirituality a major dimension in their lives and is more likely to be affiliated to religious bodies than do those in the helping field.

Integrating spirituality with culture

In response to these gaps the process of integrating a cultural framework, which recognizes the multitude of dimensions in a client's world without exclusions, provides an opportunity for practitioners to explore and understand the breadth of spirituality (Pellebon and Anderson 1999). Considering spirituality within a cultural framework may also clarify that there are many spiritual perspectives in a multicultural society (Pate and Bondi 1992).

When spirituality is considered as part of culture it opens up possibilities for it to be part of identity development (Rappaport and Simpkins 1991; Sheridan, Charlotte and Atcheson 1994). This inclusion then narrows the gap evident in the literature and practice by integrating spiritual identity as an equal to identity related to class, ethnicity, age and gender when evaluating health.

STRENGTHENING SPIRITUALITY'S PRESENCE

Spirituality understood as part of identity signals its centrality to all facets of a person's human development including political, social and economic dimensions and that it cannot be separated from oppressive or liberating conditions in society (Michel 1996; Myers and Speight 1994). It follows that an important task for any practitioner using this framework is to assess need based on clients' individual and collective spiritual identity (Canda 1988b; Myers et al. 1991).

UTILIZING WORLDVIEW

What is apparent from earlier discussion regarding a multicultural debate is a struggle to comprehend differences and commonality amongst people. The multicultural literature highlights that all client contact in the helping field may involve universal, cultural-specific and unique elements (Ibrahim 1991; Speight *et al.* 1991). The concept of worldview, which is common in cultural literature, is useful in identifying client understanding about their world. This concept can be used to clarify someone's relationship to nature, others, institutions, objects, and the metaphysical (Brown and Landrum-Brown 1995; Martsolf and Mickley 1998). Worldview then becomes helpful in disentangling differences and commonality with others.

The introduction of worldview to culture necessitates that practitioners develop sensitivity and competence in understanding many aspects of a client's life (Saleebey 1994). Factors such as class, ethnicity, gender, age and spiritual life contribute to a person's worldview. Even the concept of self appears subject to cultural conditions (Carter 1991; Hoare 1991; Sanders 1998). For example, in the Western world self-contained individualism is more common whereas non-Western cultures tend to see self more collectively and defined by one's interactions with their cultural group and community (Durie 1995). Overall worldview provides a means to tackle complexity without resorting to generalizations and stereotypes.

COMPETENCE WITH MULTICULTURAL ENVIRONMENTS

Given cultural diversity in most environments today, a practitioner needs to strive toward a generic competence and sensitivity to effectively work with a multitude of cultural groups. The challenge to a practitioner is likely to be more significant when s/he is perceived as culturally different to the client. In these cases it means addressing universal, cultural-specific and unique client qualities (Carter 1991; Patterson 1996; Speight *et al.* 1991). These are the efforts needed in order to avoid excessive use of stereotypes or generalizations and to be attuned to diversity within any given cultural group. Given that cross-cultural practice may also include perceptions of power differences between people it may be necessary to be sensitive to any form of alienation and to conditions such as coloniszation or slavery that may have negatively shaped one's personal and/or social-relational life (Mack 1994; Myers and Speight 1994).

There are many challenges to multicultural practice but the focus remains on using connection based on one's commonality and difference with the other to build support and trust. The capacity to connect cross-culturally can increase a sense of belonging and cooperation and mitigate against differences being a force for division or exclusion (Stewart 1999). Making connections can be done through finding areas of mutual belief and value between client and practitioner or in the establishment of a common set of goals and expectations in the helping process. There can also be a bond that develops between people when sharing ideas, even if opposing, in an atmosphere of unconditional acceptance between people. Connecting to the other through differences and similarities can become a source of vitality and a means of empowerment (Stewart 1999).

FINDING AN INCLUSIVE PERSPECTIVE

Practitioners need to avoid identifying spirituality with a particular set of beliefs, or religious framework. Generic definitions of spirituality offer the best position to minimize excluding anyone due to his or her perspectives. Such definitions are likely to convey respect to a wide range of individual differences in spirituality by affirming a personal set of beliefs arising innately within each individual. In so doing spiritual perspectives conceptualised individually and collectively as well as perspectives that negate a spiritual life altogether can be recognized and valued (Canda 1988a; Everts and Agee 1994; Ingersoll 1994).

Some religious groups still reject generic definitions despite their inclusive nature. For them inclusiveness is achieved by relying on a secular rationality to explain the existence of social institutions ordained by God. Innate spirituality can also be viewed by some as only giving preference to the individual by arguing that they subjugate social institutions to personal needs. Finally generic definitions have been criticized as describing faith in relative rather than in singular terms since they can be expressed through one of many religions. These views are usually present with groups defined as fundamentalists (Heise and Steitz 1991).

Pursuing self-knowledge

Practitioners' self-inquiry into their beliefs, values and philosophies develops their spiritual life and affords more insight into clients' spirituality. This insight may encourage respect for diverse religious and spiritual commitments. Bergin (1991) says 'spiritual values help to ground mental health values in terms of universals and the spiritual perspective makes it easier to establish a moral frame of reference because it views the world in value laden terms' (p.398). At the same time it is important to retain the capacity to reflect upon the potential for both benefits and harm that may arise from one's beliefs and values (Sheridan *et al.* 1994). Practitioners also need knowledge about utilizing techniques like prayer, meditation, and ritual to facilitate wellness. These techniques have the potential to attune themselves and the client to beneficial spiritual qualities, experiences and ultimate reality (Mariechild 1981; Strohl 1998). These techniques may also offset Western cultural tendencies to only focus on expanding conscious knowledge, by fostering instead what is termed 'negative capability'. This is an ability to stay with mystery or doubt without any irritable reaching for fact or reason (Fukuyama and Sevig 1997; Ingersoll 1994). The capacity to embrace mystery is essential to openness and unity with the unknown and to improving well-being (Cody 1994).

Connecting health to person-in-environment

Holistic and interactive processes typical in spiritual themes suggest a profound level of interdependence between people and the natural environment regarding fulfillment and health (Canda 1988b; Patterson 1998). Interdependence with all things raises our awareness about the importance of balance and harmony between people and the environment. Global consciousness also brings with it a sense of crisis with the apparent environmental destruction cited in modern times. These destructive forces have the potential to denigrate the planet and human well-being and increase human vulnerability to environmental disasters. Some have argued that human and environmental disaster, although undesirable, may in the end accelerate the shift to holistic, expanded planetary consciousness (Harman 1998). The debate about committing to planetary healing is becoming more urgent given the alarm expressed in credible scientific circles which are conservatively estimating that we have only 30 years in which to avoid significant social disruption due to planetary destruction (Strong 2000; Wesselman 1998). Under the circumstances some practitioners may be propelled into social and ecological activism in order to respond to this sense of future uncertainty.

Identifying spirituality in practice

The therapeutic field is significantly developed today but research indicates some reluctance to identify spirituality in practice. There are many comprehensive approaches available to practitioners, each with its set of assumptions and beliefs. Many of the existing approaches that incorporate holistic processes have heightened sensitivity to quantum physics and eco-systems theories. This opens more possibilities to the metaphysical realm but still neglects or avoids the spiritual component (Cowley and Derezotes 1994). Some practitioners and distressed clients often desire help consistent with a spiritual frame of reference (Bergin and Jensen 1991). Even so, this current environment leaves a gap for practitioners who want to address spirituality in their work. The avoidance or denial of religious and spiritual matters reduces our ability to understand modern maladies (Cowley and Derezotes 1994). Graham, Kaiser and Garrett (1998) contend that the social work profession has been ambivalent and even avoided spirituality. They argue that naming the spiritual dimension is essential to a more complete understanding of human behavior.

In the face of practitioner bias against spirituality a few writers are taking up the challenge by adding more clarity and usefulness to this misunderstood and minimized concept. For example Kilpatrick and Holland (1990) have proposed a model to begin to reflect upon the importance of the spiritual dimension. Their model suggests that it is a distinct dimension permeating all aspects of life. For them it is an aspect that extends to individuals committing themselves to the values of social justice and implementing these values in our economic and political systems. For these authors a person tends to function at a lower level when any dimension of their life is diminished or discounted. Graham *et al.* (1998) have also contributed to demystifying the spiritual dimension in practice. They have developed a simple framework to help practitioners identify spiritual issues. My own research has made efforts to clarify spirituality by comparing perspectives and their possible influences on practice (Stewart 1999).

Summary

Spirituality influences the helping professions to take notice of spiritual matters and shapes their motivation, theory, styles and techniques of helping. It is a key dimension to enhancing connection without demanding compliance to any particular belief system. The helping relationship runs parallel to the spiritual relationship in its orientation to self-determination of client healing, transformation and justice. For practitioners, awareness of spirituality's synchronicity with helping means it can be a prime consideration in the alleviation of many mental health problems, emotional despair and critical life events. It is apparent that practitioners from various faiths and spiritual orientations can respond sensitively to diverse spiritual needs and modes of expression by clients. They can do this by utilizing a common pool of skills such as empathy, careful listening and loving acceptance. Further to this, practitioners' specific spiritual techniques and approaches are a direct way of knowing more about relationships, sacred experiences, and ultimate reality.

Spirituality is a critical ingredient often excluded but necessary to understanding culture and worldview. It plays an important role in contributing to valuing both difference and commonality between people and finding our connection to a communally shared spiritual essence. One's spiritual identity development provides a potential conduit to empowerment and belonging with self, others, nature and the transcendent. It also facilitates meaning and transformation with suffering minorities, colonized, oppressed and excluded peoples. In spirituality our differences do not translate into barriers but are part of a natural unfolding that enriches our interdependence and interconnection with all.

There are many spiritual perspectives and paths to follow and perhaps many destinations. There are also many secular and non-secular influences in society shaping these pathways. The relativism of the postmodern view encourages greater respect for diversity and individual difference. As a postmodern society we are challenged to affirm all perspectives with no one path standing above the other. The strength of this relativist view is its inclusiveness but is less forceful regarding the bonds and inspiration that can link people together. In the face of this, spirituality offers an opportunity for healthier interconnection by valuing differences and commonality, promoting acceptance and self-determination and creating places of belonging and commitment.

References

Adams, N. (1995) 'Spirituality, Science and Therapy.' *Australian and New Zealand Journal of Family Therapy 16*, 6, 201–208.

Aponte, H.J. (1998) 'Love, the Spiritual Wellspring of Forgiveness: An Example of Spirituality in Therapy.' *Journal of Family Therapy 20*, 1, 37–58.

Barasch, M.I. (Nov–Dec 2000) 'Night Eyes.' *Utne Reader 102*, 66–71.

Benland, C. (1988) 'The S-Factor: Taha Wairua.' In *The Royal Commission on Social Policy, Future Directions*. Wellington, New Zealand: Mayfair House.

Bennett, C. (1996) *In Search of the Sacred: Anthropology and the Study of Religions*. New York: Cassell.

Bergin, A. (1991) 'Values and Religious Issues and Psychotherapy and Mental Health.' *American Psychologist 46*, 4, 394–403.

Bergin, A.E. and Jensen, J.P. (1991) 'Religiosity of Psychotherapists: A National Survey.' *Psychotherapy 27*, 1, 3–7.

Bishop, R. and Glynn, T. (1992) 'He Kanohhi Kitea: Conducting and Evaluating Educational Research.' *New Zealand Journal of Educational Studies 27*, 2, 125–135.

Brown, M.T. and Landrum-Brown, J. (1995) 'Counselor Supervision: Cross-Cultural Perspectives.' In J.G. Ponterotto, J.M. Casa, L.A. Suzuki and C.M. Alexander (eds) *Handbook of Multicultural Counseling*. London: Sage.

Bulhan, H.A. (1988) *Frantz Fanon and the Psychology of Oppression*. New York: Plenum Press.

Byrd, E.K. and Byrd, P.D. (1993) 'Religion and Rehabilitation: A Listing of Biblical References to Healing that May Be Useful as Bibliotherapy to the Empowerment of Rehabilitation Clients.' *Journal of Rehabilitation*, July–August, 46–50.

Campbell, J. and Moyers, B. (1988) *The Power of Myth*. New York: Doubleday.

Canda, E.R. (1988a) 'Conceptualizing Spirituality for Social Work: Insights from Diverse Perspectives.' *Social Thought*, Winter, 30–46.

Canda, E.R. (1988b) 'Spirituality, Religious Diversity, and Social Work Practice.' *Social Casework: The Journal of Contemporary Social Work 69*, 4, 238–247.

Carroll, M. (1998) 'Social Work's Conceptualization of Spirituality.' *Social Thought: Journal of Religion in the Social Services 18*, 2, 1–14.

Carter, R.T. (1991) 'Cultural Values: A Review of Empirical Research and Implications for Counseling.' *Journal of Counseling & Development 70*, 1, 164–173.

Christ, C. (1989) 'Rethinking Theology and Nature.' In J. Plaskow and C. Christ (eds) *Weaving the Visions: New Patterns in Feminist Spirituality.* New York: HarperCollins.

Cody, W.K. (1994) 'Meaning and Mystery in Nursing Practice.' *Nursing Science Quarterly 7*, 2, 48–51.

Cornett, C. (1992) 'Toward a More Comprehensive Personology: Integrating a Spiritual Perspective into Social Work Practice.' *Social Work 37*, 2, 101–102.

Cowley, Au-Deane, S. and Derezotes, D. (1994) 'Transpersonal Psychology and Social Work Education.' *Journal of Social Work Education 30*, 1, 32–41.

Donaldson, E.L. (1996) 'Imaging Women's Spirituality.' *Comparative Education Review 40*, 2, 194–204.

Durie, M. (1989) 'A Move that is Well Overdue: Shaping Counseling to Meet the Needs of Maori People.' *New Zealand counseling and Guidance Association Journal 2*, 1, 13–23.

Durie, M. (1995) *Whaiora: Maori Health Development.* Auckland: Oxford University Press.

Elkins, D.N., Hedstrom, L.J., Hughes, L.L., Leaf, J.A. and Saunders, C. (1988) 'Toward a Humanistic-Phenomenological Spirituality.' *Journal of Humanistic Psychology 28*, 4, 5–18.

Everts, J.F. and Agee, M.N. (1994) 'Including Spirituality in counselor Education: Issues for Consideration, with Illustrative Reference to a New Zealand Example.' *International Journal for the Advancement of counseling 17*, 291–302.

Flaskas, C. (1994) 'Postmodernism, Constructionism and the Idea of Reality: A Contribution to the "Ism" Discussions.' *Australian and New Zealand Journal of Family Therapy 16*, 3, 143–146.

Fox, M. (1981) 'Meister Echart on the Fourfold Path of a Creation-centerd Spiritual Journey.' In M. Fox (ed) *Western Spirituality: Historical Roots, Ecumenical Routes.* Santa Fe, New Mexico: Bear & Co.

Fukuyama, M. (1990) 'Taking a Universal Approach to Multicultural Counseling.' *counselor Education and Supervision 30*, 6–17.

Fukuyama, M.A. and Sevig, T.D. (1997) 'Spiritual Issues in Counseling: A New Course'. *counselor Education and Supervision 36*, 3, 233–244.

Genia, V. (1994) 'Secular Psychotherapists and Religious Clients: Professional Considerations and Recommendations.' *Journal of Counseling & Development* 72, 395–398.

Graham, M., Kaiser, T. and Garrett, K.J. (1998) 'Naming the Spiritual: The Hidden Dimensions of Helping.' *Social Thought: Journal of Religion in the Social Services* 18, 4, 49–62.

Harman, W. (1998) *Global Mind Change*, 2nd edn. San Francisco: Berrett-Koehler Publishers.

Heise, R.G. and Steitz, J.A. (1991) 'Religious Perfectionism: Versus Spiritual Growth.' *Counseling and Values 36*, 11–18.

Heliotrope, H. (1997) 'Paganism: A Faith for Feminists?' *Broadsheet 213*, 47–49.

Hoare, C.H. (1991) 'Psychosocial Identity Development and Cultural Others.' *Journal of Counseling & Development 70*, 1, 45–53.

Ibrahim, F.A. (1991) 'Contribution of Cultural Worldview to Generic Counseling and Development.' *Journal of Counseling & Development 70*, 1, 13–19.

Ingersoll, R.E. (1994) 'Spirituality, Religion, and Counseling: Dimensions and Relationships.' *Counseling and Values 38*, 98–111.

Kilpatrick, A.C. and Holland, T.P. (1990) 'Spiritual Dimension of Practice.' *The Clinical Supervisor 8*, 2, 125–140.

Lukoff, D., Lu, F. and Turner, R. (1998) 'From Spiritual Emergency to Spiritual Problem: The Transpersonal Roots of the New DSM-IV Category.' *Journal of Humanistic Psychology 38*, 2, 21–50.

Luoma, B.B. (1998) 'An Exploration of Intuition for Social Work Practice and Education'. *Social Thought: Journal of Religion in the Social Services 18*, 2, 31–45.

Mack, M.L. (1994) 'Understanding Spirituality in Counseling Psychology: Considerations for Research, Training and Practice.' *Counseling and Values 39*, 15–31.

Mariechild, D. (1981) *Mother Wit: A Feminist Guide to Psychic Development*. New York: Crossing Press.

Martsolf, D. and Mickley, J.R. (1998) 'The Concept of Spirituality in Nursing Theories: Differing World-Views and Extent of Focus.' *Journal of Advanced Nursing 27*, 2, 294–303.

May, R. (1975) 'Values, Myths, and Symbols.' *American Journal of Psychiatry 132*, 7, 703–706.

May, R. (1991) *Cosmic Consciousness Revisited: The Modern Origins and Development of Western Spiritual Psychology*. Milton, Brisbane: Element Books.

Merchant, N. and Dupuy, P. (1996) 'Multicultural Counseling and Qualitative Research: Shared Worldview and Skills.' *Journal of Counseling & Development 74*, 6, 537–541.

Michel, C. (1996) 'Of Worlds and Unseen: The Educational Character of Haitian Vodou.' *Comparative Educational Review 40*, 3, 280–294.

Mindell, A. (1996) 'Discovering the World in the Individual: The World Channel in Psychotherapy.' *Journal of Humanist Psychology 36*, 3, 67–84.

Moore, T. (1996) *The Re-enchantment of Everyday Life*. New York: HarperCollins.

Morell, C. (1996) 'Radicalizing Recovery: Addiction, Spirituality, and Politics.' *Social Work 41*, 3, 306–312.

Myers, L.J. and Speight, S.L. (1994) 'Optimal theory and the Pychology of Human Diversity.' In E.J. Trickett, R.J. Watts and D. Birman (eds) *Human Diversity: Perspectives on People in Context*. San Francisco: Jossey-Bass Publishers.

Myers, L.J., Speight, S.L., Highlen, P.S., Cox, C.I., Reynolds, A.L., Adams, E.M. and Hanley, C.P. (1991) 'Identity Development and Worldview: Toward an Optimal Conceptualization.' *Journal of Counseling & Development 70*, 1, 54–62.

O'Hara, M. (1995) 'Carl Rogers: Scientist and Mystic.' *Journal of Humanistic Psychology 35*, 4, 40–53.

O'Hara, M. (1997) 'Emancipatory Therapeutic Practice in a Turbulent Transmodern Era: A Work of Retrieval.' *Journal of Humanistic Psychology 37*, 3, 7–33.

Park, K.M. (1996) 'The Personal is Ecological: Environmentalism of Social Work.' *Social Work 41*, 3, 320–323.

Pate, R.H. and Bondi, A.M. (1992) 'Religious Beliefs and Practice: An Integral Aspect of Multicultural Awareness.' *Counselor Education and Supervision 32*, 108–115.

Paterson, R. and Trathen, S. (1994) 'Feminist Interventions in Family Therapy.' *Australian and New Zealand Journal of Family Therapy 15*, 2, 91–98.

Patterson, C.H. (1996) 'Multicultural Counseling: from Diversity to Universality.' *Journal of Counseling & Development 74*, 3, 227–235.

Patterson, E.F. (1998) 'The Philosophy and Physics of Holistic Health Care: Spiritual Healing as a Workable Interpretation.' *Journal of Advanced Nursing 27*, 2, 287–293.

Pedersen, P. (1991) 'Multiculturalism as a Generic Approach to Counseling.' *Journal of Counseling & Development 70*, 1, 6–12.

Pedersen, P. (1996) 'The Importance of Both Similarities and Differences in Multicultural Counseling: Reaction to C.H. Patterson.' *Journal of Counseling & Development 74*, 3, 236–241.

Pellebon, D.A. and Anderson, S.C. (1999) 'Understanding the Life Issues of Spiritually-Based Clients.' *Families in Society: The Journal of Contemporary Human Services*, May–June, 229–238.

Prest, L.A. and Keller, J.F. (1993) 'Spirituality and Family Therapy: Spiritual Beliefs, Myths, and Metaphors.' *Journal of Marital and Family Therapy 19*, 2, 137–148.

Rappaport, J. and Simpkins, R. (1991) 'Healing and Empowering through Community Narrative.' *Prevention in Human Services 9*, 29–50.

Reed, P.G. (1992) 'An Emerging Paradigm for the Investigation of Spirituality in Nursing.' *Research in Nursing & Health 15*, 349–357.

Regush, N. (July/August 1995) 'Brain Storms and Angels.' *Equinox 82*, 63–73.

Ritter, K.Y. and O'Neil, C.R. (1989) 'Moving through Loss: The Spiritual Journey of Gay Men and Lesbian Women.' *Journal of Counseling & Development 68*, 1, 9–15.

Saleebey, D. (1994) 'Culture, Theory, and Narrative: The Intersection of Meanings in Practice.' *Social Work 39*, 4, 351–359.

Sanders, B. (1998) 'Why Postmodern Theory may be a Problematic Basis for Therapeutic Practice: A Feminist Perspective.' *Australian and New Zealand Journal of Family Therapy 19*, 3, 111–119.

Sheridan, M.J., Charlotte, M.W. and Atcheson, L. (1994) 'Inclusion of Content on Religion and Spirituality in the Social Work Curriculum: A Study of Faculty Views.' *Journal of Social Work Education 30*, 3, 363–376.

Sims, A. (1994) '"Psyche" – Spirit as Well as Mind?' *British Journal of Psychiatry 165*, 441–446.

Speight, S.L., Myers, L.J., Cox, C.I. and Highlen, P.S. (1991) 'Redefinition of Multicultural Counseling.' *Journal of Counseling & Development 70*, 1, 29–36.

Stewart, B. (1999) *Spirituality in counseling: Assisting counselors and the Depressed.* Unpublished master's thesis, Massey University, New Zealand.

Strohl, J.E. (1998) 'Transpersonalism: Ego Meets Soul.' *Journal of Counseling & Development 79*, 397–403.

Strong, M. (2000, May 22) 'Cry the Beloved Planet.' *The Globe and Mail*, A11.

Van de Castle, R. (1994) *Our Dreaming Mind.* New York: Ballantine Books.

Weinrach, S.G. and Thomas, K.R. (1998) 'Diversity-Sensitive Counseling Today: A Postmodern Clash of Values.' *Journal of Counseling & Development 76*, 115–122.

Wesselman, H. (1998) *Medicinemaker: Mystic Encounters on the Shaman's Path.* New York: Bantam Books.

Witmer, J.M. and Sweeney, T.J. (1992) 'A Holistic Model for Wellness and Prevention over the Life Span.' *Journal of Counseling & Development 71*, 2, 140–148.

PART TWO

Walking the Talk

Chapter Three

Vocation and Social Care

Mary Eastham

The meaning of vocation

Since the term 'vocation' is Jewish in origin, it is useful to place it in its cultural and historical context before discussing its relevance to practitioners in professions of social care. The ancient Hebrews were the first people to think of their lives, both individually and collectively, as a vocation, a response to a direct invitation from God (Cahill 1998, p.3).

This invitation had unique contours. The Hebrew people were to journey with God in history. In contrast with deities of ancient Sumer who were archetypal expressions of the cosmos and cycles of fertility, the God of the Hebrews was personal, dialogical and historical, and yet also 'wholly other' (Otto 1923, p.25). This God called his people to live in a covenant relationship. They were to accept the daunting task of becoming a new kind of human being and to establish their individual and community life on rigorous ethical principles. Their personal destiny was to be a people set apart to bear witness to a totally new experience of God. Provided they were faithful to God's covenant with them as it was revealed in various dramatic hierophanies, they would survive as a unique people in history.

At issue was fidelity, the willingness to trust in a God who could not be controlled or placated or domesticated as were other deities of the ancient Near East. No better example could be cited of the Hebrew concept of fidelity than Abraham himself, the father of the Jewish nation. The poignant story of his willingness to sacrifice his only son, Isaac, is well known. The story is even more touching given the fact that Isaac was conceived when both Abraham and Sarah were well past the age of childbearing. Could the faithful God who called him to be the father of a great nation really be asking him to sacrifice his beloved son? Could the Hebrew people become a unique people in history if the patriarch himself left no offspring? According to the story's narrator, the issue was not if God would go through with it, but rather if Abraham trusted God enough to know that God would never betray him.

The Jewish concept of vocation is religious in the traditional sense of the term, for the very word religion, *religare*, means to 'bind back'. The Hebrew people were bound to God in a unique covenant relationship which demanded unconditional fidelity in exchange for a unique role in history as God's chosen people. This relationship was never easy. It was fraught with all the risk of a people taking a huge step into an unknown future but somehow deeply confident that a faithful, loving Father was guiding them throughout history and would sustain them in times of trial. To be sure, a dynamic experience of faith, hope and trust underpin the Jewish concept of vocation.

Invitation, journey, ethics, fidelity, trust, personal destiny... If applied to a people's understanding of who they are and what their lives are intended to be, these concepts would tend to produce very self-confident people. People who conceive their lives in relationship with a transcendent source which anchors them in history and society do not suffer from identity crises; far from it[1].

James Hillman's acorn theory of personal destiny

Because the concept of vocation, personal destiny or calling is as powerful psychologically as it is religiously, Jungian psychologist James Hillman believes it should be retrieved and rehabilitated in the interests of happier children and healthier adults. In *The Soul's Code: In Search of Character and Calling*, Hillman traces its roots in Western philosophy and psychology (Hillman 1996, pp.7–11). The concept of calling, which Hillman develops fully in his 'acorn theory', means that everyone is born with a unique personal destiny, a 'uniqueness that asks to be lived and that is already present before it can be lived' (p.6). The philosopher Plotinus maintained that this pre-existent entity, the soul, not only chose its parents but also its time and place. Moreover, once the soul was embodied, each person was also given a guardian spirit to protect and guide it throughout its life[2]. Whether the term was translated as *genius* (Roman), *daimon* (Greek), or *guardian angel* (Christian), only by attending to its demands could one become truly human and whole.

The theory of calling appeals to Hillman because it stresses the power and resiliency of the human spirit. People need never see themselves as victims of circumstance because many people have risen above less than ideal circumstances in the belief that they were 'called' to do so. Hillman puts forth his 'acorn theory' to explain this spiritual process with a metaphor drawn from nature. Just as the tiny acorn falls from the mighty oak, each person comes into the world with a personal destiny. This personal destiny is imprinted on the person's soul in the same way that the mighty oak is imprinted on the little acorn. But the acorn needs to 'grow down', to firmly fix its roots in a specific soil, a time, a place, a circumstance.

So too human beings. To 'grow down' into their vocation, they too must be firmly rooted in their own time, place and circumstance. Indeed, people realize their destiny or fall short of it to the extent that they consciously follow a path consistent with their soul's code. This code is not just about honing one's talents but also about character formation. Once aware of our personal destiny, our task is to 'grow down', to live out our vocation. Our guardian spirits are a constant presence, giving us glimpses as children about who we are and what we have been called to do in this place, at this time. This notion of personal destiny stresses the importance of particularity in living out one's vocation. Vocation involves not just the inner dynamism of faith, hope and trust but also an acute awareness of our outer world. Inner and outer must co-evolve simultaneously.

Hillman believes that history is replete with examples of extraordinary people whose lives can be interpreted in this way. In his book, he documents the lives of Eleanor Roosevelt and Judy Garland among others. In the first instance, we see a lonely and unhappy girl. Eleanor's parents died while she was very young, compounding her sense of isolation. But according to Hillman, she survived her childhood because of her intense fantasy life. Her recurrent 'vision' was of living with her father as 'the mistress of his large household and companion in his travels' (p.21). Hillman concludes that her 'fantasies of attending to "Father" were a preliminary praxis into which she could put her call, her huge devotion to the welfare of others' (p.22). They were a manifestation of her *daimon* giving her glimpses of her personal destiny as the first activist First Lady during the tumultuous years of the Great Depression and World War II.

The story of Judy Garland, of course, is very different. Like Eleanor Roosevelt, her *daimon* manifested itself at a very early age. However, because she had no private life, no space or time to nurture her spirit or attend to her soul, she never learned to express her enormous gift and hold her humanity intact at the same time. Judy Garland belonged to her public, to the people who managed her career and to the demands of her adoring fans. Hillman even suggests that it may have been 'her acorn not only to sing and dance in the theatrical spotlight, to be the magical child and enact the otherworld's presence as the white-faced clown, but also to be the representative of exile and its longings' (p.57). Without a doubt, this would suggest that the *daimon* is not always about 'happily ever after'. Life is a mystery unfolding in ways that cannot be controlled.

Hillman's discussion of the term 'vocation' is psychological in the traditional sense of the term, for the very word *psyche* means soul, the depth dimension of the person. To realize one's destiny requires an arduous process of 'growing down' into the person one was destined to be. This process is as fraught with all the risk and uncertainty as the journey of God's chosen people through history. For we must consciously cooperate with the *daimon* that gives us clues to our purpose in life but never controls us. To 'grow down' is a spiritual journey of self-understanding that will take us to the roots of our soul in order to discover spiritual gifts of life and love that can be shared with others.

Taken in themselves, both understandings of vocation convey a powerful sense of personal and professional identity. Practitioners who conceive of their work as vocation are not just doing a job. They are engaged in a project involving the total orientation of the person – mind, body and spirit. Vocation is greater still than a career, for career can be conceived solely in terms of skills training, knowledge, and monetary gain. However, if one's work is conceived as a vocation, one is professing a unique sense of individuality in the service of community.

These ideas are intensely spiritual and moral. They touch people at the core of their being. They demand a response. To know who you are at such a deep level is almost as if you have no choice. Indeed, you have already made the most important choices in your life. Your life means fidelity to this path, not a casual flirtation with passing fancies. Your path is to embody and profess certain ideals in the world. These ideas convey a unique sense of freedom – freedom for greater commitment; freedom from distraction. In *The Beatitude of Truth: Reflections of a Lifetime*, Donald Nicholl explains the nature of spiritual authority in this way: 'To "command" means to leave no choice but to obey; and its application here becomes intelligible when we bear in mind the roots of the word "obedience", because this word has its roots in the Latin word for hearing' (Nicholl 1997, p.158).

During times of personal crisis, the idea of vocation as an innate spiritual authority can sustain practitioners just as it sustained Abraham in his fateful walk up the hill with Isaac, bewildered why God would ask him to commit such a grotesque act, yet trusting all the while that the God he loved would somehow reveal to him the greater good. During times of professional crisis, these ideas can nurture practitioners just as Eleanor Roosevelt's *daimon* nurtured her spirit and soul so that she could realize her unique personal destiny as one of the most influential and compassionate women in North American politics. I will now discuss how these insights can enrich the professional and spiritual development of practitioners.

Social work as a healing vocation

In the preface to *Social Work in Action*, veteran New Zealand social worker Merv Hancock defines social work as 'a profession, a community of people who share a common goal of always seeking new ways to assist people' (Hancock 1994, p.9). It also carries a kind of stigma because social workers deal with dependent people who are not able to make their own way. Third, the profession is 'sedimented' within the task of renewing the welfare state, because its dismantling in 1974 has resulted in great hardship for the disadvantaged in New Zealand. He concludes that social work in New Zealand has an 'uncertain future':

> The future holds as much uncertainty as the past. It is very important to live with uncertainty and to accept it. The uncertainty of the world economy is always present, and anybody who suggests that it is not uncertain is a rogue and a vagabond. However, although uncertainty is the order of the day, the future is in a sense what one makes of it. Social work can make a contribution to defining the kind of society we live in. Therefore it needs to maintain a level of optimism about itself. (p.13)

Although Hancock nowhere employs the word 'vocation', the language he uses clearly conveys the inner and outer dimensions of the concept. The inner orientation of the person includes a strong ethical commitment, a willingness to trust in the goodness of life, and the need to 'grow down' into one's profession despite an uncertain future. The outer orientation includes the commitment to restore the welfare state. One hears echoes of the religious and psychological dimensions of vocation as a commitment to realize a very special destiny despite all the difficulties involved.

Moreover, in Part Three of *Social Work in Action*, practitioners discuss the therapeutic nature of their work. They critically reflect on their healing techniques in various fields of practice, which include work with older clients, the deaf community, people with disabilities, women in need of abortion, victims of sexual abuse, abusing mothers, etc. (Munford and Nash 1994). This critical reflection is not just about developing more effective therapeutic techniques, but, as Janet May (1994) describes it, about 'exploring the blocks of awareness within ourselves that we come to identify in the course of our work' (p.329). In 'Developing an Integrated Approach to Practice: A Christian Perspective', May refers specifically to areas of cognitive dissonance between the Christian worldview and contexts for therapy. As her title suggests, she believes that Christian counselors must develop an approach to their practice which is 'articulate enough to reflect [their] distinctive world view in ways which do not over-simplify or distort the complex difficulties [they] encounter in social work and counseling contexts' (p.348). In this way, a harmonious integration can occur between these two important areas of their lives. The article describes how she accomplished this integration in her own work with adult survivors of childhood sexual abuse.

This process of exploration also bears a distinctive resemblance to the dynamism of 'growing down' into one's vocation, even if May does not use the phrase. For May, the 'growing down' is not simply a matter of religious commitment but also professional ethics. Clearly, one must be rooted in one's personal and professional identity. Now if social workers can apply concepts to themselves and their work which have distinctive religious and psychological meanings, they may consider themselves a kind of religious personality. In so doing, they can draw on ideas and practices that can enrich their personal and professional development.

Practitioners as self-healed healers

In their article 'Some Central Ideas in the "Just Therapy" Approach', Charles Waldegrave and Kiwi Tamasese describe the therapeutic conversation as a

> sacred encounter, because people come in great pain and share their story. The stories they share are nearly always deeply personal and very exposing. These are the sort of stories people normally only share with their closest friends and family. For us, the story is like a gift, a very personal offering to the therapist given in great vulnerability. It has a spiritual quality. (Munford and Nash 1994, p.117)

Note the distinctively spiritual language to describe the therapeutic conversation. For an encounter to be sacred implies that one is in the presence of the divine where great power resides – both positive and negative. Indeed, in almost every wisdom tradition, symbols such as wind, water and fire describe the way the divine works in human life and history. Now wind, water and fire are the mutable elements. They signal that powerful changes are taking place, and that these changes involve death and rebirth[3].

What could these insights mean to social workers engaged in a therapeutic encounter? When counselors listen compassionately to a client's story of pain and suffering, has it ever happened that they too may suddenly feel quite vulnerable? Apart from the phenomenon of transference[4], has it ever happened that counselors may also experience feelings of anger, fear, sadness and grief? If so, what could explain this phenomenon?

When clients speak about their pain and hope, they are speaking from the depths of their being, their soul. If practitioners listen *com*-passionately, that is to say, suffer with them, they too will be touched at the depths of their being, their soul. In a very real sense the soul of the client touches the soul of the practitioner. They are now both moving in the realm of the spirit, the divine, the source of all life. In the intimate encounter of soul touching soul, an unexpected psychic wire may be tripped for practitioners, and uncomfortable feelings may suddenly emerge. The vulnerability may reveal unresolved personal conflicts of which they were not consciously aware.

In *When the Spirits Come Back*, Janet O. Dallett documents a therapeutic encounter that opened psychological wounds she thought were healed sufficiently for her to facilitate the healing journey of her patient. She discovered however that the intensity of the connection caused powerful feelings to emerge as it activated 'godlike and demonic projections' in her dreams (Dallett 1988, p.70). Her knowledge of symbol and archetypes[5], as well as her training as an analyst allowed her to maintain a therapeutic relationship with her client when these feelings and images assaulted her. In that she devoted four chapters to this experience, we can surmise that the incident shook her to the core of her being. Indeed, much of the book documents Dallett's 'dark night of the soul'[6], in which she examined almost ruthlessly her motivation for becoming an analyst and the reasons why she wanted to continue.

What did Dallett learn? She became aware of three related issues. First, that a therapist's ability to facilitate the healing journey of a client is directly related to her progress in healing the wounds of her own life. Second, therapists will inadvertently project onto their clients any difficulties they have not yet resolved in their own lives – which can be disastrous for the client. Indeed, her client regressed as a result of her inner turmoil. Third, Dallett became aware that people are often attracted to the study of psychology because of their own 'troubled' backgrounds (pp.11–24). Their fascination with the mind and human behavior is an attempt to understand their own experiences in order to transcend them and live happy and whole adult lives. Could this also explain the 'call' to social work for some practitioners?

To borrow Hillman's language, perhaps some social workers may have heard their *daimon* whispering to them at an early age that pain and suffering did not have the last word in their lives, that it was not the totality of their existence, and that they were called to a life of healing and service to others. However, for social workers to be effective healers, they must first begin the healing journey in their own lives, as Janet O. Dallett was compelled to do. Like Dallett, their journey may also involve a kind of 'dark night of the soul'. However, if social workers understand the spiritual dynamism at work in this interior journey, they need not be afraid. With guidance and compassion for oneself and others, one always emerges on the other side – where increased awareness, love and freedom are waiting[7].

The shamanic journey: the courage to confront one's fears

In the history of religions, there is a specific name for people who are self-healed healers. They are called shamans (Eliade 1964, p.8). They are central to the health and well-being of the community because their unique function is to rescue a person from soul-loss in order to restore spiritual balance to the community.

Now the concept of soul-loss may seem foreign to social workers until we compare its meaning with the word 'diabolic'[8]. Soul-loss means that one suffers from such a profound loss of meaning and value that one is cast adrift in society and can no longer find one's way. 'Diabolic' means to throw apart (Eastham 1991, pp.205–206; Partridge 1959, p.825). How often have practitioners encountered such pain, suffering and injustice that they intuited that 'diabolic' forces may be at work? These forces are cosmic, social and personal. They tear us apart from our soul, our deepest self, that part of us that longs for health and healing.

In every society where shamanic practices endure, shamans are honored as the most balanced people in the community. Stability is imperative, for to rescue a person from soul-loss, the shaman's soul must be intact. From their teachers and their own ecstatic[9], experiences, they have learned a great deal about life, both its light and darkness, and know therefore that evil can be fatally fascinating. Once shamans rescue a lost soul, therefore, they must leave the underworld immediately, lest they too become trapped there. When the shamanic journey is complete, the act of healing and atonement (*at-one-ment*) can take place. The spiritual balance of the community is restored once the person has achieved inner peace – both within themselves and the community at large.

Shamans are able to make this journey for those unable to do it for themselves because they have found the courage and strength to make the healing journey in their own lives. This is always a perilous journey, because they must confront all the negative forces in their own life – not only their own doubts, fears and pain – but sometime also all the psychic baggage their family has never dealt with[10]. In his classic work, *The Hero with a Thousand Faces*, mythologist Joseph Campbell documents the healing journey of countless 'heroes' who have functioned as shamans for their community. He has found the structure to be similar throughout the world: 'separation–initiation–return' (Campbell 1949, p.30). The hero hears the call to be a special servant to the community, rejects the call initially, receives divine intervention to strengthen their resolve, goes into the wilderness to confront their demons and emerges victorious on the other side (Campbell 1949, pp.49–238). Campbell rightly calls it an heroic journey because it requires strength to begin it, discipline to sustain it, and courage to be faithful to it.

Consistent with our idea of vocation, shamans hear an inner voice early in their lives calling them to become healers. In many instances, elders recognize their special gifts before they themselves become aware of them. Like the *daimon* at work in every human life, elders encourage and often challenge a young person to accept his or her destiny. However, no one can be forced to do something against their will. Coercion violates the very dynamism of vocation, which is always a response in freedom to serve the healing forces of life in the universe.

Once the shamanic journey has been endured, the person is reborn. Every aspect of reality has been transfigured for them. In *Myths to Live By*, Joseph Campbell describes the 'rebirth' of a self-rescued patient on experiencing spontaneous remission: 'The grass was greener, the sun was shining brighter, and people were more alive, I could see them clearer. I could see

the bad things and the good things and all that. I was much more aware'
(Campbell 1972, pp.236–237)[11].

Note that the heightened awareness is of both good and evil. Note also
that the shamanic experience described above appears to have taken place
over a finite period of time. However, the healing experience at the heart of
the shamanic journey can occur for anyone without the dramatic intensity
of going out into the desert for 40 days and 40 nights. In *Ordinary People as
Monks and Mystics: Lifestyles for Self-Discovery*, Marsha Sinetar maintains that
anyone who seeks to become whole and healthy can accomplish this goal
by obeying the inner voice within them. Sinetar, who calls herself a spiritual psychologist, defines this process precisely as 'vocation': 'Anyone who
answers the yearning of the inner self is *called*, has a vocation, in the
original sense of that word, which was "to be addressed by a voice"'
(Sinetar 1986, p.19). Provided one is willing to dedicate a portion of each
day to attend to the inner voice calling one to wholeness, one can be
healed. This process is called contemplation.

Contemplation: healing what has been cut apart

Contemplation is not a will-o'-the-wisp activity with no practical
outcome, far from it. Contemplation requires the total engagement of the
person: mind, body and spirit. Through contemplation, one connects with
the life-giving forces of the universe in order to heal the entire creation.
This is no small order. The Greek root of the word contemplation is
temnein, which means to cut. *Contemplation*, therefore, means joining
together what has been cut apart. Through contemplation we rediscover
our innate wholeness and embody it with courage and tenacity. This
wholeness has been ripped apart by the vicissitudes of life – not only suffering and injustice but also the economic and political structures of
modern life, which cannot nurture the spiritual dimension of life.

Contemplation opens a clear space in the human heart so that the
divine or greater self can be experienced. In *A Return to Spirit: After the
Mythic Church*, Desmond Murphy defines the inner or higher self as 'the
source of inner harmony, wisdom, love, creativity, intuition and inner
promptings to integration and wholeness' (Murphy 1997, p.83). In contemplation, the inner self is awakened by lifting the mask of the ego, which

is not only socially constructed but also functions as a kind of coping mechanism to protect one from pain. Whether one is following an Eastern or Western spiritual path, contemplation is the process of letting go of fixed ideas about life or oneself, listening intently to the inner voice that is making real demands, and being willing to change. Christian Desmond Murphy calls this process 'active-passive surrender': '"Active" involves the choice to cooperate with life and not to fight it. "Passive" indicates that the ego relaxes its boundaries to allow the integration of deeper realities' (Murphy 1997, p.199).

Paradoxically, this movement from ego to self is not perceived as a loss of self, but as an encounter with the higher self at the deepest levels of one's being. Contemplatives often describe the experience with the language of paradox: finding oneself in the process of losing oneself. This language would suggest that some degree of conflict is often involved. Indeed, in some instances the inner turmoil can be excruciating. At the beginning of *The Divine Comedy*, Dante writes: 'In the middle of the journey of our life, I came to myself within a dark wood where the straight way was lost' (Sinclair 1939, p.23). The dark wood Dante entered was the totality of his life, the world of unresolved hurts and fears that lie waiting for resolution. To achieve wholeness and healing, Dante was called to integrate every dimension of his life into a harmonious whole. Indeed, *The Divine Comedy* is the artistic expression of this arduous work of personal integration which led to spiritual transformation (Nicholl 1997, p.70).

A surprising element of this personal rebirth is that one does not experience a completely new personality or even freedom from neurosis. In *After the Ecstasy, the Laundry: How the Heart Grows Wise on the Spiritual Path*, American Buddhist monk Jack Kornfield quotes a 58-year-old teacher who describes his 'awakening' experience: 'Here were these cosmic revelations and I still needed therapy just to sort through the day-to-day mistakes and lessons of living a human life' (Kornfield 2000, p.xvi). This quotation indicates that contemplation is not therapy. It does not change our personality, but it does enable us to live more compassionately with ourselves and be more true to who we really are.

The process of contemplation produces an authentically spiritual person who can celebrate the goodness of life despite its messiness, limitations and imperfections. Through contemplation, one comes to see limitations as a source of freedom. For only in recognizing that we cannot do everything or be everything can we embrace totally what we can do. Thus, contemplation results in authentic reconciliation within oneself and those closest to us. Not only have our deepest wounds been incurred within these networks of intimate relationships, but we have often hurt ourselves and others by not acknowledging limitations – either our own or others'. Contemplation heals these wounds by putting us in touch with our greatest self, and through this encounter, with the power of forgiveness.

Contemplation and social action

Every wisdom tradition teaches that contemplation leads to greater social awareness and concern. If not, the person is not truly following a spiritual path. Just as contemplation leads to social action, authentic action leads to deeper levels of reflection. This process is called 'praxis'. Through a rigorous process of fasting and prayer, Gandhi, for example, came to reinterpret the symbol of non-injury into the social ethic of nonviolent resistance by which he called the people of India to participate in the process of sociopolitical revolution (Erikson 1969, pp.395–406).

Social workers are involved with social change. Merv Hancock comments: 'If you only talk about what can be achieved by changing the structures, then you are going to miss the individual. The two are inseparable and must go hand in hand' (Munford and Nash 1994, p.9). So too the healing conversation cannot begin for victims of social injustice until they become aware of the connection between the dysfunctional elements of their lives and the unjust conditions that have created the emotional, psychological and physical illnesses: 'events such as unemployment, bad housing or homelessness, racist or sexist experiences' (Waldegrave and Tamasese 1994, pp.110–111). When these external conditions were addressed so that people did not blame themselves for illnesses caused by these events, the healing conversation could begin.

Because contemplation leads to social awareness and political action, it is imperative that social workers begin the hard work of personal reconciliation in their own lives. Too often the angry revolutionary becomes the oppressor once tables are overturned and the new regime established.

Social workers must rage in their hearts against the violence which victimizes the most vulnerable members of the community, such as children or the elderly. Thus, to be advocates of change, social workers must also be advocates of conversion and personal reconciliation. Jack Kornfield (2000) writes: 'If we want to overcome greed, racism, exploitation, and hatred, to end suffering and bring our lives into harmony with the earth, we must see that the fundamental crisis is in human consciousness' (p.274).

Is this enough? Can anyone be content with this 'limited' contribution? We may take heart from what chaos theory has come to call the 'butterfly effect' (or sensitive dependence on initial conditions). In *Seven Lessons of Chaos: Spiritual Wisdom from the Science of Change*, John Briggs and David Peat explain how 'sensitivity comes from the fact that even small increases in temperature, wind speed, or air pressure cycle through the system and can end up having a major impact' (Briggs and Peat 1999, p.33). Applied to the realm of human affairs, this would suggest that every authentic action, good or bad, has a rippling effect throughout the cosmos. Peats cites the example of Rosa Parks to illustrate how her authentic action of refusing to give up her seat on a segregated bus in Montgomery, Alabama, transformed the consciousness of the United States on the issue of 'institutionalized racism' (Briggs and Peat 1999, p.50)[12].

Contemplatives like Thomas Merton are among the most highly conscientized people in the world. They are also the most peaceful. They have learned to trust the healing powers of the universe as they have discovered their own inner reservoirs of healing and wholeness. They have also been able to facilitate the awakening and healing of countless people – not only in their lifetimes, but long after their deaths. The same man who wrote *The Seven Storey Mountain* (1948) later wrote *Conjectures of a Guilty Bystander (1968)*. The first tells the story of why a young man who had it all, in secular terms, would enter a Trappist monastery at age 26 and take a vow of silence. Why? To become whole and truly alive by becoming awake, aware and at peace. The second book is a reflection of every contemporary issue of the 20th century from the perspective of a Christian who believed fervently that peace and justice could be the way of the world.

Neither Merton nor Gandhi believed they were called to save the world all by themselves. However, each knew he was called to do his part, and if he embraced that call with integrity, it would be enough. Life would do the rest.

Strategies to nurture the nurturer

People who have assumed the responsibility for nurturing others must themselves be healthy and whole. This is easier said than done. Parents know this; working parents especially know how easy it is to forget to nurture oneself when pressed with the demands of family and work. It somehow seems selfish to nurture oneself – until one becomes ill. Then, when the family routine collapses and one is unable to carry out professional responsibilities, we reproach ourselves for our stupidity. Why didn't we pay attention to the symptoms? How can anyone think they are indispensable at work? Unique and irreplaceable, maybe; indispensable, no. There is always someone else who can take up the job. They won't do it the way you do, but they'll get the job done.

These insights are sobering. They are not intended to smash one's professional self-esteem, but rather to make the point that unless people nurture their total well-being – physical, intellectual, and spiritual – they will not be able to nurture anyone else. And this fact requires all those in the healing professions to make some serious time for themselves.

In *Ordinary People as Monks and Mystics,* Marsha Sinetar studied people who were seriously striving to lead a life they considered to be healthy and whole. She wanted to document the experiences of people who were aware of an inner call to wholeness and discover how they had to arrange their lives to make this possible. Everyone she studied, from business people to teachers, had to find some way to simplify their lives in order to attend to the yearnings of their soul. For some this meant giving up their job; for others it meant moving to the country. For still others, it meant time away from partners and children – even if some people interpreted their craving for solitude as selfish. For all, it meant dedicating their lives to the interior journey, and realiszing that this would be a life-long process. Sinetar concluded: 'Many realized that by preserving their strength and by cultivating their new sense of purpose, they would, in the long run, be better equipped to serve others' (Sinetar 1986, p.42).

If applied to social workers, these insights suggest the following practical strategies. First, though social workers may not have the luxury to work part-time or move to the country, anyone should be able to restructure their day to make room for an hour that is theirs and theirs alone. Second, contemplative work must be done in solitude and silence so that one can become well acquainted with one's heart and soul. Third, this time apart must become a daily discipline so that one can begin to experience the fruits of the interior journey: greater awareness, inner harmony and trust in the goodness of life.

Because social workers deal with people in pain, it is imperative that they embrace this difficult inner work. As Janet O. Dallett discovered, they must be faithful to the interior journey – wherever it may lead them. Some may discover that their desire to become social workers stemmed from unresolved suffering in their lives. Were it not for this pain driving them in mysterious, unconscious ways, they might have chosen a different path. They may find themselves, therefore, at a professional crossroads, where different choices become imperative. Contemplation will make them aware of their motives, strengths and limitations. Still others may come to rejoice in how the presence of pain and suffering awakened in them the desire to become a healer. Were it not for these experiences, they may have remained ignorant of their own depths. Moreover, they might never have come to see their lives as a calling: to heal themselves, others and, little by little, the wide world of troubles we all share.

Notes

1. Not all practitioners in professions of social care will be comfortable with the existentially loaded concept of 'vocation'. Moreover, many of these professionals might be among the most ethical and conscientious practitioners. The use of explicitly religious language may jar them for many reasons, not the least of which might be the single-minded zeal often associated with people who believe themselves to have a divine mission in history and society. History is replete with examples of horrific destruction when religious zeal

fuels social and political causes. We need look no further than the Middle East itself, the cradle of this powerful sense of personal and national identity, to see the intrinsic conflict of interest between the heirs of Abraham. For as we know, both Israel and Ishmael were his sons, and both believed themselves to have a holy mission in history.

For these reasons, the separation of church from state occurred for humanitarian, practical reasons in the West. After the bloody wars of the Reformation, it was the only way the public sphere could be exorcized of its religious demons. Centuries later, the West faces a different challenge. The rigid separation of church and state goes hand in hand with the ideology of secularism which makes it difficult for 'enlightened' citizens to address the spiritual and moral dimension of many public issues. Scientific and technological problems have tended to be regarded as 'secular' issues to be resolved through a scientific, technological reasoning which might be called the 'instrumental reason' (Habermas 1984). This kind of reasoning can only see what its methodology permits. It cannot see the big picture because a more holistic way of looking at human problems requires intellectual tools not available to the 'technician'. The grave crises facing human beings in the 21st century – the continued threat of nuclear war, a rapidly decaying environment, the AIDS epidemic, the widening gap between rich and poor nations, etc. – have persuaded many scholars across disciplines to conceive and address all human concerns as spiritual, moral, scientific and technological. In this way, the whole person embedded in a complex environment can be addressed.

2.   It is important to define how the words 'spirit' and 'soul' will be used in this chapter, because they are related in meaning but not interchangeable. The traditional meaning of the word 'spirit' is the life force whether it is used to describe the life force within the person or the source of life itself. If I use the word to refer to the source of life itself, I will use the term 'spirit'. The traditional meaning of the word 'soul' is the essence of one's being, what makes us who we are. It often takes a lifetime to discover who we really are because of our social conditioning and the masks we wear to survive.

3.   The negative and positive power of the spirit, the life force, can also
       be explained in psychological terms. In *The Wisdom of No Escape and
       the Path of Loving Kindness*, Buddhist nun Pema Chodron explains:
       'The basic creative energy of life – life force – bubbles up and
       courses through all of existence. It can be experienced as open, free,
       unburdened, full of possibility, energizing. Or this same energy can
       be experienced as petty, narrow, stuck, caught' (Chodron 1991,
       pp.21–22).

4.   In *A Return to Spirit: After the Mythic Church*, Desmond Murphy (1997)
       defines transference as 'the unconscious displacement of unresolved
       feelings and attitudes from a primary relationship figure to another
       significant relationship figure (in this case, therapist or spiritual
       director)' (p.210).

5.   Desmond Murphy defines 'existential archetypes' as 'inherited forms
       that distil aspects of life experienced by every human – life, death,
       birth, mother, father, and so on' (Murphy 1997, p.230).

6.   The phrase 'dark night of the soul' is usually associated with the
       Catholic mystic John of the Cross. In his writings, he describes 'the
       processes of spiritual purification, through trials and temptations and
       through deliberate detachment from external things', as he tried to
       live in union with God (McBrien 1981, pp.1067–68).

7.   In her book *Journey to Freedom*, Leslie Kenton documents 13
       quantum leaps for the soul. Her research brings together ancient
       shamanic practices with leading-edge physics, biology, systems
       theory and consciousness research to present the shamanic journey
       as a passage to greater levels of freedom and awareness (Kenton
       1998, p.1). As she sees it, the main ingredient for a successful
       passage is compassion for self and others.

8.   The high rate of suicide in New Zealand would suggest that many
       young people suffer from soul-loss. This is especially true among
       young males whose flirtation with violence suggests that they are in
       need of the kind of initiation rituals documented by Joseph
       Campbell (1949) in his classic work *The Hero with the Thousand Faces.*
       Indeed, Campbell suggests in another book, *The Power of Myth,* that
       the popularity of movies like *Star Wars* indicates that many young

men crave the kind of heroic journey Luke Skywalker undergoes in the film, but do not know how to do so (Campbell 1988, pp.144–147).

9.   The word 'ecstatic' refers to the religious experience of heightened awareness in which one feels himself or herself to be in harmony with all of creation and with God, the unknown source of it all.

10. According to Janet O. Dallett, the healing journey is often perilous because any depth encounter with the soul will touch 'the stuff of mysticism, creativity and madness, all three' (Dallet 1988, p.153). Without a doubt, this is a realm of great spiritual power, both positive and negative. Not only repressed wounds will surface but also encounters with archetypal figures like gods and demons. For this reason, the initiate does not make the journey alone. He or she is always accompanied by an elder. If not, a person could experience a psychological breakdown.

11. Note that Campbell's 'self-rescued patient' has undergone rebirth by experiencing spontaneous remission from a serious illness, such as cancer. The link between soul, mind and body is again being recognized by many in the medical establishment. For thousands of years, people believed that many physical illnesses had a spiritual component. Thus, to heal the body, one must also heal the spirit. The converse is also true.

12. Rosa Parks was a black American who refused to give up her seat on a segregated bus in Montgomery, Alabama. In so doing, she ignited a flame of bitterness and resentment that was just waiting for a spark and became a symbol of nonviolent resistance in the American civil rights movement of the 1960s.

References

Briggs, J. and Peat, D. (1999) *Seven Lessons of Chaos: Spiritual Wisdom from the Science of Change.* New York: Harper Perennial.

Cahill, T. (1998) *The Gifts of the Jews: How a Tribe of Desert Nomads Changed the Way Everyone Thinks and Feels.* New York: Doubleday.

Campbell, J. (1949/1968) *The Hero with a Thousand Faces.* New Jersey: Princeton University Press.

Campbell, J. (1972/1982) *Myths to Live By.* Toronto: Bantam Books.

Campbell, J. (1988) *The Power of Myth with Bill Moyers.* New York: Doubleday.

Chodron, P. (1991) *The Wisdom of No Escape and the Path of Loving-Kindness.* Boston and London: Shambala.

Dallett, J.O. (1988) *When the Spirits Come Back.* Canada: Inner City Books.

Eastham, S.T. (1991) *The Radix or the Original Radical Poem.* Bern/New York: Peter Lang Publishers.

Eliade, M. (1964/1974) *Shamanism: Archaic Techniques of Ecstasy.* New Jersey: Princeton University Press.

Erikson, E.H. (1969) *Gandhi's Truth: On the Origins of Militant Nonviolence.* New York: W.W. Norton and company

Habermas, J. (1984) *Theory of Communicative Action I & II.* Translated by T. McCarthy. Cambridge: Polity Press.

Hancock, M. (1994) 'Preface: A Conversation with Merv Hancock' in R. Mumford and M. Nash (eds) *Social Work in Action.* Palmerston North: The Dunmore Press.

Hillman, J. (1996) *The Soul's Code: In Search of Character and Calling.* Australia: Random House.

Kenton, L. (1998) *Journey to Freedom: 13 Quantum Leaps for the Soul.* London: HarperCollins.

Kornfield, J. (2000) *After the Ecstasy, the Laundry: How the Heart Grows Wise on the Spiritual Path.* London: Rider.

May, J. (1994) 'Developing an Integrated Approach to practice: A Christian Perspective'. In R. Munford and M. Nash (eds) *Social Work in Action.* Palmerston North: The Dunmore Press.

McBrien, R. (1981) *Catholicism.* Minneapolis: Winston Press.

Merton, T. (1948) *The Seven Storey Mountain.* New York: Harcourt, Brace and Co.

Merton, T. (1968) *Conjectures of a Guilty Bystander.* New York: Image Books.

Munford, R. and Nash, M. (eds) (1994) *Social work in Action.* Palmerston North: The Dunmore Press.

Murphy, D. (1997) *A Return to Spirit: After the Mythic Church.* Australia: E.J. Dwyer.

Nicholl, D. (1997) *The Beatitude of Truth: Reflections of a Lifetime.* London: Darton, Longman and Todd.

Otto, R. (1923/1969) *The Idea of the Holy.* London: Oxford University Press.

Partridge, E. (1959) *Origins.* New York: Macmillan.

Sinclair, J.D. (1939/1970) *Dante's Inferno.* New York: Oxford University Press.

Sinetar, M. (1986) *Ordinary People as Monks and Mystics: Lifestyles for Self-Discovery.* New York: Paulist Press.

Waldegrave, C. and Tamasese, K. (1994) 'Some Central Ideas in the "Just Therapy" approach.' In R. Munford and M. Nash (eds) *Social Work in Action.* Palmerston North: The Dunmore Press.

Chapter Four

Spirituality and Volunteers
The Leaven in the Dough

Mary Woods

Introduction

This chapter looks at the particular issues surrounding spirituality and the involvement of volunteers in spiritual care. Volunteers as board members promote an organization's vision and, as caregivers, they complement the work of professionals. Volunteers' motivations arise from a wide range of sources including spirituality. Energy from spiritual sources enables some volunteers to work with people in very hard situations. Managers need to be aware of the spiritual content of volunteers' motivations in order to make appropriate placements and to create a climate which encourages their continued effective involvement. The final section gives some practical examples of spirituality in action with volunteers.

Questions included in the text invite the reader to reflect on the ideas presented in the light of their own experience.

Volunteers in social care

Volunteers are people who choose to work for reasons other than money. They are not paid for the work they do, though, it is hoped, they are reimbursed for any expenses they incur. Volunteers in social care are found in various roles. They can be board members, administrators, fundraisers or caregivers delivering the services of an agency. They might be more than one of these. Many voluntary agencies are directed by a board made up of volunteers. They have responsibility for the continuation of the mission and work of the agency and setting the management policy. Sometimes this role extends to management duties, administration tasks and fundraising. As board members they uphold the vision that is the basis of a voluntary organization. This vision often arises from the spirituality of the people who set an organization up and those who choose to continue to be its leaders.

Many volunteers are caregivers. They are counselors on crisis phone lines, visitors and supporters of people who are housebound through age or disability, leaders in community development groups, peer supporters in self-help groups. They provide a wide range of services: companionship, transport, a listening ear, specialized counseling, physical help and care, budget advice, preparation and delivery of meals, community celebrations, information, advocacy, leadership, etc. Volunteer caregivers complement the work of paid social workers and counselors by offering different skills, or being able to give an individual person more time than a paid worker with a busy case load. Sometimes the volunteer's relationship with the person receiving help is different from that of the professional simply because they are there by voluntary choice.

Volunteers are often the people who provide a link between an institution (e.g. hospital or prison) and the community. They are also the people who first respond to specific community needs or who risk working with a new idea. Many of the larger voluntary agencies started out with total volunteer effort and later began to employ paid staff to cope with expanding demands. Volunteers are lay people or professionals in various fields. They come with their life experience, their work experience and often with training specific to their roles.

Motivation

Volunteers fill needs in their lives by their voluntary work. The image of the volunteer as a true altruist is in most cases a myth. In reality the motivation of an individual volunteer is usually complex and mixed. Some will respond to human need because of their religious or humanist spirituality. Some will see the benefit to the whole community when the neediest are empowered. Some want to develop new skills, gain work experience, feel useful, or simply make a connection with other people.

The needs that move a person to volunteer can be generalized into the need to belong and be with other people, the need to achieve, and the need for power, either personal or social (Woods 1998, pp.28–44). Motivation involves meeting a range of human needs. Significant among the range of motivators is meeting spiritual needs.

Think of your own experience or that of other people you know; what motivations have you found that people have for volunteering?

Spirituality

Spirituality is a fundamental part of being human. Its lack of tangibility makes it hard to define, yet it is experienced in very tangible ways. It is part of integration and wholeness. Stephen Covey says: 'The spiritual dimension is your core, your center, your commitment to your value system. It draws upon the sources that inspire and uplift you and tie you to the timeless truths of all humanity. And people do it very, very differently' (Covey 1989, p.292). Our spirituality drives us to seek spiritual well-being. After interviewing many New Zealanders, Eileen Shamy concluded:

> Spiritual well being is the affirmation of life in a relationship with God, self, community and environment that nurtures and celebrates wholeness. It is the strong sense that I am 'kept' and 'held' by Someone greater than myself who 'keeps' the whole of creation, giving life meaning and purpose. It is the sure knowledge that I am part of that meaning and purpose. (Shamy 1996, p.57)

Spiritual energy comes from within and without. It is tied into our culture, values and beliefs and yet is beyond them. It is part of the uniqueness of each human person. When individuals were asked what they understood about the spirituality of volunteering, they came up with words and phrases like 'compassion', 'sharing pain', 'sharing joy', 'growth', 'sharing resources', 'interdependence', 'walking beside', 'connectedness', 'rooted in time, place and personal story' and 'rooted in history'. It involves gifting to and receiving from. It requires respect and reverence for people. It grows from a sense of wonder, honoring the gifts of life and creation (Woods 1998, p.40). The ability to forgive and be reconciled is a spiritual gift.

What words would you use to describe the spirituality of volunteering?
Spirituality involves the recognition of a 'God' beyond our humanity, or a 'higher power' outside of ourselves, however we choose to describe that higher power. In Christian terms it is the spirit of God acting in our lives. It is about freedom and growth.

But is spirituality always a positive force?
Is there a negative spiritual force or does negativity simply result from the absence of spiritual well-being? Volunteers will come to an organization with a range of spiritual needs. They may be spiritually well or spiritually unwell. This will also be true of the people they care for. Sometimes the spiritual attributes in people's lives are not positive ones: hurts are nursed and held on to, personal power is wielded over people to belittle them in relation to self and a person's own needs are met at the expense of others.

A negative spirit may be overt and expressed in a group's declared values. Or it may be covert and hidden in the environment of a charitable organization or religious group or culture that promotes judgement of, and damnation for, those who are outside its realm. It shows itself in racism, sexism, ageism or any movement that oppresses another group in society. In an individual such negativity can grow from life experiences that have stunted spiritual and personal development.

Spirituality and organized religion

Because people often equate spirituality with religion, it is important to separate these two. While many people choose to express their spirituality through religion, organized religion does not encompass the whole of spirituality. Spirituality is a universal human aspect. Some very religious people would not limit their spiritual expression to church observance.

Many other people understand and express their spirituality totally outside any religious affiliation. For some, organized religion is the antithesis of spirituality and some people who describe themselves as atheists may also claim a spiritual base for their volunteer work in the community.

Church members often exhibit a range in their volunteering. Some choose to volunteer within the church community or in the wider community in the name of their church. It is easy to identify a religious element and assume a spiritual component in such work. However, many church people are committed to causes outside their church and this commitment also has a spiritual base. When church people are inspired by their spirituality to volunteer outside their church community they may or may not be intent on proselytizing or trying to convert people. Unfortunately proselytizing does sometimes happen but in the provision of effective social care, spirituality can give transcendence over the need to convert and lead to attitudes of respect and reverence towards each person.

Spirituality as a motivator of volunteers

As humans, body, mind and spirit are all interwoven in our being as part of how and why we do things. The whole concept of volunteering acknowledges the need of people to work for goals that are not material. To leave spiritual goals out of this is to be incomplete. For many volunteers their motivation and source of energy is spiritual and this operates alongside other motivators.

Spirituality is a source of life-giving energy that goes beyond ordinary commitment. It goes beyond working for gain, even non-financial gain. It goes against the predominant culture of many societies. But its acknowledgement is important in the universe of volunteer work because it is a significant motivator and source of energy for many volunteers. Exceptional people like Mother Teresa of Calcutta, who cared for the sick and dying regardless of their beliefs, can be seen as motivated by a spirituality which transcends their own personal need. They are our beacons. But there are also lots of ordinary folk too who work from a spiritual base when they volunteer.

A person's desire for spiritual well-being is often behind their choice of the cause they volunteer to work for. 'To love my neighbor as myself' inspires people to volunteer in caring situations. Wanting to 'right a wrong' can motivate people to work with the victims or survivors of various sorts of abuse. The need to make reparation for a previous perceived wrong can motivate a choice. Liberation theology that came from South America is the spiritual force that drives many who work to right injustice. Spirituality will inspire people to give their cause energy far and beyond what might seem 'reasonable'.

How the spirituality of the carer affects their view of the receiver of service

A volunteer who is in touch with their own spirituality is more likely to recognize the spirituality of the person they may be caring for. This can result in the receiver of help being treated with a greater respect and reverence. Spirituality does influence and grow from how we relate to the people around us and how we view our participation in our community. And while it may not be valid to give directions of causation, spirituality is a factor in why people undertake to do really difficult caring work where they see no returns for their efforts. These are the people who grapple with the hard issues of life – the volunteer who sits with a person dying of AIDS, the volunteer who sings to a person whose intellectual disability prevents them from responding in any recognizable way, the volunteer who drives an incontinent elderly person to see a garden in spring. It is the spirituality of the carer which recognizes the spirituality of the person they are caring for and allows them to look beyond the inevitable end, the lack of response, and the messed-up car seats. It is also the spirituality of the carer that enables them to recognize the spiritual needs of the other – the need for someone to be with them especially on the final journey of life, the need for music even if they can't sing and the need to be in a beautiful environment especially when life is messy.

How does your spirituality shape how you view the people you care for?

Spirituality in the management and selection of volunteers

Any person in an organization who has responsibility for managing volunteers needs to know and understand their motivation. The manager needs to explore with volunteers how their motivation fits with the tasks they are to do and the people they are to serve, remembering that motivation is usually mixed.

A good manager will take their volunteers seriously by ensuring that all the tasks of managing them are carried out. They will have clear job descriptions, orientation processes, training and supervision. They will encourage communication and take the trouble to ensure that both paid staff and volunteers are aware of where they interface and complement each other's work. There will be funds available to reimburse expenses incurred in being a volunteer. They will acknowledge the contribution made by their volunteers and let them know they are appreciated. They will create an affirming atmosphere for volunteers, that recognizes the spiritual aspects of their motivation and their work.

In selecting people to do caring work a manager needs to understand motivations of volunteers. While a wide range of acceptance of differing motivations is needed, sometimes the motivation of a volunteer will be an indicator of their unsuitability for a particular sort of work. This is particularly true of spiritual motivations and the crossover point between spiritual and religious motivations if the helper has an agenda of converting the person being helped to their own particular brand of spirituality. Often this exhibits itself in an inability to listen and accept difference. A rather negative story demonstrates this point:

> Penny was tired and sick. She was a mother alone with three preschoolers. Her house was messy and dirty and she couldn't work up enough energy to get beyond the mess. A volunteer came to help her clean her house, but, shocked at the state of her fridge, chose to tell her that if she just prayed all her problems would be solved. Penny's response was that she had prayed for someone to help her clean her house!

This is the sort of story that gives volunteers a bad press. The helper was putting her own spirituality on the person she was there to give practical help to. She was also failing to listen to the simple practical request, let alone the far more complex needs that were beneath the basic request.

The problem here is not the spirituality of the helper. Many very constructive workers support their work with prayer, but it is their own prayer in their own belief system. The problem here is the mismatch between the helper's spirituality and her role as carer. She was trying to impose her own spiritual solution on another person whose spirituality was different and whose need from her at this point was purely practical. This can be a rather difficult area and calls on the person with responsibility for selecting volunteers to have the skill to identify a mismatch of spiritual values without indulging in religious discrimination.

It requires that volunteers have a clear job description outlining roles and boundaries and good ongoing training and supervision support. If spirituality is recognized in these processes, the closely related issues of spirituality and values can be worked upon and the volunteer can develop their sensitivity and skill. If they can't then maybe a hard decision is called for. Volunteers offer what they have to give, but if what they are offering does not fit the need of the person receiving the service it is unwise to accept the offer. Inappropriate help is at best a disservice and at worst can be damaging. A good manager of volunteers knows that it is fine to refuse a volunteer's offer of help or to dismiss a volunteer. In fact sometimes it is irresponsible not to.

Creating a climate which encourages spiritual well-being

Spirituality is by its nature intangible. Yet essentially we experience it and express it in very practical ways. In living our spirituality we use all of our senses. It is easier to do spirituality than to talk and write about it. Can an essay on poetry ever adequately describe a poem? Can a chapter on spirituality ever do justice to the breadth of spirituality? Human needs are physical, psychological, social and spiritual. These do not function separately in our lives but in wholeness interacting at all times and in all situations. To deny the influence of a person's spiritual well-being on their lives is to deny part of themselves. Burnout develops from such a denial.

Spirituality is acknowledged when the importance and uniqueness of each volunteer is recognized. Time is given to recognize people, to greet them, to show an interest in their work and at appropriate times to thank them genuinely. Significant events are celebrated or commiserated with. Individual volunteers' needs are acknowledged by their peers and the people in the organization who have responsibility for them.

How volunteers are received into an organization will shape how they will treat the receivers of the service. Volunteers will be encouraged and perform well if they feel their spirituality is being recognized. They will experience this in the atmosphere created within their organization. Groups can create a climate of hospitality, which encourages the spiritual well-being of their members. Hospitality nurtures spirituality in making a person feel welcome, whether it is the volunteer or the person receiving the service. It involves stopping to welcome the person who arrives, giving them undivided attention and making them feel they are right to be there. It often includes sharing food or drink. Hospitality is a truly spiritual action.

How do you recognize when you are being spiritually nurtured?
The nurturing of spirituality needs time and suitable space. In an organizational setting, diverse spiritual needs have to be met in such a way that is relevant to the needs of the individuals and the focus of the group. Physical surroundings can impact on the spirituality of the people working in them.

Think of the room where volunteers work or gather. Does it have windows? Is there a view of sky or sea or hills or trees? Or is the view of the back of another building? Maybe the room is totally closed-in giving a feeling of imprisonment.
The place where volunteers gather is important. Often they are working for organizations that are on a tight budget in low rental rooms. Spending money on decor with a corporate image would be at odds with the philosophy and culture of their organization. But there are other ways of bringing nature in and indicating that people matter. Flowers, candles, symbols, photos and pictures that relate to the spirit and purpose of the group create an atmosphere that enhances spiritual development. Even stones and water can introduce a spiritual atmosphere. Volunteers are likely to want to make their own contributions, such as flowers from their own gardens or pieces of their own artwork or a joint effort such as a collage or

a quilt. Photos of volunteers doing their work or coming together for celebrations all record their participation and create for them a sense of
belonging and acknowledgement. These are spiritual attributes.

Allowing time and opportunity to enjoy nature can also nurture spirits.
Maybe part of a team-building exercise or a celebration could be carried
out at a park or a garden or a beach. A lunch time walk outside in the fresh
air can both renew jaded spirits and encourage reflection. Smell is spiritually evocative. The smell of incense has spiritual meaning for someone
who grew up attending a church that used lots of incense in its ceremonies.
But influenced perhaps by Eastern religions the burning of incense has
become quite commonplace to create a spiritual atmosphere:

> Kate had a sense of disturbance in the room she worked in and felt it
> needed to be spiritually cleansed. She proposed to do this by burning
> incense – a simple acceptable spiritual action.

Spirituality has its own language and jargon; 'cleansing the room' has a
spiritual connotation different from 'cleaning the room'.

How would you choose to nurture spirituality in the volunteer workplace?
The general ambience and way people treat each other in an organization
affirm the spirituality of volunteers and other people involved in giving
and receiving the service. But there are other more specific ways that the
spirituality of volunteers can be nurtured. These are by reading, reflection
and ritual, and a brief overview of each approach follows.

READING TO NURTURE SPIRITUALITY

Anne Wilson Schaef says 'Our spirituality is experiential, and it is intimately connected with who we are' (Schaef 1990, 'February 6' page). Different people will choose different ways of identifying their own spirituality and what actions they need to take to nurture it. This may be a style of
prayer or meditation or it might be in reading what others have written.
One way spirituality is nurtured is by sharing insights with people who
come from a similar belief system.

Essential to my own spirituality is the acceptance that others equally
are entitled to their own forms of spirituality. But I find that in being

general and inclusive I am not expressing the passion that fuels my spirituality, so for a moment I want to cast off generality and write about the particular books that nurtured my spirituality as a volunteer. Books gave me access to the thoughts of writers across the world. As a Christian woman I look to the Bible, but I look also to the insights of practitioners who have considered the Christian spirituality of caring. There are three writers whose works I have read and re-read as their ideas resonate with my own experience: Jean Vanier, Sheila Cassidy, and Fran Ferder.

Jean Vanier is a French Canadian. The son of a governor general, he left his career in the Navy to live in community with two people with intellectual disability at Trosly Breuil in France. From this beginning has grown the worldwide movement of L'Arche – homes for people with intellectual disability living in community with their carers. In *Be Not Afraid* he uses stories from his work to draw meaning from the Christian scriptures (Vanier 1975). His message of unconditional love affirmed my own work at the time.

Sheila Cassidy is an English doctor who came to fame initially when she was tortured in Chile for giving medical treatment to a wounded revolutionary. Since then she has worked in hospices in Britain. In *Sharing the Darkness* Cassidy explores the spirituality of caring in the light of Christianity (Cassidy 1988). She looks at the issues that face the carer – not only what it takes to give good care but also the problems the carer encounters such as overwork, depression and burnout. It is a book of hope and encouragement.

Fran Ferder is an American Catholic sister with a doctorate in ministry and clinical psychology. In *Words Made Flesh: Scripture, Psychology and Human Communication*, she reflects on the different skills of communication in the light of the Christian scriptures (Ferder 1986). She seeks the common ground in scripture and psychology rather than seeing them as polarized either/or choices. This book brought spiritual insights to my work as a carer and trainer of carers.

Each of these writers related the Christian scriptures to the caring work they were doing. As I read I recognized that there was someone else out there that shared my spiritual insights and in a sense gave them validity. This reading was an important step in affirming my own developing spirituality of caring as part of my Christianity. Because of the particular and personal nature of spirituality, care needs to be taken when recommending books for different people. There is a wide range of material available and the aim is always a successful match between an author and the spiritual needs of the reader.

What books do you read to nourish the spirituality of caring?
Organizations can usefully ask their volunteers to bring and share books that they find are spiritually nourishing, as a way of affirming the spirituality of their volunteers and encouraging them to understand and, it is hoped, accept their different perceptions.

NURTURING SPIRITUALITY BY REFLECTION

Reflection happens when a group of volunteers comes together on a regular basis to share their experiences as carers. They reflect on these experiences in the context of their own lives and explore the implications of them. An inevitable contributor to this process will be each person's own spirituality. Whether this is formally expressed or not, it will color each person's perception of what goes on. Because a group such as this has a reflective exploratory nature it allows each member the freedom to claim their own spirituality without having one imposed on them. It recognizes diversity. This of course sounds very like group supervision, and indeed Michael Carroll (2001) described supervision as a spiritual process in his keynote address to the Supervision: From Rhetoric to Reality conference in Auckland, July 2000.

Another variation of the reflective process is for a group to gather on a regular basis to reflect on a reading chosen by one of them and relate it to their volunteer work. Various books like Anne Wilson Schaef's *Meditations for Women Who Do Too Much* (Schaef 1990) or Henri Nouwen's *Bread for the Journey* (1996) give a meditation for each day of the year. Joy Cowley's *Psalms Down-Under* (1996) gives a New Zealand flavor to reflection, while *Life Prayers* edited by Elizabeth Roberts and Elias Amidon (1996) uses sources from all round the world. From Australia Michael Leunig's *The Prayer Tree* (1991) combines his skills as a cartoonist and a poet to reflect on life. In fact a good cartoonist can often give insights that lead to reflection on many serious matters and the cartoon from the daily paper could well be used as a focus.

What would you choose as a focus for reflection?
The reading or cartoon acts as a focus, but the reflection comes from each member's response. Our spirituality is activated by what we see and read. While beauty of nature and art and the wise words of literature and poetry can affirm and inspire, the dark times of suffering of self and others can also be a source of spiritual inspiration. The important aspect of this activity is both the content of the reflection, and the acknowledgement of the worth of each participant's contribution.

In situations where volunteers are dealing with difficult realities, it is often their spiritual motivation that gives them the strength to continue. This is nurtured by sharing with others. A reflective process has many benefits: it gives volunteers feedback that may not be available to them from the people they are caring for, it enables them to check out the appropriateness of what they are doing and it affirms their own spirituality as being a factor in their ability to do hard work. It also gives them the moral support of being part of a group. Ideally such a group would operate within the volunteer's agency. But if this is not so, many volunteers find it beneficial to meet informally with others from similar fields to reflect and nourish their spirituality.

RITUALS AND SYMBOLS

Groups quickly form their own rituals. They can range from how the group deals with conflict to whether its members meet at the pub on Friday nights. The rituals are the formalized ways of dealing with a wide range of situations. Rituals can be a way of nurturing spirituality.

> The group, in its formation stages, was polarized over a fundamental issue. The dinner break came and members drifted off in small groups to the pub down the road. Then they started to drift again away from the pub but up the street to the church. This was not a religious group but clearly many of its members were religious. That night spiritual needs were probably met in both places – the social atmosphere of the pub and

the quiet reflection and prayer in the church. The meeting reconvened and a solution was found.

Was it the spirituality of those people that carried them through that night and has them (and their successors) still offering a constructive service to families 25 years later?

Celebrations of the organization's milestones or cultural and community events are important rituals because celebration is part of expressing spirituality. A significant part of celebration is the sharing of food. Even a training meeting where lunch is shared has a different feel to one where people bring and eat their own lunch. The ritual of sharing food fulfills a spiritual as well as a nutritional need.

Occasions that give opportunity for reflection on the vision, the history, the context, the purpose and the work of the organization all help acknowledge what is spiritual in volunteers. It is often in the vision and the history that the volunteer recognizes the congruence between the spirit of the organization and their own spirituality. An important spiritual ritual can be making time to remember and acknowledge a volunteer, or a person being cared for, who has died. Creating an opportunity for volunteers to express their grief at the passing and acknowledging their contribution to the group is a spiritual action. Such rituals are important in the informality within a group as well as attending a funeral.

Symbols are often used in rituals. They can be culturally based and it is important to check out the meanings of specific symbols where volunteers come from a variety of cultures. A caring organization's logo can have a spiritual significance for its members. It is much more than just a tool for advertising. The logo has often been designed to express the spirit of the mission of the organization in a visual form. Like much of spirituality, it speaks without words.

Figure 4.1 Logo of Community Liaison Chaplaincy

Community Liaison Chaplaincy sets out to meet the spiritual needs of people with intellectual disabilities who have left an institution to live in the community. Their logo, a forget-me-not, is a prompt to remember these people and not let them be submerged by the community they live in. Remembering is a spiritual attribute.

Figure 4.2 Logo of Pregnancy Help Inc

Throughout New Zealand, Pregnancy Help gives support to pregnant women and new mothers. The Pregnancy Help logo incorporates the images of mother and child. The central 'koru', which is the name of the design of the unfolding fern, is the Maori symbol for new life. Here it relates to the child before and shortly after birth. The extended arms surrounding the logo are the arms of the volunteer whose unconditional, practical caring is the work of this organization. Unconditional love and caring are the spiritual values of Pregnancy Help.

Groups sometimes celebrate their links in the making of a quilt. A relevant theme is chosen and members participate in the making. The quilt stands as a symbol of the group's service and connectedness.

Practical experiences of spirituality in action

Community Liaison Chaplaincy for people with intellectual disabilities is commissioned to work ecumenically with churches to provide support for the spiritual needs of people with intellectual disabilities who have recently moved into their neighborhoods. In reality this means working with small groups of church volunteers who visit. The visitors sometimes just sit with people, or provide music, or take people for walks, and very occasionally include those who want to participate in some of their local church activities. They are being asked to meet spiritual needs by being community to intellectually disabled people in their neighborhood.

This has required of the church volunteers that they recognize the spirituality of people having severe intellectual limitations, many being unable to communicate verbally and some who also have challenging behaviors. They are challenged to expand their own vision of spirituality beyond organized religion which has very limited relevance for most of these people, and overcome their own fears of dealing with people who are different.

Just as the church people are charged with supporting the spiritual needs of the intellectually disabled people, it is the role of the community liaison chaplains to support the volunteers who do the work in a practical way that acknowledges their spirituality. Two examples of how this has been done are the Spring Festival and 'Who is My neighbor?' groups.

The Spring Festival was a one-off event to encourage the involvement of church volunteers. Church members were invited to attend a spring festival at the center for People with Intellectual Disability, which was in the process of being deinstitutionalized. Residents of the center were invited too. The aims for the day were for church people to have the opportunity to meet and interact with the residents, to participate in some learning and to have a good social and spiritual experience.

The program for the festival included a short church service, workshops on various aspects of the work church people were being recruited to do, and afternoon tea – worship, education and sharing food. The scene for the spring festival theme was set with lots of flowers, candles and balloons. The church service was short, simple and encouraged participation from the very mixed congregation. The workshops included a game of softball with the residents and a music lesson where illiterate residents taught the church people a song.

This event met spiritual, social and educational needs of the people who were part of it. All participants – those with disabilities and those without – were treated with equality and the spirituality of all was recognized and acknowledged.

The 'Who is my neighbor?' groups are part of the ongoing support process for church volunteers who visit people with intellectual disability in their neighborhood. It involves regular meetings of church visitors in a particular locality with their community liaison chaplain. They come together from different denominations to talk about the work they are doing and share their successes and frustrations. Each meeting begins with some spiritual reflection or prayer which the members take turns to prepare and lead. Often it is based round the season of the year, or something relevant that someone has found and wants to share with the group.

The spiritual needs of these volunteers are met by their coming together, the spiritual focus of the reflection and the practical and down-to-earth work they do. The members tend to form a close bond with each other. As the churches involved cover a wide range of denominations the volunteers are called on to be sensitive to differing theological views among their group members as well as differing ways of meeting spiritual needs among the people they are serving. Needless to say food is also shared at these meetings.

The examples above are taken from experiences of working with church members who could be expected to respond positively to some spiritual content. The next example was used with the board of a caring organization which was not in any way church related.

> The national board of a voluntary organization, which offered a caring and support service for women, was meeting for its half-yearly two-day meeting. The president invited all members to have their feet washed. The symbol of foot washing has strong Christian connections but it also can stand in its own right as a way for carers to get in touch with what it feels like to be cared for.
>
> While a poem relating feet to the work of the group was being played in the background, the leader washed and dried the feet of each member. The water was warm and perfumed and towels were clean and soft. Afterwards people were given an opportunity to comment on the experience.

The responses were mixed. The words used were 'spiritual', 'humbling', 'embarrassing', 'nurturing', 'revealing', 'relaxing'. Some still talk about it as a significant event in their lives.

Spirituality is nurtured in very practical ways. These are just some examples that I have experienced in groups of volunteers.

Can you create or find activities that fit your group?

Conclusion

Spirituality is an integral part of how and why people choose to work as volunteers in the field of social care. It is a source of motivation that can draw volunteers to work in difficult situations. Recognizing and acknowledging their spirituality will encourage volunteer caregivers to do the same for the people they care for. Identifying the spiritual aspects of a group's vision will inspire volunteer board members to support it with energy.

Spirituality is an issue for those who manage volunteers. Does the individual's spirituality match the ethos of the agency? Are the boundaries of a volunteer's work clearly stated so that carer and client are safe? Spirituality is nurtured in very practical ways by creating a climate that affirms volunteers and by encouraging them to read, reflect in groups, and recognize and use rituals and symbols, appropriate to the people and the situation.

Any person in an agency can contribute to creating a climate that nurtures spirituality – board members, managers, volunteers and paid staff who interact with volunteers. The words that come to mind are from the song Bread and Roses: 'yes it is the bread we fight for, but we fight for roses too'.

How can you enhance the spirituality of volunteers in social care?

References

Carroll, M. (2001) 'The Spirituality of Supervision'. In L. Beddoe and J. Worrall (eds) *Supervision: From Rhetoric to Reality.* Auckland: College of Education.

Cassidy, S. (1988) *Sharing the Darkness: The Spirituality of Caring.* London: Darton, Longman and Todd.

Covey, S.R. (1989) *The Seven Habits of Highly Effective People.* New York: Simon and Schuster.

Cowley, J. (1996) *Psalms Down-Under.* Wellington: Catholic Supplies (N.Z.) Ltd.

Ferder, F. (1986) *Words Made Flesh: Scripture, Psychology and Human Communication.* Notre Dame, Indiana: Ave Maria Press.

Leunig, M. (1991) *The Prayer Tree.* Victoria: Collins Dove.

Nouwen, H. (1996) *Bread for the Journey.* London: Darton, Longman and Todd.

Roberts, E. and Amidon, E. (1996) *Life Prayers from Around the World: 365 Prayers, Blessings and Affirmations to Celebrate the Human Journey.* New York: HarperCollins.

Schaef, A.W. (1990) *Meditations for Women Who Do Too Much.* New York: Harper and Row.

Shamy, E. (1996) *More Than Body, Brain and Breath.* Aotearoa New Zealand: ColCom Press.

Vanier, J. (1975) *Be Not Afraid.* Dublin: Gill and Macmillan.

Woods, M. (1998) *Volunteers: A Guide for Volunteers and their organizations.* Christchurch: Hazard Press.

Chapter Five

Being, Loving and Contributing

Ksenija Napan

Central to the advancement of human civilisation is the spirit of open enquiry. We must learn not only to tolerate our differences. We must welcome them as the richness and diversity which can lead to true intelligence. (Albert Einstein 1991, p.79)

Introduction

I would like to invite you to imagine that you are a cabbage. A nice, green cabbage in a cabbage patch. Imagine that you can feel the sun's warmth and the refreshment that rain brings. You have no eyes so you cannot see the caterpillar eating your leaves nor can you see a farmer coming and enriching the soil with all you need to become a big and healthy head. But, you can feel it. You have no ears so you cannot hear when the farmer's wife comes and sings in the garden, but you can feel the resonance of her voice. You do not know and you do not try to explain if your farmer is a god or your guardian angel and you do not know what role is played by the farmer's wife or what kind of scientific experiment she is conducting while singing. You do not know whether they will eat you at the end or will the caterpillars be faster, but it does not really matter, because you are who you are and you are expressing the life force in its complete beauty. You are doing your best – you are being, loving and contributing in your unique way.

Have you ever noticed, as a human, the beauty of the cabbage head, the perfection of the leaves enveloping one another? Is there any way of relating this experience to social practice? Is there a way of relating it to the main principles we are guided by? Let us open our minds like parachutes and go exploring. Who knows in whose cabbage patch we are growing? I believe that there is more to life than what we can see, hear, touch, taste and smell, and that an important part of our evolution is in discovering these additional dimensions.

When I was invited to write this chapter I was delighted with the idea to have the opportunity to put on paper ideas that shaped my being in this world. The initial enthusiasm was replaced with anxiety when I was faced with difficulties of writing about something, which is beyond the three dimensions we can easily perceive with our five senses or explain with reason. Maybe this anxiety was just an excuse to focus and create a paper, which does not come only from my head, which gained me more degrees than a thermometer, but from my whole being. How challenging and how disclosing…

My interest in spirituality is probably as old as I am. At the age of three or four I invented (or got in touch with) my own 'God' – a loving and omniscient source of wisdom and practical advice who assisted me in my inquiry about life. He communicated to me his name (or I gave him the name), spelled it to me and although it looked like a misspelled male name, I accepted it. I was aware that he could take any shape or form and his presence was beyond gender, culture, or any other polarity that we use to explain our realities. There was no ritual about my experience of the divine, it was just my direct experience and communication with the higher source. My mum used to ask me about him, assuming that I had an imaginary friend, but even at the age of four I was able to deny that and say that he was much more than an imaginary friend.

For me 'Oswaild' was a source of all knowledge and an immaterial being who could travel through space and time without limitations. To me he was a creator, a friend and an omniscient being who emanated love and wisdom. He was part of me and I was part of him. He permeated everything I could imagine and I had the privilege of having a direct line to him. Every time I would have a question, I would ask him and he would give me answers, but as far as I can remember he would never impose any actions on me. He would give me the information and my actions were always my choices. This was so empowering.

I was brought up in an atheistic family where allowance was given to matters spiritual and respect was given to various religions. However, religion and spirituality were generally viewed by my family members as beautiful myths and legends but not as reality. Reality was something that can be seen, or heard, or touched, or at least smelled and tasted by the majority. It had to be tangible. My bedtime stories were from all over the world – from Greece to Japan and around the globe – and very early I was puzzled about why they called their gods different names; was 'Ookuninusinomikoto' just another name for 'Zeus', or did different people just invent different gods to justify their actions? Why did some cultures have only one god and others many? Why were all these gods external and I felt mine strongly within? Because of my direct connection, I experienced the divine as external and internal at the same time and I left open the possibility that I was just making Oswaild up. But, the issue of realness was not really important to me. Oswaild would come when I was in need and I knew that I could rely on him. He was never intrusive, nor would he come uninvited, so I was never labeled as being delusional. Nevertheless, only people closest to me knew about my communication with him, because I did not want to be perceived as too different from the crowd.

My experience of the divine can be best described by the metaphor of a drop of water, which came out of the ocean, and just when observed separately it is called a drop. When the very same drop falls in the form of rain in a river, and when it eventually joins the ocean, we call it ocean again. Only the separation that we as observers create gives it a separate existence. The essence of the ocean was always in the drop and the essence of the divine is always with us. It seems that rivers serve as connecting factors, and our rivers are our lives and ways we choose to live them (Singh 1996). This is how we co-create and participate in our evolution. This is how we contribute and bring forth the world with our thoughts, sharing and actions. For me spirituality is about having a participatory relationship with the divine, which permeates all that is. It is about inhaling and exhaling the life force in its complete beauty, it is about reverence for all life, it is about the connection with our living planet and the living universe, it is about the connection with others, people, plants, animals and rocks. The more connected I am the more likely it is that I will live in accordance with my highest self. Paradoxically, the more connected I am, the better I express my uniqueness.

In my teenage years I started exploring religions and philosophies. I wanted to 'scientifically' prove or disprove my experience of the divine. I wanted to find a holy book or a person, which or whom I would accept completely and find answers from outside. I started questioning the authenticity of my own experience, because the majority of people thought about spirituality differently. Practical spirituality was generally seen as organized religion (like going to church on Sundays) or talking with ghosts (which was seen as being weird and dangerous by the majority). I disagreed with this rigid and limited understanding and wanted to find a way to explain and understand my spiritual needs differently. This was a long journey and I learned a lot, but my major questions stayed unanswered and I did not find refuge in any formal religious group. My perception of the dogmatism in Christian churches turned me away as well as awareness of wars, oppression and discrimination condoned by the church contributed to my alienation from mainstream Christianity. I always believed in Jesus as a historical person who lived in accordance with his god and his higher self, but I did not like the way his teachings had been distorted and manipulated during the last 2000 years. However, his message of love and teaching through parables somehow became implanted in my worldview and very visible in my teaching style. Experiencing Jesus directly and communicating with him in meditation was enlightening, but that contact never pushed me closer to organized religion.

Growing up in a socialist country (Croatia) and being a feminist by inheritance (my mum was a feminist) minimized my interest in Islam because of my perception of the oppression of women in Muslim countries – as if it were easier to perceive oppression 'out there' than in 'my tribe', where women were expected to be well educated, earn the same wages as men, drink and smoke as much as men, but cook, clean and iron as well as grandma did, and still be fully responsible for the children's education and upbringing.

I have spent years exploring ancient Greek, Roman, Tibetan and Egyptian beliefs and was impressed by their similarities. Buddhism and Hinduism were presented to me through the idea of reincarnation, which was very compatible with my ecological heart – always keen to recycle and see nature dynamically, in cycles and spirals. But, being born with the 'karmic debt' (the paying of debts collected from previous lives) and the idea of passive resistance and acceptance of whatever happens were not in accordance with my radical and critical social work worldview. Action is my passion and I was not able, nor patient enough, to see much action in the East. Perhaps I explored Hinduism and Buddhism too early in my life and perhaps I was unable to comprehend the depth of their teachings.

At the same time, experience of spirituality through tarot cards, crystal balls and clairvoyance were not something that my scientific heart could take seriously. Being a scientist and a social worker enabled me to see spirituality as something that needs to be cherished (unconditional positive regard) and explored (scientific curiosity). I realized that religion is not what I needed in order to be able to put my social practice in perspective. I knew that there was more to social practice than mere problem solving, I needed a place where I could discuss and explore the meaning and purpose of life and analyze my own spirituality with the aim of being able to accept my clients' and students' spiritual needs as well as their other needs. I wanted to be able to support them to improve the quality of their life in a way that would be in harmony with their social, psychological, physical and spiritual needs. To be able to do that competently I needed to balance myself and my own spiritual needs.

With this problem of belonging or devoting my soul to one organized belief system, I was left to explore my own spirituality experientially, utilizing my five (or more) senses, intuition and the knowledge available in books and on the internet. Especially valuable are rare and meaningful discussions with colleagues and direct contact with 'universal consciousness' (whatever that may mean) or the principle that connects 'all that is', and that provided the context in which my spirituality could be free to flourish, evolve and develop. Being a scientist did not help at all until I discovered action research. Finally, I encountered a methodology which allows the researcher to be a part of the process; at last, a method which describes a process of research in the form of a spiral not a flat line. Action research enabled me to explore my own spirituality through experience, reflection, abstract conceptualization and active experimentation. Experiencing, reflecting, conceptualiszing and experimenting with the divine has become part of everything I do, privately and professionally.

I experience spirituality as integrative and permeating all that is in life. It is an integral part of everything I do, even though I may not be consciously aware of it. I believe that the more aware we are of our spirituality the more we are evolving consciously. Conscious evolution integrates science and spirituality, body, mind and spirit, humans and their environment, psychology and ecology, individual and the wider contextual considerations. Conscious evolution integrates mindful actions, which bring forth the world. It is compatible with the science of the 21st century, which needs to integrate technology and ethics, psychology and ecology, concrete and abstract, observer and the observed, spirituality and the material world. Spirituality is related to direct experience of the meaning and purpose of life, transcendence, connectedness, love and integrity. It is connected to the feeling that there is more to life than mere existence, there is more to life than it seems. There are some coincidences in our life that happen too often to be irrelevant. There is a connectedness between all beings on our planet, and when one suffers, the others may feel it too. This very down-to-earth view of spirituality is closely linked to what Albert Schweitzer (1969) called 'reverence for life'. To me everyday spirituality is about being, loving and contributing. Everyday spirituality is about being who you are, loving the fellow beings on this planet including the planet itself and contributing in the best way you can. To make this contribution as simple as possible, let's focus just on *being, loving* and *contributing* in relation to social practice and teaching.

Please note that the statements that follow are personal statements open to challenge, discussion and further exploration. They do not present any 'universal truth', they are evolving and gliding through the realm of ideas and anchoring themselves in actions guided with the intent of making a meaningful contribution.

Being

Being is about life, coherence, harmony and uniqueness. The need to live, grow and develop permeates our planet. Life sprouts where it is least expected – witnessing creation in every living being on this planet could not leave me untouched. Our curiosity and reverence for life have carried us through the millennia. We are still asking the same questions: *Who am I? Where did I come from? Where do I belong? Why am I here? Where am I going?*

After all these years of searching we still do not have a definite answer or at least one that most of us would agree with. But maybe that *is* the answer. Our purpose is in searching, experiencing, growing and developing. Our purpose is in searching and experiencing not in finding; our purpose is in being who we really are – because then we feel most fulfilled. Our purpose is in being, loving and contributing.

No matter how much I tried and how much my parents, teachers, partners, children or bosses tried, I could not avoid being who I really am: I am the best at being me – nobody can do it better. The more I practice the art of being who I really am and the more I am aware of my contribution to my evolution the more likely it is that I will be in the right place at the right time. It seems that, when I achieve that state of awareness, I start to develop the ability to read the clues that I was previously unaware of and then I can 'ride the thermals' like all wise birds do and glide seemingly effortlessly through life making a meaningful contribution. In that state of being, enthusiasm grows and tasks seem to be easy, because I am who I am and I do not waste time and energy manipulating others or trying to please or be somebody else. Life seems easier because I am energized by my purpose and I strive for quality and doing my best. Focusing on quality in my thoughts and actions motivates me intrinsically and it increases my self-esteem and effectiveness, which in turn encourages me to undertake new and meaningful tasks.

Being who I really am is energizing. People like Mother Teresa, Albert Einstein, Jesus, Albert Schweitzer, St Francis of Assisi, Jane Goddall, Nikola Tesla, Gandhi, Stephen Hawking, the Dalai Lama and many others demonstrated incredible energy in realiszing their vision and contributing to the growth of humanity. When they encountered obstacles or difficulties, they perceived them as challenges and continued being who they were, while acting with integrity. They 'rode the thermals' and used their life mission to bring forth the world.

Teaching as well as social work is more a vocation than a mere profession. As Elizabeth Soper noted: 'Social work is having the vision, staircasing the vision, "partnershiping" the vision, making the change the vision brings. Vision with clients is electric and challenging. Vision without empowerment is blindness. Social work is the rainbow of the vision laced with strong dollops of empowerment' (Soper 2001). If I, as a social practitioner, embark on social practice just to avoid dealing with my personal problems and if I continuously project them onto my clients, I am not doing harm only to them but to my personal evolution too. If I am unaware of that, it is likely that I will further damage myself because I am not addressing what I need to address in this life cycle. Therefore, I propose providing the opportunity for students to become aware of this common phenomenon early in their education. Then they are presented with the opportunity to leave with dignity or find ways to heal their 'wounded child' (Heron 2001) during their professional training, before entering the profession.

I argue that quality education is personal, professional and social and that it focuses on knowledge, skills, attitudes and values. During the process of teaching and learning professional practice it is necessary to allow the space and time for exploration of a whole range of issues that could impact on effectiveness. I find experiential learning very effective, but only when the whole learning cycle is equally represented, as envisaged by David Kolb (1984). It allows students to have concrete experience of the subject they focus on, to have an opportunity to reflectively observe, to conceptualize and integrate it with theories and to actively experiment with new ideas, skills, values or attitudes. Learning how to be open to a client's pain and how to let it go is an essential skill for any effective social practitioner. Becoming aware of our own projections and unresolved issues may be a good pathway to becoming an effective practitioner.

When I was 22, I worked with Dianne, who was the same age as me. She was using a wheelchair and was barely able to speak, using a very weak voice. It was obvious that talking was a great effort for her. She had very limited use of her arms and hands. She could not feed herself and had difficulties swallowing. She had beautiful brown eyes and a strong need to communicate. Dianne told me that she had lost most of her abilities after a car accident, which happened while she was riding a horse. In the middle of her sentence spoken with great effort, I said 'Excuse me' and ran to the toilet where I could not stop myself from crying. I thought that I felt sorry for her and I did not want her to see me feeling sorry. I wanted to 'protect' her from my feelings of being sorry or I wanted to protect myself from her seeing me being vulnerable. I had learned in my social work training that we cannot help our clients if we feel sorry for them or openly express our feelings, so I tried to suppress them, but my unconscious evolutionary process was stronger. My need to sort out my own issues was too strong to be repressed.

After being alone for a few minutes in the toilet cubicle, I realized that I did not actually feel sorry for Dianne. I became aware of my projection. I had worked with many brain-damaged people and feeling sorry was not my usual way of feeling about them. I focused on their strengths and listened to their pain with empathy, not pity. The situation with Dianne was different. I rode horses and was pretty wild at the time (playing with danger was my favorite game) and there she was sitting in front of me: gentle, brave and proud, very mentally able, very physically disabled and dependent on others. To lose my independence and my ability to express myself would be my worst nightmare! Quickly realizing what I believed was the reality of the situation, I went out of my insightful toilet cubicle, wiped my tears, apologized again and continued talking with Dianne. This time it was on a different level – without feeling sorry, without shame and guilt, without my social worker's hat: it was soul to soul with love and compassion. We laughed and cried together and we healed parts of each other. Thank you Dianne for teaching me a lesson on projection that I was unable to learn from books and my social work theory teachers. (More than 15 years later I fell off a horse and almost lost my ability to walk; was my reaction to Dianne's story my projection or my intuition?)

Education is the process where students discover that learning a new theory, skill or changing an attitude will contribute to their quality of life. Until they discover this they will not be motivated to learn, neither to contribute (Glasser 1998). If the students' true beings do not resonate with the process and the content of what is taught, it is not likely that they will benefit. Similarly, in social practice – until our clients discover that what we are doing with them will improve the quality of their life, and until they resonate with the content and the process of our practice, it is not likely that they will benefit from interactions with us.

Supporting clients in their discovery of their true being is a big task and it requires patience, openness, humbleness and focus. Allowing professionals to do the same requires that the same qualities permeate the teaching environment. We need to develop reflective practices where we can 'ride the thermals' of unavoidable change and steer students into creative and purposeful directions.

For a young social practitioner, discovering and being who he or she is is essential for his or her effectiveness and well-being. It relates to discovering one's calling and real reasons for joining the profession. At the same time, one of the main tasks of effective social work is to encourage clients to find their answers to the very same questions. A client who lives in harmony with his or her true being is likely to improve his or her quality of life and use available resources better. This of course does not mean that all problems imposed by inadequate policy, oppression and discrimination will be solved – but they will be addressed with more focus, passion and willingness, so that imposed injustices may be challenged and changed.

Quality living and enhancing quality of life is the purpose of social practice. We are in the business of being, but not mere being; we are in the business of living according to our highest standards and doing our best. For each individual client, this will be expressed in their unique ways, and without the soul-to-soul contact social practitioners would not be able to comprehend this. I believe that this is the essence of quality social work, quality caring and quality teaching and learning.

Loving

This idealistic view of the social work profession and teaching can easily be overturned if the context in which it is practiced is permeated with fear as opposed to love. As a consequence social actions may become driven by fear and become defensive, which will only contribute to victimization of the client or practitioner. 'Loving' refers to my understanding of everyday spirituality, which means performing every activity with reverence and devotion. It refers to sharing the gift of love with people, expressing it through activities and ideas. Love energizes. Love melts the fear. Love allows fear to express itself through focused questions as opposed to violence. Love allows curiosity and softens rigidity. Love is the choice and an internal need that drives our actions. Because it is essential for our being, when suppressed or not accessed love can be transformed into fear leading to violence or self-destruction.

Love is divine energy transformed into human action. Love is the expression of our true being shining towards others, ideas, goals, processes, things and nature. William Glasser (1998) talks about the need for love and belonging as a basic need, and love is even more than that. Love transcends and love energizes, love motivates and love encourages. Love is internal but we engender it through our connection with the universe, ideas and fellow beings on this planet. Love is self-creative. It creates and spreads and it shows itself beyond our five senses. It is real and illusive at the same time.

When teaching social practitioners, the prerequisite for addressing the idea of spirituality is development of the atmosphere of trust. Trust seems to be essential because our understanding and experience of spirituality touches us at the core of our being. Having a class of students with the whole range of spiritual beliefs and views on a range of topics perfectly mirrors the reality in which they will work in future. Trust has to be mutual, I need to trust my students first and only then can I hope that they will trust their peers and me. Collaboration and cooperation during the class is essential for development of trust. Personal and professional involvement is equally important. To me, learning all the names of the students in the first few weeks of the course, as well as noticing the strengths of each, is essential for the development of trust. In a class of 50 students, it becomes really challenging, but it is still fun and it keeps my brain cells regenerating. True benefits are always mutual. Trust is the core virtue for social practice. Short-term, over the counter, quick fix methods of social practice are not conducive to trust or the integration of spirituality in everyday practice.

I learned about trust when I worked with a deaf and blind seven-year-old girl. After only two days of being together in a residential environment we went together on a water slide, her sitting on my lap. She laughed sliding down and she taught me about trust. That happened 20 years ago and I worked with her for only a week. I still remember her name and her smile. Trust is a prerequisite for love. Thank you, Rachel.

'Life sucks and in the end you die' – this was told to me by a suicidal teenager, and he was right. He was equally as right as Rachel when she enjoyed her first ride on a water slide: without expectations. Our experience of life is dependent on our perception. Our perception is dependent on our thoughts, quality of life is dependent on the quality of our thoughts, and we are the only ones who can control them. This does not imply that our thoughts create reality, as some 'new agers' might say. It implies that thoughts and perceptions shape our *experience* of reality. My actions are led by my experiences and thoughts and I am the only person who is in charge of them. Maybe I am just a former cabbage whose dreams have come true: to move, to influence, to see who the farmer is and to consciously participate in the farmer's wife's experiments, or maybe I am just a future cabbage and I will understand more about God and nature when I learn how to grow roots and leaves and feed caterpillars with my body.

I am not grateful to the people who oppressed me, but I am grateful for my learning and many will be grateful because the experience of oppression prepared me to react to oppression as soon as it shows itself. It would be senseless to encourage our clients to be grateful for the oppressive systems they are involved in but we can focus on their strengths and encourage them to stand up for themselves or help them create the context where they can leave the oppressive situation. We can advocate and make individual situations public to create social change and challenge oppression. If we work effectively, when our clients learn to stand up for themselves, they will be grateful, not to us but to their strengths – and that is the true meaning of 'empowerment'. When they become interested in (as opposed to fearful of) the process of living and being, they will be better able to experience love. When we experience love for fellow humans, animals, nature and ideas we develop an urge to contribute, we feel that we belong and we contribute from our hearts and from our true being.

Contributing

No matter how much I try, I cannot avoid contributing. It is an internal urge to participate and co-create realities. From the moment each of us arrives and our parent(s) or caregivers greet us, we turn their lives around. The love they feel for us gives them incredible energy to survive sleep deprivation, physiological, hormonal and lifestyle changes. Their need to contribute to our life is equally strong and it enhances our willingness to grow, develop and to pass the same love on to future generations. Our contribution is visible from the first moment and we contribute just by being who we are – a tiny, unique brand new baby.

When I am in tune with my real being and when my actions are motivated by love, my contributions engender love and promote empowerment. When I am motivated to help others just to distract myself from the pain I feel because I do not deal with the personal issues that I need to deal with, my contributions engender fear, confusion and disempowerment. In other words, if I am not truly being I am not truly contributing.

Curiosity did not kill the cat, it kept her alive. If the cat were not curious it would never catch the mouse. If God were not curious the world would not exist. If the universe were not restless the Big Bang would never have happened. If we were not curious our lives would be dull, boring and stale. If there is no passion, nor interest in the field of inquiry, studying can become terribly boring. Do we want our students to become indifferent, detached bureaucrats or do we want them to go out there and make a difference? Questions like Why have you chosen social work as your profession? What interests you in your work with this particular group of clients? How do you learn best? How would you like to contribute? can help students to focus on the vision of their mission, but only if the atmosphere of trust is already established. When the teaching environment is permeated with fear and competition, we will get clichés for answers.

I am interested in my students as human beings. I am interested in their contribution because their contribution changes my world too. We are all interconnected – we all swim in the same river towards the same ocean – but it is just that our swimming styles differ. I am interested to learn from my students. I encourage them to challenge my ideas and I challenge theirs. We create the course together in the same way they create their realities and in the same way that they will support their clients in creating theirs. The classroom is a laboratory for effective social practice. If we do not practice it in the classroom it is not likely that it will be practiced in their professional life. The classroom offers safety to explore, practice, challenge, construct and deconstruct; it is a place for inquiry, not for dogmatic preaching, and the same can be said for social practice.

> Every living thing needs to contribute in some meaningful way, through some essential work or activity, in order for the larger systems of Earth and Universe to benefit and grow. In exchange for the opportunity of life, I believe we are required to give back our talents, skills, and wisdom to make the world a little bit better. If you feel unfulfilled in your work life, then consider whether or not the efforts of your spirit are reflected directly, indirectly, or in any way at all in your current job, career, and volunteer or community activities. (Young-Sowers 1993, p.201)

Our contributions are meant to bring forth the world and we cannot avoid it; even when our contributions are destructive, in an indirect way, they will contribute to someone confronting us and helping us to become more in tune with our real being and to contribute in more creative ways. The kind of contribution we choose to make is not as important as the fact that it should be purposeful and of benefit either to the individual or the community. In professional practice external supervision provides a safe space for the exploration of the potential consequences of our contributions.

Contribution and the idea of mission in life are not an obsessive-compulsive drive to constantly do what we must or ought to do. Healthy contribution relates to the balance of times to be active and times to observe and it relates to acceptance of life cycles. This is probably best illustrated by a story about the artist who was sitting in his garden gazing at birds and leaves when a neighbor asked him: 'You are relaxing today, aren't you?' The artist answered: 'No, I'm working.' The next day he was standing by his easel painting and his neighbor asked: 'You are working today, aren't you?' And the artist said: 'No, I am relaxing.'

Teaching students and clients to accept paradoxes and contradictions in life enables them to become aware of what they can change and what they cannot, what they have influence over and what they have not. Their contributions then become relevant and meaningful and they start bringing forth the world. Being relates to who I am. Loving relates to my relationships to other beings, events, situations and ideas and contributing relates to my actions and to how I express my being and my loving. And this is just the beginning of a spiritual journey a social practitioner may undertake to understand the context, the other, the self and the process in order to learn how to 'ride the thermals' like all wise birds do.

Instead of conclusion

I would like to invite you to imagine that you are a butterfly and that you have one day on this planet to make your contribution. What would you do?

References

Einstein, A. cited in Shields, K. (1991) *In the Tiger's Mouth: an Empowerment Guide for Social Action*. Newtown, NSW: Millennium Books.

Glasser, W. (1998) *Choice Theory*. New York: Harper and Row.

Heron, J. (2001) *Helping the Client*, Fifth Edition. London and New Delhi: Sage.

Kolb, D.A. (1984) *Experiential Learning: Experience as the Source of Learning and Development*. New Jersey: Prentice Hall.

Schweitzer, A. (1969) *Reverence for Life*. New York: Harper and Row.

Singh, S.T. (1996) *The Journey Within: Encounters with Sant Thakar Singh*. Video recording.

Soper, E. (2001) Presentation in the course 'Just Practice', Bachelor of Social Practice program, UNITEC, School of Community Studies, 8 August.

Young-Sowers, M. (1993) *Spiritual Crisis: What's Really Behind Loss, Disease, and Life's Major Hurt*. Walpole, NH: Stillpoint.

Chapter Six

Spirituality and Social Work in a Culturally Appropriate Curriculum

Mary Nash

This chapter contextualizes the teaching of spirituality for social work students in New Zealand, briefly looking at recent literature including that exploring faculty practices and student receptiveness. The cultural imperative for including this topic in the writer's own Bachelor of Social Work (BSW) degree is discussed and the curriculum described. Issues to do with introducing students to indigenous spirituality are explored with reference to the writer's experience.

Introduction

This chapter considers the place of spirituality in the New Zealand social work curriculum. It contextualizes New Zealand social work, introducing key principles guiding the Aotearoa New Zealand Association of Social Workers (ANZASW) in relation to the Treaty of Waitangi (1840). Recent international literature indicates a growing interest in the relationship between social work and spirituality. Definitions of spirituality, including Maori perspectives, are discussed and a distinction is drawn between spirituality and religion. Reference is made to research on faculty and student views on the place of spirituality and religion in good social work education programs as well as practical material concerning fieldwork, assessment and intervention.

In New Zealand, teaching social work students and practitioners about the meanings and significance of the spiritual dimension in practice requires, among other features, a culturally appropriate curriculum. Different approaches to spirituality can be found among social work practitioners, faculty members and students, depending on whether they come from a Maori (indigenous), European, or Pacific Island background. Maori and non-Maori students are likely to be positioned differently in relation to both spiritual understandings and clients. In a class where all three cultural groups are present a sensitively designed curriculum is required in order to prepare students for working with Maori clients.

For eight years, there has been a spirituality module in the second year of the BSW degree at Massey University in New Zealand. Culturally appropriate social work practice entails an understanding of the spiritual dimension, hence its place in the degree. Mainstreaming and/or modularization are options for the inclusion of spirituality in the curriculum. This chapter discusses levels of student interest, and future developments for teaching in this area, mindful of innovative courses elsewhere, in particular at the Inter-University center for Post-graduate Studies in Dubrovnik.

Social work in New Zealand: the Treaty of Waitangi and the professional association of social workers

The Aotearoa New Zealand Association of Social Workers (referred to below as either ANZASW or the Association) is the professional social work organization for social workers in New Zealand. The Association, formed in 1964, sets professional standards for its members which reflect the special nature of social work in Aotearoa New Zealand while at the same time meeting international standards. Several features give the ANZASW a particular profile differentiating it from many professional associations of social workers in other parts of the world.

Membership criteria have consistently been inclusive of practitioners and based on occupational status regardless of certificated tertiary qualifications. Originally, this was a largely pragmatic decision, based on the fact that there were too few professionally qualified practitioners in the country.

In 1985, a ministerial advisory commission chaired by a well-respected and professionally qualified Maori social worker found widespread dissatisfaction on the part of the Maori community, comprising clients, advisers, practitioners and citizens, concerning the workings of the Department of Social Welfare and its treatment of Maori children. The report, referred to as 'Puao-te-Ata-tu' (daybreak), is commonly regarded as marking a watershed in social work services in Aotearoa New Zealand (Ministerial Advisory Committee on a Maori Perspective for the Department of Social Welfare 1986). The Government accepted its recommendations, which were practical and far-reaching. It called for more Maori social workers, together with recognition of Maori expertise and retraining for non-Maori social workers, particularly around anti-racism and cultural competence.

The Association responded by affirming its inclusive approach to membership and developed its own set of practice standards in which candidates for membership have to demonstrate their competency. One of these practice standards states: 'The social worker demonstrates a commitment to practicing social work in accordance with the bi-cultural Code of Practice and an understanding of the Treaty of Waitangi' (ANZASW Board of Competency 1997). To demonstrate this competency, candidates are asked, among other things, to describe how they work with Maori clients and what is different about working with them. In this chapter it is argued that an important difference is recognition of and respect for spirituality because it holds great significance for Maori people and the way in which they live their lives.

Key social work values of client self-determination and linking personal troubles to wider social, political, cultural and economic issues have particular implications for social work in Aotearoa New Zealand. The first three objects of the Association illustrate this point and are worth quoting here, for they expect social workers:

(a) To promote an indigenous identity for social work in New Zealand and to assist people to obtain services adequate to their needs.

(b) To ensure that social work in New Zealand is conducted in accordance with the articles contained in the Treaty of Waitangi.

(c) To advocate for full social justice in New Zealand and address oppression on the grounds of race, gender, disability, sexual orientation, economic status and age. (ANZASW 1993, p.9)

The Treaty of Waitangi was signed in 1840, between the Crown and Maori chiefs, and has constitutional status. It guaranteed that all signatories, as citizens, should have the same rights and be protected from harm. It guaranteed to the chiefs: 'The unqualified exercise of their chieftainship over their lands, villages and all their treasures' (Treaty of Waitangi, Article 11).

In the Maori version of the Treaty, the term 'tino rangatiratanga' meaning 'sovereignty' is used instead of 'chieftainship'. The Association's constitution (1990) acknowledges the importance of the Treaty of Waitangi for social workers and charges its members with practicing in accordance with its principles. Social workers interpret 'tino rangatiratanga' as referring to Maori self-determination relating to Maori well-being and for Maori this is based explicitly on a spiritual as well as practical relationship to the world around them, to the land they belong to and to their extended family, past, present and future.

Social workers, therefore, whatever their culture of origin, need to be informed about the spiritual dimensions of practice in relation to Maori clients. It is only a small step, and one in tune with the now burgeoning literature (Canda and Furman 1999; Okundaye, Gray and Gray 1999; Russell 1998; Sermabeikian 1994) to recognize that the spiritual dimensions of social work practice in Aotearoa New Zealand actually encompass not only indigenous clients but potentially all clients and their social workers.

The spiritual dimension in social work: a review of the literature

A review of the literature covering the interface between spirituality, religion and social work shows that during the last 15 years there has been an increased interest in the topic. Kilpatrick and Holland (1990) review the spiritual dimensions of social work practice, sketching a brief history of the relationship between social work, spirituality and religion. Founded, as it partly was, in religious, charitable and philanthropic organizations, by the 1920s social work had begun to adopt a more scientific and clinical approach, informed by psychoanalytic theory. Many social workers aspired to seeing their discipline elevated to professional status. Social workers have always been pulled between clinical and conservative practice on the one hand and social justice, social action and community development on the other, the 'cause and function' debate, as it is known in the USA (Ehrenreich 1985).

Today, these strands continue to be part of the social work and social care tradition. The growing interest in spirituality, manifested in the secular sphere as well as within social work, now adds a new dimension to social care. This picture is endorsed by studies of the attitudes of faculty, students and practitioners to the place of religion, spirituality and social work in both practice and the curriculum. Surveys of faculty suggest that there are significant levels of interest in including elective courses covering spirituality and religion in the social work curriculum. These studies find a high proportion of practitioners and students who are interested in exploring the spiritual dimension in their work. They also signal a dearth of teaching resources and theoretical material (Canda 1989; Derezotes 1995; Dudley and Helfgott 1990; Russell 1998; Sheridan and Amato-von-Hemart 1999; Sheridan *et al.* 1992).

The study of spirituality and religion has been strongly advocated by Canda (1988a) who has conceptualized spirituality for social work and been proactive in the development of an appropriate curriculum with rich resources for graduate social work programs (Canda 1988b, 1989; Canda and Furman 1999). Most articles in this area are quick to define spirituality as distinct from religion and, from a Western standpoint, many students find this helpful. Spirituality is defined as 'the human search for life meaning, morally fulfilling relationships and the understanding of the reality that has the greatest significance to you' (Canda and Furman 1999, p.313). In their view, spirituality does not necessarily entail a belief in either a personal god or a supernatural being, and therefore it is a concept, which is accessible to those of secular and humanist ways of thinking. Religion is distinguished as 'an organized set of beliefs, values and practices, shared by a community, that focuses on spirituality. Therefore, a person's spirituality may or may not be expressed through religion' (Canda and Furman 1999, p.313).

The points made here provide common ground for discussion between people with widely ranging ideas about spirituality and religion in relation to social work. The authors argue that 'spirituality is the heart of helping. It is the heart of empathy and care, the pulse of compassion, the vital flow of practice wisdom and the driving force of action for service' (Canda and Furman 1999, p.xv). 'The heart of helping' is an apt phrase and applicable to so much of the spiritual in social work. The work of Sheila Cassidy (1988) in particular comes to mind, as does hospice work throughout the world.

A variety of other understandings about spirituality occur in the literature and are reflected by the authors contributing to this book. In his study of hardiness and spiritual well-being as predictors of self-esteem for social work students, Kamya (2000) identifies several recurring themes among descriptions of spiritual well-being in the literature. These include having a satisfying relationship with a higher being, together with developing a sense of purpose and meaning in life (Ellison and Smith 1991, in Kamya 2000, p.232).

At the 2001 Symposium on Spirituality and Social Work in Dubrovnik, discussion about how to define spirituality in a meaningful and inclusive fashion ranged far and wide. For some, the points already mentioned were important, but also moments of beauty and great joy were seen to be significant for providing spiritual experiences. Spirituality was described as being about the candle lit to remember a loved one, the saying of grace before a meal, or simply being aware of the present moment (Rennebohm 2001). Children dancing, experiencing joy in discovery and learning from the elements were important features for one member of the symposium working closely with children affected by the 1992 war in former Yugoslavia. Spirituality is recognized to be an elusive, subtle and complex concept, and personal definitions will vary and need to be respected. At the same time, helpful definitions as offered by Canda and Furman (1999) above are a valuable foundation on which to build.

A reflective article by Sermabeikian (1994) considers a theoretical framework for understanding the place of spirituality in the individual, based on Jung's analytic psychology and his recognition of the importance of the relationship between therapist and worker. Jung emphasized the need to respect spirituality when working with people and explored the links between the physical, mental and spiritual dimensions in each individual (Sermabeikian 1994). Spirituality is widely recognized as a core ingredient in a person's worldview. This approach is familiar in New Zealand, where Maori traditions shed further light on the meanings of spirituality. Henare (1988) wrote about the foundations of Maori society for the Royal Commission on Social Policy. The terms of reference for this Commission were that it should ask the people of New Zealand what kind of social policies they wanted in the future, and the values on which these should be based.

For those Maori who are brought up with traditional knowledge, 'wairuatanga', the spiritual dimension, is part of collective everyday awareness. It is defined and expressed differently according to tribal traditions, but there is a broad general consensus of meaning. There is no separation between the spiritual and the non-spiritual, for, traditionally, the Maori world and all that was part of it was imbued with spirit (Henare 1988). It is with this understanding of culture that Maori refer to their 'taha wairua' (their spiritual side) and they are profoundly influenced by it. From a Maori perspective, appropriate social policy as it affects Maori people should have a 'wairuatanga' (spirituality) as well as a temporal aspect central to its formulation and practice. The integration of 'te wairuatanga' forms a central and significant aspect of Maori aspirations for social reform (Henare 1988, pp.15–16).

Coloniszation destroyed much that is sacred for Maori, with the result that 'the life forces in society are debased and all life is impoverished' (Jenkins 1988, p.494). Traditional Maori society relied heavily on the protection of 'wairuatanga' (spirituality) to conserve and preserve its cultural lifestyle (Jenkins 1988). In acknowledging descent lines connecting them to the land, Maori, like the ancient Celts, see themselves as belonging to the land with a responsibility to act as good stewards of the environment. Instead of a hierarchical and dominating position in relation to creation, their ideal has been one of respect and collective care. It has been argued that 'the separation of the spiritual and the secular in everyday life is the most significant effect of colonization on Maori in general and on women in particular, undermining the traditional status of Maori women' (Calligan 2001, p.7).

Current statistics of Maori women show that they have the highest rates of breast cancer, unemployment, smoking, high blood pressure and as victims of domestic violence. Many lack qualifications, they have a low rate of home ownership and they head up the highest proportion of single parent families (Calligan 2001, p.7). A series of high profile child deaths involving Maori women has indicated new depths to the difficulties experienced by them. Calligan's argument is that while not condoning these tragedies, society must understand the causes in order to effect change. Social workers claim to work at the interface of personal and social change. I would argue therefore that they need to make the connection between the disproportionately high statistics of poor Maori health and the fact that so many Maori are 'spiritually out of sync with self, others, environment and Atua/atua [God]' (Calligan 2001, p.7).

Through colonization, and industrialiszation, some, but by no means, all Maori have become estranged from their ancestral lands and knowledge of their territorial tribal affiliations. The cultural, social and economic results are to be seen in the high proportion of Maori in general, in the statistics for illiteracy, imprisonment, alcohol and drug abuse as well as unemployment and child abuse. For social workers, therefore, Maori well-being and the spiritual dimension of life are closely associated and form a bridge within the curriculum, connecting social justice and the psychosocial dimension in social work and social care.

The great religions of the world call for justice and compassion. The Christian churches have strong traditions of social justice and Christian social teaching. Speaking in South Australia at the Pan-Aboriginal Spirituality Conference (1990) the Aboriginal leader and activist Kevin Gilbert argued: 'You can't divorce yourself, your politics, your colour or human rights from spirituality' (Gilbert 1996, p.62). He continued, suggesting that instead of responding to the appalling injustices suffered by Aboriginal Australians with hatred, they might rather guide the white man to look differently at the world, to see the sacred in creation and to value it above material wealth. The challenge of retaining social justice within the heart of social work and acknowledging and studying it as a spiritual dimension in our work requires a braver response from social workers. It tends to be nurtured, if at all, within the community development movement.

In summary, definitions of spirituality and spiritual well-being vary, but recurrent themes indicate how this is an important aspect of human life, related to but different from religion. Similarly, many reasons for including spirituality and religion in the social work curriculum have been identified. Of these, three stand out. First, the safe and confident practitioner needs to know his or her personal approach to spirituality and religion. Second, clients may have particular religious or spiritual difficulties or worldviews about which the social worker needs to be knowledgeable. Finally, the client with strong cultural traditions in which spirituality is a key element has the right to a culturally competent social care worker.

Once it is accepted that there should be coverage of spirituality and religion in the social work curriculum, what should social work students be taught, who should be teaching them and what boundaries should be in place to ensure that curriculum content is appropriate and safe for the students concerned? Canda (1989, 1999) has developed suggestions for curriculum content in an elective paper on religion and spirituality. His work is carefully researched and is based on an inclusive approach respecting religious and spiritual diversity. He stresses the value in educating to extend practitioner self-knowledge and promote the principle of client self-determination. These ideas are very much in tune with the (compulsory) module taken by undergraduate BSW students at Massey University in New Zealand, described below.

The Bachelor of Social Work (BSW) degree and the spirituality module

Using the 1996 census, Statistics New Zealand (1998) indicates a continuing decline in the conventional Christian denominations, and a 55 percent growth in Pentecostalism, sometimes referred to as fundamentalism. Non-Christian religions, namely Buddhism and Islam, have more than doubled, although their actual numbers are still very small. A quarter of the population indicated that they have no religious affiliation. The majority of people in New Zealand have some form of religious belief, though the population is becoming more diverse in terms of what these religious beliefs are and there is ongoing change in this area.

The BSW degree is a four-year undergraduate course available through the School of Sociology, Social Policy and Social Work at Massey University, New Zealand. For eight years it has included a short module on spirituality and social work within one of its core (compulsory) second year papers. This module developed out of two earlier ones introducing students to existentialism and religious (specifically Christian) material related to social work. It came about as part of an ongoing process of curriculum adaptation to changing circumstances, two of which were particularly significant.

It was recognized that a good proportion of students were very interested in their Christian faith journey and this was a motivating factor in their studies to become social workers. However, this was not something they felt they could address in their academic studies. Students with a deep commitment to their Christian faith may struggle to discover where evangelization ends and social work begins. It is important that this issue is explicitly addressed with students, rather than remaining an unspoken, but powerful, driving force.

At the same time, other students had little or no energy for religion and found existentialism conceptually very foreign. If social work students are to enter the workforce as balanced practitioners, it is important for them to have the opportunity to examine their motivation and their values and measure these up to the principles of practice upheld by the professional association. It was felt that spirituality was a wide enough concept to attract both groups of students without promoting any one set of beliefs or values.

The second reason for the change was the need to ensure that Maori approaches to spirituality were also covered. These add another dimension to spirituality, in accordance with the principles of the Treaty of Waitangi. Because Maori spirituality underpins the Maori worldview, Maori and non-Maori students and their future clients will gain greatly from an explicit study of it. The composition of students reflects the proportion of Maori in the general population, being around 14 percent. Not all Maori students will have been brought up to be familiar with their indigenous spiritual traditions, which vary according to their 'iwi' (tribal group).

Designing culturally appropriate curriculum content for a varied group of students is a challenge. For some, the spirituality module is familiar territory, for others it is new and perhaps uncomfortable terrain. The students who are already well versed in their Maori worldview may find the content elementary. Care must be taken to ensure that the concepts explored are treated with respect and that the more sacred aspects of Maori spirituality are introduced, if at all, by Maori lecturers who will be able to manage these sensitive areas.

Bearing in mind these two reasons for adapting the second year curriculum, the module introduces students to definitions of spirituality, both Maori and non-Maori, and the distinction between spirituality and religion is made clear. By the time the module is studied, students will have completed an assignment in which they place themselves in the context of the family within which they grew up, examining their family practices, culture and values (Nash 1993). This provides an excellent platform from which to look at some of the key existential questions which spirituality addresses, such as: 'Who am I?' and 'Why do I exist?'

The aims of the module are to help students to examine their own spirituality and that of others and to clarify the place of spirituality in social and community work. It is intended that they will become more grounded in their outlook and will deepen their understanding of why they are becoming social workers. Thus the module encourages students to consider questions around creating a relationship with 'God', creation, others and ourselves, so that when working with clients, students will have reflected on their own position on such matters. Spiritual explanations for basic events and happenings such as birth, death, love and pain have implications for our relationships and these will vary according to different spiritual traditions. Students need to be aware and to accept that their own understandings of these matters may be quite different from those of their clients. They need to learn how to hold them both respectfully in their minds.

Students also look briefly at the diversity of religions and their implications for practice. Canda and Furman (1999) have introduced an excellent and comprehensive text for the study of spirituality in social work. The space allocated to spirituality in our undergraduate program is too small to allow for such an informative program of study as that which they offer, but the standard they set is one to aim for.

Other tertiary institutions in New Zealand have different approaches to how they address spirituality in the social work curriculum. For some, perhaps most, it is mainstreamed and is referred to in the context of culture, ageing, grief and loss. The modular approach is still rare, but we find that it prepares students for their study of the above mentioned topics by providing them with critical tools for analysis. I know of no published New Zealand research into the place of spirituality in the social work curriculum. Apart from its assured place in Maori culture it is barely mentioned in any of the basic minimum standards available.

Discussion

The preparation of a curriculum for spirituality and social work in an environment where indigenous spirituality is alive and respected raised four issues which have been significant for me in developing this module. These issues are: the position of students in relation to what is taught, authority to teach, having respect for sacred knowledge, and practical applications for what is taught. Other concerns have also been important such as how to balance coverage of Western approaches to the topic, including diversity in religious and spiritual traditions, but space does not allow much discussion of them.

An example of what experience has taught me shows how at times a happy conjunction of opportunity and readiness to learn can transform one's understanding. Some years ago I was asked by the Maori staff in our school to facilitate a tutorial consisting of Maori social work students, all of whom had considerable life experience. The topic for discussion was social work interventions with Maori using Maori concepts of genealogy, connection, narrative and metaphor.

For Maori, knowledge of one's connection to 'whanau' (extended family) and genealogy has tremendous significance for mental health. This knowledge imparts a sense of identity and belonging. It connects a person to their wider family and to their ancestors, and each ancestral tree has as its foundation a spiritual being. This spiritual being or 'atua' imparts to each person their 'mauri' (life force) and their 'mana' (dignity and authority) which constitute their grounds for respect. By 'grounds' I mean both justification and, literally, territorial land or 'turangawaewae' – the place where 'tangata whenua' (people of the land) can stand as of right.

As the tutorial discussion got underway, my place was largely that of an outsider and the students needed little facilitation from me. Their discussion focused on ways of working with Maori clients using Maori creation narratives and relating these highly spiritual stories to their clients' lives and their sense of belonging to their extended family and to their land. It became clear to me that in most situations it would be inappropriate for non-Maori practitioners to attempt to practice in this way. Their clients would regard them as having no legitimate connection to that particular world. My outsider position then was, and still is, one of goodwill, learning and, where necessary, referring on in an appropriate way.

Student position in relation to what is taught

In New Zealand, the term 'Maori' is a non-indigenous category which recognizes the indigenous population in a homogeneous manner. Maori prefer to call themselves 'tangata whenua', people of the land, and to identify as members of their 'iwi' (tribe) and 'hapu' (sub-tribe) and 'whanau' (extended family). The students enrolled for the spirituality module are a diverse group. Some are school leavers, others are older adults, often with children and other dependents. Some will be studying part-time and at a distance while holding down a job. There will be Maori students from the local 'iwi' and they are regarded as 'tangata whenua', people of the land. Other Maori students from 'iwi' outside this area will have a different status, as 'manuhiri', or visitors. The third and largest category of students is non-Maori students of Pacific Island, European or Asian origin.

Teaching such a diverse group of social work students together means several different cultures need to be acknowledged and catered for. Students need to feel safe and respected in this environment. Every spiritual tradition has its sacred areas. The tutor who introduces sacred material into the curriculum will need to do so with care and will need to ensure that as far as all members of the group are concerned, they have the authority to do so, and can keep the group spiritually safe.

A classroom with 'tangata whenua' from the area and Maori from other tribal areas as well as students who have non-indigenous status is one where students are positioned differently in relation to what they are being taught and who teaches it. Some Maori students may be introduced to ideas and concepts that they can use directly with their clients, which could be inappropriate or even dangerous for non-Maori to use in their work. Nevertheless, all the students need to be well-informed in order to assess safely and be a useful source of referral for clients.

Authority over information

This leads to the question of who has the authority to teach students, both Maori and non-Maori, about Maori cultural traditions and beliefs. Our course sets an assignment (mentioned above) in which students are asked to describe and reflect on their family of origin and what values and beliefs have been passed on to them. Recently, a Maori student handed in his assignment late. We had discussed some of his issues about writing it, issues to do with setting boundaries, safeguarding personal privacy and respecting the information of one's elders. In the assignment, students are asked to discuss what they have learned and the processes they go through to get the required information. This student stated very clearly that his grandfather, still living on the 'marae' (meeting place), had objected strongly to information about the student's 'whakapapa' (family tree) and extended family being put on paper for the sake of an academic grade.

My response was to acknowledge his concerns but also to point out that the academic grade (though significant) was not what most concerned me. The point was rather to know that the student had grappled with his sense of identity, knew who he was in relation to his family, and knew his family values and their implications for his work. A Maori teacher originally set this assignment, at a time when students could spend longer preparing their work. She used to insist that students include their entire family tree. Some of the Maori students objected strongly to this, because their family tree was regarded either by themselves and/or their elders as 'tapu' (sacred), and for some, particularly the women or younger brothers, it was simply not accessible. This practice of restricting access to 'whakapapa' (family tree) has been explained as follows:

> Such knowledge is tapu: refraining from teaching the young too much too soon protects them against unwitting blunders. The custodians of whakapapa should test young enquirers for ability and commitment, select the most promising and mature, and teach them in installments appropriate to their stage of development. (Metge 1995, p.91)

When I took on sole charge of this assignment, I dropped the family tree requirement, not having the inside knowledge and authority to negotiate such an exercise with students. Students are still expected to refer to the family values with which they were brought up, and this regularly leads to discussion about religion and spirituality. They now are only expected to present and discuss their parents' and grandparents' generations.

Respecting sacred or 'tapu' knowledge

I became aware that some students, especially the older ones with traditional Maori backgrounds, had concerns over the extent of spiritually charged information that was being communicated to students. On one occasion two Maori students approached me after a class which was taken by a new Maori lecturer. They felt he had shared information that was not appropriate in a non-Maori academic setting. They recognized his desire to share important and useful information, but felt he was, as it were, giving away information that should be restricted.

Others have provided feedback that to examine students' understanding of certain concepts was culturally inappropriate. Traditionally, children picked out by the elders as having particular aptitudes would be groomed and educated in these areas. Only some people would be considered worthy of receiving certain types of knowledge, and they in turn would become guardians of that knowledge for future generations. Older Maori students with knowledge of their traditional customs were anxious lest restricted knowledge was being transmitted to all and sundry and thereby being debased or misused.

In a modern university setting, this may be a difficult and sensitive area calling for debate in arranging and communicating the curriculum. I take advice here and have to be able to reassure students for whom there are issues at stake. Some people might be inclined to ridicule the notion that any ideas or knowledge should constitute a no go area. The debate is worth having, and there will be limits to what a non-Maori social worker, possessed of 'sacred' knowledge, can safely do with that knowledge without causing distress or offense.

Consideration of the practical applications of what is taught

The fourth issue to raise here follows on from the previous issue. Who is entitled to use the information being taught and how can they put it to use? How can one be sure that the knowledge being shared is safe in the hands of those 'iwi' to whom it may not belong or, perhaps more importantly, with non-Maori? Associated with these questions is a further one which is often raised, whether non-Maori social workers should be working with Maori clients at all. There are no simple answers to these questions. A high proportion of clients are of Maori origin and a high proportion of people working as social workers are not. Whether Maori clients have links to the traditional or classical Maori worldview is yet another matter. Those who have lost that worldview and the ties of responsibility, namely belonging and reciprocity that go with it, may prefer to work with non-Maori. Some Maori social workers argue that it is precisely these clients, more than any others, who need to have that consciousness and those links restored to them. Who is most likely to be able to do this?

These are problems for any neo-colonial country and its indigenous people. Has the time come when the insights and willingness to address them constructively have ripened and can be put into practice? The answer will differ from country to country, and within countries there will be a variety of viewpoints. In New Zealand, when non-Maori social workers work with Maori clients, some models for culturally appropriate practice have been developing. Similarly, models of practice which can be used by Maori with Maori clients are available and culturally skilled non-Maori might, under certain circumstances, draw on these as well.

One of the most popular of these cultural models for practice is known as the 'whare tapa wha' (four-sided house) model. This grew out of the 1970s when Maori called for more holistic assessment in health and mental health settings. A prominent Maori mental health academic has taught this model to many students (Durie 1995). According to Durie, the model compared health to the four walls of a house, all four being necessary to ensure strength and symmetry, though each represents a different dimension: 'taha wairua' (the spiritual side), 'taha hinengaro' (thoughts and feelings), 'taha tinana' (the physical side) and 'taha whanau' (family) (Durie 1995, p.71).

The concept of health and well-being presented by this model is one which encompasses what many people would agree to be the core features of good health when found in balanced harmony. It resonates well with Jungian insights mentioned earlier. Students, whether Maori or not, study the meaning of these four concepts and their implications for assessment and intervention with Maori clients. Some will recognize that these ingredients have universal application. Whether these students are Maori or not, they can use this model and it will assist in reducing the cultural harm which Maori clients face from the culturally inept. At the assessment stage, it alerts the social worker to the importance of an holistic exploration of a client's situation. At the intervention stage it points up the need to work to restore balance in the client's life, by addressing all four aspects of their world: the spiritual, the physical, the psychological and emotional as well as the familial.

Summary and concluding remarks

This chapter has reviewed some of the core literature about spirituality in the social work curriculum. It has introduced the aims and main areas covered in the BSW second year spirituality module and discussed four issues, which I have had to work through in teaching the course. There are many questions that could be raised and reflected on in relation to developing and teaching modules on spirituality for social workers. Are social work students on an undergraduate program ready for and interested in such a topic? My experience suggests that many are very keen to pursue this area, judging by the numbers who choose it as their elective examination question, and they cover the ground very well. The area appeals not only to indigenous students but also to non-Maori students with a strong faith and commitment to Christian beliefs.

There are several important questions about what it feels like for non-Maori students studying the spirituality module if they themselves do not feel a strong sense of their own spiritual life. Might they be intimidated, inspired or silenced by the strength and richness of Maori spirituality when comparing this with their own? There is a need for research here, as in so many areas connected with preparing social work students for work in this field.

What future developments, if any, are called for and how well equipped are social work educators, personally and professionally, to teach this material? In view of the growing interest in this area, research and theory need attention so that practitioners and educators can expand their knowledge and practice skills appropriately. Perceptions of spirituality in connection with social work studies within academic and practice circles will vary. In New Zealand there is respect and interest within the professional association of social workers (ANZASW), which ran a well-received workshop ('Wairuatanga and the Spiritual Dimension in Social Work') on the topic during its 2000 conference. In other fields, interest can also be seen by conferences covering topics such as spirituality and disability and spirituality and ageing.

Perhaps the last point should come from Erenora Puketapu-Hetet, a traditional Maori weaver, regarded by Patterson (1992) as an inspiration for his work exploring Maori values and beliefs. As a weaver, she has talked and written about the need to respect the materials used:

> It is important to me as a weaver that I respect the mauri (life force) of what I am working with. Once I have taken it from where it belongs, I must give another dimension to its life force so that it is still a thing of beauty. I am talking about a whole way of living in harmony with natural things – nature itself, natural lines, natural movements and being at one with these things. (Puketapu-Hetet 1986, p.40)

Can you see any connections between this approach to living in the world and how you or your clients aspire to live? It is imbued with respect for the other in one's life, be that material, human, spiritual, or all three at once. It is, I believe, profound in its simplicity and capable of transforming the person who implements what it means. Whether or not one's imagination is caught by spirituality as an appropriate area for social workers to be involved with, the notion of respect for all around one is widely accessible. How one understands 'mauri' or life force is up to each person. It is possible to take much or little of the idea and still to be touched with an attitude to life that bodes well for the continuity of human beings in a world where, for survival, everything must be respected.

Acknowledgements

In writing this chapter, I wish to acknowledge the help of Dr Ephra Garrett, a Maori woman of great standing in New Zealand; Mrs Vapi Kupenga, my one-time colleague, who challenged me to think about the issues discussed here. Also acknowledged are my colleagues, Dr Leland Ruwhiu, Mrs Rachael Selby and Mrs Wheturangi Walsh-Tapiata. This paper is adapted from my presentation at the 2001 Symposium on Spirituality and Social Work in Dubrovnik.

References

Aotearoa New Zealand Association of Social Workers (1993) Code of Ethics. Dunedin: ANZASW.

Aotearoa New Zealand Association of Social Workers Board of Competency (1997) Practice Standards. Dunedin: ANZASW.

Calligan, T. (2001) Keynote Speech. Report of Auckland conference of women scholars of religion and theology. *New Zealand Catholic,* 11/3/2001,7.

Canda, E.R. (1988a) 'Conceptualising Spirituality for Social Work: Insights from Diverse Perspectives.' *Social Thought,* Winter, 30–46.

Canda, E.R. (1988b) 'Spirituality, Religious Diversity and Social Work Practice.' *Social Casework 69,* 4, 238–247.

Canda, E.R. (1989) 'Religious Content in Social Work Education: A Comparative Approach.' *Journal of Social Work Education 25,* 1, 36–45.

Canda, E. and Furman, L. (1999) *Spiritual Diversity in Social Work Practice: The Heart of Helping.* New York: The Free Press.

Cassidy, S. (1988) *Sharing the Darkness: The Spirituality of Caring.* London: Darton, Longman and Todd.

Derezetes, D.S. (1995) 'Spirituality and Religiosity: Neglected Factors in Social Work Practice.' *Arete 20,* 1, 1–15.

Dudley, J.R. and Helfgott, C. (1990) 'Exploring a Place for Spirituality in the Social Work Curriculum.' *Journal of Social Work Education 26,* 287–294.

Durie, M. (1995) *Whaiora: Maori Health Development.* Auckland: Oxford University Press.

Ehrenreich, J.H. (1985) *The Altruistic Imagination. A History of Social Work and Social Policy in the United States.* Ithaca and London: Cornell University Press.

Ellison, C. and Smith, J. (1991) 'Toward an Integrative Measure of Health and Well-Being.' *Journal of Psychology and Theology 19,* 1, 35–48.

Gilbert, K. (1996) 'God at the Campfire and that Christfella.' In A. Pattel-Gray (ed) *Aboriginal Spirituality: Past, Present and Future.* Australia: HarperCollins Religious.

Henare, M. (1988) 'Standards and Foundations of Maori Society.' In *Royal Commission on Social Policy.* Vol III, Part One. Wellington: Government Print.

Jenkins, K. (1988) 'The Spiritual Link: a Maori Perspective on the Spiritual Dimension of Social Wellbeing.' In *Royal Commission on Social Policy.* Vol III, Part One. Wellington: Government Print.

Kamya, H.A. (2000) 'Hardiness and Spiritual Well-Being among Social Work Students: Implications for Social Work Education.' *Journal of Social Work Education 36,* 2, 231–240.

Kilpatrick, A.C. and Holland, T.P. (1990) 'Spiritual Dimensions of Practice.' *The Clinical Supervisor 8,* 2, 125–140.

Metge, J. (1995) *New Growth from Old. The Whanau and the Modern World.* Wellington: Victoria University Press.

Ministerial Advisory Committee (1986) *Puao-te-ata-tu. The Report of the Ministerial Advisory Committee on a Maori Perspective for the Department of Social Welfare.* Wellington: Department of Social Welfare.

Nash, M. (1993) 'The Use of Self in Experiential Learning for Cross-Cultural Awareness: An Exercise Linking the Personal with the Professional.' *Journal of Social Work Practice 7*, 1, 55–61.

Okundaye, J.N., Gray, C. and Gray, L.B. (1999) 'Reimaging Field Instruction from a Spiritually Sensitive Perspective: An Alternative Approach.' *Social Work 44*, 4, 371–383.

Patterson, J. (1992) *Exploring Maori Values.* Palmerston North: The Dunmore Press.

Puketapu-Hetet, E. (1986) (Interview) Nicholas 1986. In J. Patterson (1992) *Exploring Maori Values.* Palmerston North: The Dunmore Press.

Rennebohm, C. (2001) Spirituality and Social Work Conference, Dubrovnik. Personal communication.

Russell, R. (1998) 'Spirituality and Religion in Graduate Social Work.' In E.R. Canda (ed) *Spirituality and Social Work: New Directions.* New York: The Haworth Pastoral Press.

Sermabeikian, P. (1994) 'Our clients, ourselves: The spiritual perspective and social work practice'. *Social Work 39*, 2, 178–183.

Sheridan, M.J. and Amato-von-Hemart, K. (1999) 'The Role of Religion and Spirituality in Social Work Education and Practice: A Survey of Student Views and Experiences.' *Journal of Social Work Education 35*, 1, 125–142.

Sheridan, M.J., Bullis, R.K., Adcock, C.R., Berlin, S.D. and Miller, P.C. (1992) 'Practitioners' Personal and Professional Attitudes and Behaviors toward Religion and Spirituality: Issues for Education and Practice.' *Journal of Social Work Education 28*, 2, 190–203.

Statistics New Zealand (1998) *New Zealand Official Yearbook.* Wellington: Statistics New Zealand.

Chapter Seven

Integrating Western and Aboriginal Healing Practices

Romeo Beatch and Bruce Stewart

Introduction

Aboriginal communities in North America often display significant problems related to depression, suicide, addiction, family violence and incarceration. Western-trained counseling practitioners have attempted to assist Aboriginal people to reduce levels of maladjustment but this cultural group has not easily endorsed a Western rehabilitative process (Blue and Annis 1985). Those in the helping field, particularly counseling practitioners, are likely to be challenged in dealing with possible causal links to distressed behavior given the appearance of widespread community malaise and impoverishment within Aboriginal communities. Frustration on the part of cross-cultural practitioners in finding effective treatment is likely to raise a question about what kind of perspective and treatment is needed to reduce a sense of deep-seated alienation and suffering.

This chapter acknowledges the level of distress among Aboriginal people in the Canadian Arctic, which is comparable with that found in southern Canada and in North America. Its presence suggests urgency in providing effective help and explores culture and spirituality within culture as significant factors in developing effective therapy. These views will be presented through themes and issues identified in the literature sources and direct knowledge from the writers' cross-cultural experience in the Canadian Arctic. We argue that enhancing cultural development will improve well-being and that Aboriginal cultural loss through colo-niszation and assimilation by Western influences has contributed to wide-spread malaise. Based on this view, effective treatment necessitates a recovery of cultural knowledge and practices and finding common ground with Western practitioners dedicated to healing. To this end sto-rytelling, mythology, symbol and ceremony and partnership of Western practitioners with traditional healers will be highlighted.

Connecting Western and Aboriginal practices

Respecting similarities and differences

Non-Aboriginal trained practitioners are likely to rely primarily on Western thinking and practices in their work (Sue and Sue 1990). This means secular beliefs, modern science and expertise derived from academic training will influence their work. This background has a prefer-ence for rationality, impartial service delivery and investigating individuals apart from their community (Harman 1998). However, the therapeutic value of Western individualistic concepts is likely to be incomplete in alle-viating suffering and alienation for collectivist and land-based culture groups (Herring 1996).

Traditional First Nation perspective has a preference for ecological systems, holistic processes, belonging at the community level and reliance on traditional beliefs and values (Herring 1996). This view includes recogniszing that a spiritual connection to sacred knowledge is an integral part of the well-being of individuals and communities (Deloria 1995). Cultural beliefs and values, which underpin sacred knowledge, often assert respectful connections to land, heritage, ancestry, and spirit world to promote harmony and balance within and beyond oneself (Canda 1988, pp.33–34).

Understanding healing perspectives

Aboriginal healing includes strengthening cultural belonging, identity and community-based self-determination (Cordova 1996; Rappaport and Simpkins 1991). Healing is a holistic process involving the person's connection to their environment and removes people's isolation from one another and their cultural heritage (Hobday 1981). This heritage may be depicted by the medicine wheel, which highlights the elements of earth, fire, air and water and guides individuals to balanced living (White 1996). The elements embody the 'Ceator's' spirit that is alive in all things. The medicine wheel is also used to identify the four dimensions of the human person: mental, emotional, physical and spiritual (Canda 1983, p.16; Herring 1996, p.544). When alienation and suffering are present both within and outside the person healing occurs by respecting the wisdom of the 'Creator' and by searching for harmony or balance within or with the forces depicted by the medicine wheel (Hart 1996). Harmony is achieved by participating in traditional rituals and ceremonies, which evoke individual and community strength. The rituals and ceremonies involve such things as daily or regular cleansing ceremonies or 'smudges' (Sun Bear, Wabun Wind and Mulligan 1991), drum dances, healing circles, and sweat lodges (Hart 1996, p.64). Physical journeying to places considered sacred and where the healing spirit of the 'Creator' is evoked may also take place (Carmody and Carmody 1996). The latter is often achieved through mystical and non-ordinary experiences by individuals who participate in vision quests, dream interpretation, and guided trance (Bynum 1993, p.29).

Western counseling also embraces the concept of healing. Healing can be a blanket term for the outcome of any caring activity or an intentional activity by a helper, which may or may not involve energy exchange. It can also occur as an unintentional experience(s) in a helping relationship and frequently is depicted as presence, tenderness or an inherent quality from the therapeutic relationship (West 1997). Many Western methods focus on resolving personal and interpersonal conflicts through such approaches as solution focused, cognitive-behavioral, and rational-emotive therapy. These approaches are helpful in addressing bio-psychosocial problems but can be incomplete for individuals looking for help with their spiritual reality.

Some Western practitioners take a wider view of individual healing by looking at balance through ecological and holistic wellness (Graham, Kaiser and Garrett 1998; Park 1996). Here healing is understood by balancing mind, body, emotions and spirit in one's environment (Cowley 1993). Counselors that embrace this approach often heal by inherent qualities in the therapeutic relationship and facilitating connections to the outside world (Canda 1998). The helper may act as a vehicle to transfer healing energy between client, counselor and the greater world by spiritually oriented techniques such as prayer, ritual and meditation to enhance healing. Other therapists may use Western hypnotic techniques to create an altered state of mind that provides the same insights leading to healing as those experienced in indigenous shamanic ordeals, vision quests and ritualized ceremonies (Hammerschlag 2000, p.16). Western healing experiences unlike Aboriginal activities tend to be confined to one's workplace and home and only rarely involve direct links to the physical environment (Park 1996, p.322).

Utilizing unseen power

Western helpers and traditional healers may have some common ties to a belief that well-being is improved by harmonious relationships with a living world. It is a view of the world where all things are interdependent and interconnected by a universal life force. Attuning oneself to the principles of a nurturing earth is a fundamental belief system common to many in the non-Western world (Lee and Armstrong 1995). Similar views can be found in such sources as ancient European history, perspectives in ecological wellness or spiritually and holistic influenced helping models (Cowley 1993).

In the earth power concept health arises through respecting the inherent life force of 'Mother Nature' and living according to her laws (Park 1996). By respecting the earth's life patterns, human beings are provided with a capacity to derive power and healing from the earth (Estes 1992). Not living with respect for nature creates imbalance and sickness by disconnecting us from the earth's healing power and permits destructive forces to be unleashed on the planet (Christ 1989; Durie 1995; Starhawk 1989). A concrete picture of healing by living in harmony and abiding by earth's laws is evident in the Aboriginal 'sacred hoop' (Richardson 1981, p.223). The hoop symbolizes that all people and things contained in it benefit by living in balance with one another. In pre-Christian

Europe its spiral and circular motifs represented a primary nurturing force. These images also encouraged people to revere the land and its cycles in order to be supported by earthly powers (Meadows 1996, pp.9, 319).

Spirituality's inseparability from culture
Acknowledging the non-visible world

There is significant evidence that practitioners working cross-culturally with Aboriginal groups in Canada's Arctic are likely to see direct reporting of phenomena that are extraordinary and paranormal. The reports usually occur when there is rapport and trust between client and practitioner. Our experience in these situations is that frequent reference is made to some kind of contact with the spirit world through unusual signs, sensations, sounds and energy surges in nature or in one's community. Some individuals also describe dramatic visionary experiences of 'spirit helpers' or beings from another world. Others tell of psychic knowledge concerning the whereabouts of people missing on the land, the occurrence of future events and acquiring healing abilities from a greater power. Many of these stories seem highly exceptional from a Western rational perspective but this is mitigated by the sincerity and credibility of the people telling us about first-hand accounts with a spirit world. It is evident that in most cases the accounts do not reflect human pathology but are a cultural interpretation of some actual events. In many cases practitioners are unprepared to comprehend or validate these interpretations given the influences of Western scientific thinking. Where Western and positivist thinking are still dominant in the practice field, spirituality is considered non-verifiable and excessively subjective (O'Hara 1997). However, learning to value the accounts of the spirit world can be developed by becoming more involved with the living style of Aboriginal people.

Participating in Aboriginal practices

Effective cross-cultural practice may necessitate partnership and involvement in Aboriginal practices (Trimble and Lafromboise 1987). Further, Western practitioners who show a willingness to learn the belief systems of a particular Aboriginal group and actively participate in their traditions may begin to operate with more personal confidence and gain legitimacy as effective healers. In the following chapter, Ross Wheeler presents an example of such a practitioner. This legitimacy is also demonstrated by showing an interest in how Aboriginal people experience their daily life. It means understanding the spiritual significance of such daily activities as hunting, fishing, sewing and social gathering. It also includes appreciating the collective sense of obligation and responsibility to family, elders, and community. The practitioner may become more openly accepted by participating in many meaningful practices that arise in daily living. At the same time, Aboriginal people are not all the same in their breadth and depth of adherence to traditional beliefs. Therefore the practitioner is also likely to discover spiritual diversity within the Aboriginal community itself and needs to adapt to the practices that stem from this diversity.

Integrated practice

This section focuses on integrating Western and First Nation healing for the benefit of clients and practitioners. It shows a theory and approaches often used and illustrates how symbol, ritual, travel on the land and 'Elder' guidance are all important in the process. The setting is a correctional facility involving the treatment of adult males convicted of sexual offenses but the approach could apply to many other population groups in northern Canada. In this situation the majority of offenders are First Nation individuals from a variety of cultural backgrounds including Dene, Inuit, Metis and Inuvialuit.

Conventional offender treatment draws on a common body of knowledge developed by professionals largely informed by Western knowledge, practice and science. The primary goal of treatment for individuals convicted of sexual offenses is to decrease the potential for the individual to re-offend in a sexual manner. This body of knowledge suggests that a cognitive-behavioral approach to treatment tends to provide the best results (Marshall and Williams 2000, p.42). Furthermore there are specific issues or factors that have been identified as critical in determining the level of risk and which guide treatment initiatives for the individual. There are historical and dynamic factors that determine the level of risk and guide the treatment initiatives (Wong *et al.* 2000). Historical factors include such things as the number of previous charges and/or convictions for sexual offenses, who the victim is in relation to the offender, whether there was any non-sexual violence at the time of the sexual offense and whether the individual ever lived with a partner for two years or more. Dynamic factors include such things as the individual's ability to understand the cycle of events that were part of the build-up to the offense, the lifestyle of the individual, community support and response to treatment. Effective assessment and treatment is usually influenced by the nature of the therapeutic alliance between the practitioner and client. This holds true for this case study as well and possibly even more so. For an individual to talk about his personal sexual behavior requires a high degree of confidence in the person to whom he is talking.

The medicine wheel in context

It is important when using Western knowledge and practices with a specific First Nation population to retain respect for their traditional knowledge, values and beliefs. Therefore incorporating some of their fundamental symbols into the treatment process is necessary. In this example treatment is provided within two possible contexts, either a traditional teepee or a tent frame.

THE TEEPEE

The teepee is a tent used traditionally for living and gathering by Aboriginal people. Its use predates settlement by European people of North America. The teepee's circular shape symbolizes the importance of interconnection and the cyclical nature of life (Northwest Territory Dept of Education, Culture and Employment 1993, p.xix). In the spiritual realm it may allude to wider themes of achieving wholeness through the circle of life and being connected to a universal spirit through the symbol of the circle (Meadows 1996). The circle is often found through healing circles formed on the open land. In these situations it is evident that those gathered can follow a tradition of walking clockwise to show respect for the seasons and cycles of the earth. Fire is often at the center of many circular gatherings with a circle of stones surrounding it. The fire becomes a focus of attention in offering prayers to the 'Creator'. Walking behind anyone sitting in the circle is necessary to respect whoever may be praying or speaking to others sitting in the circle. Walking in front of a person in a healing circle is avoided in order that the connection and communication between individuals, others and the 'Creator' is not disrupted.

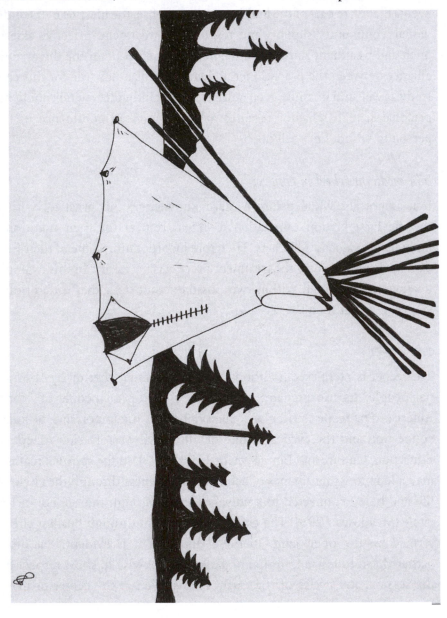

Figure 7.1 The teepee

THE TENT FRAME

Another traditional structure is the tent frame. It is a wooden structure with a floor, skeleton walls and roof covered by a heavy canvas specifically designed for this square structure. Northern First Nation people commonly use it when living on the land. A small tin stove that provides very quick heat for warmth and cooking heats the structure.

The teepee and tent frame are now seen as important places where programs and traditional ceremonies can take place and have been built within the grounds of the correctional center. Providing treatment within these two traditional spaces removes individuals from the negative attitudes often found in correctional facilities. Both environments are well known to First Nation people and are frequently experienced as positive settings in which they can be productive, respected and can experience a strong connection to their traditional values and beliefs.

The treatment program for sexual offenders is placed within the values and beliefs of First Nation people, which are often symbolized by the medicine wheel (Bopp *et al.* 1984). The fundamental values at the heart of the medicine wheel are respect for all things and living in harmony with all that is around and within oneself. When individuals begin to explore the causes of their offending behavior they begin to realize that their offense is the ultimate contradiction of their value system. It shows a complete disrespect for themselves as well as the victim. They also realize that they have often set aside many of the positive practices supporting their beliefs and values. For example, individuals talk about how they had stopped participating in community drum dances. Or an individual can trace how he gradually shifted his interest and responsibility in being a drummer and singer within his community to becoming more involved with individuals whose primary interest was drugs and alcohol.

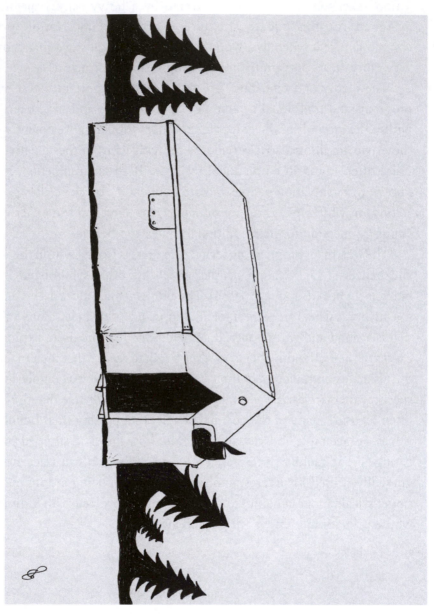

Figure 7.2 The tent frame

CLEANSING PRAYERS

The program begins with a cleansing ceremony and prayer. The cleansing ceremony involves the burning of sweet grass, sage and tobacco (Hart 1996, p.68). These items are burned in a dish that comes from the earth such as a large seashell. Sometimes the 'Elder' who provides instruction on the meaning of the various plants that are used leads this ceremony. The smoke rising from the burning sweet grass, sage and tobacco is gathered up in one's hands and poured over the head, arms, chest, and legs. The sacred smoke is also brushed over one's eyes, ears, and mouth, cleansing one's thoughts, clearing one's ability to hear the words spoken around the circle and giving the courage to speak the words that one must speak at the appropriate time. The cleansing ceremony can be used at any time and in any place. When one goes on to the land, the cleansing ceremony takes place, cleansing all of one's body including the soles of one's feet. In this way one is reminded to walk respectfully upon the earth. The belief is that in participating in a respectful relationship with the earth the necessary mental, emotional, physical and spiritual healing can take place within a person.

A case study: the land-healing journey

An important part of the treatment process is that group members should take responsibility for their abusive behavior. Each member of the group is first asked to do a written exercise describing the events leading up to his offense and then the actual offending behavior. They then present this information in the group where they can receive feedback and questions of clarification from other group members. This often generates feelings of shame, guilt and remorse. A sense of heaviness settles over the group. Sometimes their disclosures trigger memories of past experiences of abuse an individual himself might have experienced. This only adds to the already heavy mood settling in on the group.

With the support of the Elder, a day on the land is planned after all group members have had the opportunity to talk about their offenses. This day on the land is led by the Elder. When possible traditional foods such as caribou made into stew, sausages or hamburger, fish or dried meat will be prepared and shared among the participants. Group members then work together to load the supplies and to set up the campsite. On the way to the campsite, the Elder will choose a location to stop for a traditional ceremony. This location is often near a waterfall, the shore of a nearby lake or river. At this location the group members are allowed to have some time with their own reflections. Then they are called together for a cleansing ceremony led by the Elder. Once again the traditional symbols of sage, sweet grass and tobacco are used. The Elder understands the struggle they have recently come through, the negative feelings and the negative memories of what they have done and what may have been done to them. Participants take a little tobacco in their hands. The Elder prays, reminding the group members of the need to be connected to the earth and the many gifts it can offer.

The group is also reminded of their weaknesses and the need to be connected to the strength, support and power of the 'Creator'. When there are drummers among the group, a drumming prayer is sung. And then each person is invited to individually make his prayer while placing the tobacco he holds in his hand into the water of the river. In this way he is invited to cleanse himself of all the negative thoughts, feelings and behaviors while inviting new strength to come from the water and earth on which he stands. During the winter and spring seasons when the water is frozen, the campfire becomes the center of the circle. The same ceremony as described above takes place with the individuals placing the tobacco in their hands in the fire.

With the completion of these ceremonies, the group moves on to a location that is selected by the Elder as the place where a campsite can be established. The group members actively participate in preparing the campsite, collecting the necessary wood, building the fire and preparing the food. The entire day is spent within the context of remembering, appreciating and experiencing the benefits of reconnecting with the earth.

This case example has parallels with similar methods in use in other parts of the world, such as New Zealand, where indigenous people are involved on both sides of the social care divide (Ruwhiu 1994). One of the challenges it poses is how to work at this level with those who have left their cultural and territorial place in the world, whose indigeneity has been transformed so that they have become migrants or refugees. This case study signals a number of ways in which spirituality influences good practice in social care.

Spirituality's impact on practice
Recognizing spirituality supports cultural diversity

Given demographic changes and technological advancements there is increasing cross-cultural interchange in Western society. Practitioners are now realistically confronted with a diversity of cultures in their work (Pellebon and Anderson 1999). This places an increasing need upon practitioners to develop an effective client-centered approach in their work. Spirituality often plays a significant role in the lives of many cultural groups (Lukoff, Lu and Turner 1998). Therefore openness to and familiarity with the diversity of spiritual worldviews is a necessity. The spiritual aspect of culture can be critical in reflecting fundamental beliefs and values of clients. Practitioners tolerant of different client beliefs and values create an environment with potential for exploration and understanding of differences between client and counselor. The practitioner's own spiritual development is also important and does not need to be compromised in the process of being open to client views. In fact the counselor's own personal spiritual development is an asset to enhancing competence and willingness to address the spiritual dimension (Canda 1998).

The literature indicates that only recently have there been efforts to introduce spirituality into counseling (Kilpatrick and Holland 1990). In the past, secular influences in society have minimized or devalued the spiritual elements in the helping field. Now there seems to be a renewal of interest in integrating spirituality with counseling (O'Hara 1997). This is evident by a growing acceptance in society about the reality of increased cross-cultural contact and more recognition of the potency that one's cultural-spiritual view has on human behavior. From a helping perspective, it is becoming more acceptable for counseling to use a bio-psycho-socialspiritual model.

The spiritual dimension heightens awareness

Current counseling research supports the notion that spiritual perspectives can benefit clients. Past bias to excluding spirituality in practice is likely to lessen with growing awareness that it plays a significant role in under-standing a client's worldview, decision-making and behavior. Spirituality is increasingly being associated with improving healing, relieving depression and adding to empowerment. Developing a spiritual perspective is also significant in helping people to deal with issues of death, day-to-day coping, and developing constructive meaning to significant life events that have caused alienation and suffering (Sermabeikian 1994). These benefits occur in part due to spirituality's link to cultural beliefs and values that strengthen identity and self-determination (Canda 1988).

Many of the traditional beliefs and values for First Nation people associated with identity and self-determination were lost through colonization (Ivey 1995; Saleebey 1994). In North America colonization resulted in acculturation by increased cultural vulnerability from genocide, removal to boarding schools and conversion to Christianity by the early European missionaries (Brown and Vilbert 1996, pp.xxii–xv). The acculturation process has resulted in significant social and psychological problems in Aboriginal communities (Choney, Berryhill-Paapke and Robbins 1995, pp.77–80). Today Western psychology clearly reflects its cultural orientation to individualism, modern science and secularism. Despite its adherence to helping others, these beliefs and values influential in counseling may not reflect collectivist cultures. The helping field therefore needs to be careful about impositions, spiritual or other, on culturally different groups to avoid contributing to even subtle forms of colonialism (Gergen 1994).

Spirituality raises issues about integration

There are many positive aspects to integrating spirituality into practice; however, there are also some cautionary notes. In regards to culture, the multicultural field indicates that spirituality is part of cultural identity and as such, subject to the same influences that create significant identity difference within a culture. Assimilation, cross-cultural interchange and influences from the global economic-technological community all appear to create cultural differences within Aboriginal communities (Hart 1996). The result is that each individual can vary in terms of the depth and relevance that their cultural teaching has for them. Therefore practitioners need to be careful in making assumptions that if a person is part of a cultural group that they will have a specific set of spiritual beliefs and values.

For practitioners, acceptance of a client's worldview is essential. Therefore interpreting spirituality broadly can facilitate acceptance and inclusion of many views. Tolerance needs to extend to traditional Aboriginal healers who may have beliefs and approaches divergent from more common thinking associated with Western science and Judeo-Christianity. At the same time, Aboriginal helpers and their practices may have their own imperfections and are not above being constructively criticized. Traditional healers/shamans are often just as ethnocentric as many Western helping professionals and certain treatments may be harmful (Canda 1983, p.20). Western and non-Western therapies both need to be critiqued and mutually improved for facilitating wellness.

Spirituality can be conceptualized as a life journey for meaning, interconnection and belonging to something deep within and/or beyond oneself. Yet the very belief systems that generate these significant developments can spark intolerance from those who feel challenged by different views. If the challengers are in the minority (as is often the case with indigenous people whose spiritual beliefs are at stake) they may suffer from negative criticism or psychological harassment and their potential for positive self-determination is weakened. Therefore the nature of any spiritual system needs to be carefully considered for its potential to heal, empower and to nurture relationships (Canda 1983).

Conclusion

Aboriginal communities often reflect much of the land-based spirituality from their culture. However, Western colonialism has historically produced a significant loss in their beliefs, values and lifestyles that has reduced this spirituality. The impression is that this loss in Aboriginal communities increases destructive behavior due in part to culture fragmentation and spiritual malaise. Western-oriented treatment programs are inadequate in fully reaching these communities unless they can significantly integrate their approach with traditional beliefs and values and are focused on relieving alienation and suffering from cultural loss. In terms of a treatment process it may mean participating in holistic healing approaches designed to recover and re-integrate traditional beliefs, values and practices. It also means working collaboratively with traditional healers in open dialog regarding strengths and weaknesses inherent in each therapeutic system.

References

Blue, A.W. and Annis, R.C. (1985) 'Counseling Native Canadians: Issues and Answers.' In R.J. Samuda and A. Wolfgang (eds) *Intercultural counseling and Assessment of Global Perspectives.* Toronto: C. J. Hogrefe.

Bopp, J., Bopp, M., Brown, L. and Lane, P. Jr. (1984) *The Sacred Tree.* Twin Lakes, WI: Lotus Light Publications.

Brown, J.S.H. and Vilbert, E. (1996) 'Introduction.' In J.S.H. Brown and E. Vilbert (eds) *Reading Beyond Words: Contexts for Native History.* Peterborough, Ontario: Broadview Press.

Bynum, E.B. (1993) *Families and the Interpretation of Dreams: Awakening the Intimate Web.* New York: The Haworth Press.

Canda, E.R. (1983) 'General Implications of Shamanism for Clinical Social Work.' *International Social Work 26,* 4, 14–22.

Canda, E.R. (1988) 'Conceptualizing Spirituality for Social Work: Insights from Diverse Perspectives.' *Social Thought,* Winter, 30–46.

Canda, E.R. (1998) 'Afterward: Linking Spirituality and Social Work: Five Themes for Innovation.' *Social Thought: Journal of Religion in the Social Services 18,* 2, 97–106.

Carmody, D.L. and Carmody, J.T. (1996) *Mysticism: Holiness East and West.* New York: Oxford University Press.

Choney, S.K., Berryhill-Paapke, E. and Robbins, R.R. (1995) 'The Acculturation of American Indians: Developing Frameworks for Research and Practice.' In J.G. Ponterotto, J.M. Casa, L.A. Suzuki and C.M. Alexander (eds) *Handbook of Multicultural Counseling.* London: Sage.

Christ, C. (1989) 'Rethinking Theology and Nature.' In J. Plaskow and C. Christ (eds) *Weaving the Visions: New Patterns in Feminist Spirituality.* New York: HarperCollins.

Cordova, V.F. (1996) 'Doing Native American Philosophy.' In S. O'Meara and D. West (eds) *From Our Eyes: Learning from Indigenous Peoples.* Toronto: Garamond Press.

Cowley, Au-Deane, S. (1993) 'Transpersonal Social Work: A Theory for the 1990's.' *Social Work 38*, 5, 527–534.

Deloria, V. (1995) *Red Earth, White Lies: Native Americans and the Myth of Scientific Fact.* New York: Scribner.

Durie, M. (1995) *Whaiora: Maori Health Development.* Auckland: Oxford University Press.

Gergen, K.J. (1994) 'Exploring the postmodern: Perils or potentials?' *American Psychologist 49*, 5, 412–416.

Graham, M., Kaiser, T and Garrett, K.J. (1998) 'Naming the Spiritual: the Hidden Dimensions of Helping.' *Social Thought: Journal of Religion in the Social Services 18*, 4, 49–62.

Hammerschlag, C.A. (2000) 'Ericksonian Psychology and the Shamanic Journey.' *Milton H. Erickson Foundation Newsletter 20*, 1, 16.

Harman, W. (1998) *Global Mind Change* (2nd edn). San Francisco: Berrett-Koehler.

Hart, M.A. (1996) 'Sharing Circles: Utilizing Traditional Practice Methods for Teaching, Helping and Supporting.' In S. O'Meara and D. West (eds) *From Our Eyes: Learning from Indigenous Peoples.* Toronto: Garamond Press.

Herring, R.D. (1996) 'Synergetic Counseling and Native American Indian Students.' *Journal of Counseling & Development 74*, 6, 542–547.

Hobday, M.J. (1981) 'Seeking a Moist Heart: Native American Ways for Helping the Spirit'. In M. Fox (ed) *Western Spirituality: Historical Roots, Ecumenical Routes.* Santa Fe: Bear & Co.

Ivey, A.E. (1995) 'Psychotherapy as liberation: Toward specific skills and strategies in multicultural counseling and therapy'. In J.G. Ponterotto, J.M. Casa, L.A. Suzuki and C.M. Alexander (eds) *Handbook of Multicultural Counseling.* London: Sage.

Kilpatrick, A.C. and Holland, T.P. (1990) 'Spiritual Dimensions of Practice.' *The Clinical Supervisor 8*, 2, 125–140.

Lee, C.C. and Armstrong, K.L. (1995) 'Indigenous models of mental health intervention: Lessons from traditional healers'. In J.G. Ponterotto, J.M. Casa, L.A. Suzuki, and C.M. Alexander (eds) *Handbook of Multicultural Counseling.* London: Sage.

Lukoff, D., Lu, F. and Turner, R. (1998) 'From Spiritual Emergency to Spiritual Problem: The Transpersonal Roots of the New DSM-IV Category.' *Journal of Humanistic Psychology 38*, 2, 21–50.

Marshall, W.L. and Williams, S. (2000) 'Assessment and Treatment of Sexual Offenders.' *Forum on Corrections Research 12*, 2, 41–44.

Meadows, K. (1996) *Earth Medicine: Revealing Hidden Teachings of the Native American Medicine Wheel.* Shaftesbury: Element Books.

N.W.T. Department of Education, Culture and Employment (1993) *Dene Kede-Education: A Dene Perspective.* Yellowknife: Education Development Branch.

O'Hara, M. (1997) 'Emancipatory Therapeutic Practice in a Turbulent Transmodern Era: A Work of Retrieval.' *Journal of Humanistic Psychology 37*, 3, 7–33.

Park, K.M. (1996) 'The Personal is Ecological: Environmentalism of Social Work.' *Social Work 41*, 3, 320–323.

Pellebon, D.A. and Anderson, S.C. (1999) 'Understanding the Life Issues of Spiritually-Based Clients.' *Families in Society: The Journal of Contemporary Human Services*, May–June, 229–238.

Rappaport, J. and Simpkins, R. (1991) 'Healing and Empowering through Community Narrative.' *Prevention in Human Services 9*, 29–50.

Richardson, E.H. (1981) 'Cultural and Historical Perspectives in Counseling American Indians.' In D.W. Sue (ed) *Counseling the Culturally Different: Theory and Practice.* New York: Wiley.

Ruwhiu, L. (1994) 'Maori Development and Social Work.' In R. Munford and M. Nash (eds) *Social Work in Action.* Palmerston North: The Dunmore Press.

Saleebey, D. (1994) 'Culture, Theory and Narrative: The Intersection of Meanings in Practice.' *Social Work 39*, 4, 351–359.

Sermabeikian, P. (1994) 'Our Clients, Ourselves: The Spiritual Perspective and Social Work Practice.' *Social Work 39*, 2, 179–183.

Starhawk (1989) *The Spiral Dance: A Rebirth of the Ancient Religion of the Great Goddess.* New York: HarperCollins.

Sue, D. and Sue, D. (1990) *Counseling the Culturally Different: Theory and Practice* (2nd edn). New York: Wiley.

Sun Bear, Wabun Wind and Munnigan, C. (1991) *Dancing with the Wheel:The Medicine Wheel Workbook.* New York:Simon and Schuster.

Trimble, J.E. and Lafromboise, T. (1987) 'American Indians and the Counseling Process: Culture, Adaptation, and Style.' In P. Pedersen (ed) *Handbook of Cross-Cultural Counseling.* New York: Praeger.

West, W. (1997) 'Integrating Counselling Psychotherapy and Healing: An Inquiry into Counsellors and Psychotherapists whose Work Includes Healing.' *British Journal of Guidance and Counselling 25*, 5, 291–311.

White, L.O. (1996) 'Medicine Wheel Teachings: In Native Language Education.' In S. O'Meara and D. West (eds) *From Our Eyes: Learning from Indigenous Peoples.* Toronto: Garamond Press.

Wong, S., Olver, M., Wilde, S., Nicholaichuk, T.P. Gordon, A. (2000, July) *Violence Risk Scale (VRS) & Violence Risk Scale-Sex Offenders Version (VRS-SO)*. Paper presented at the 61st Annual Convention of the Canadian Psychological Association, Ottawa, Canada.

Chapter Eight

'Talk Story'
Interview with Ross Wheeler

Bruce Stewart and Ross Wheeler

Introduction

Dr Ross Wheeler is a physician and addiction specialist with Stanton Yellowknife Hospital located in a small city in Canada's sub-Arctic. While he works with people of Aboriginal and European origins, many Aboriginal people who seek psychological recovery frequently request his assistance. Bruce Stewart therefore interviewed him to find out more about his approach to practice and what it is that attracts them. The interview portrays his individual journey toward personal healing and professional development. He began his career as a medical doctor but became more interested in the value of cross-cultural exchange in resolving the mental health issues commonly observed in his medical practice. Today Ross Wheeler's journey has taken him beyond a fundamental emphasis on physical medicine to alleviating mental health and addiction problems. His perspective now is pointedly spiritual and comes after much reflection, work experience, and his own struggles with alcohol addiction. The interview sheds light on the forces influencing his development and it documents his personal beliefs about his identity, direction, and purpose in life.

The chapter consists of material drawn from the interview with Ross Wheeler, together with some commentary. It has been edited so that the story and its key themes unfold in a developmental fashion; the names of his colleagues have been changed. Wheeler describes his practice and the nature of the problems he addresses. He has an office on the psychiatric ward at the hospital where he is a consultant. He also sees people who would be seen through the outpatient mental health clinic. Wheeler gets direct referrals from clients, as well as from agencies. This means that people don't have to be admitted to the hospital in order to see him, nor do they have to go through the doctor when they are feeling low. When he works from his downtown office at the mental health clinic or with Yellowknife health and social services, referrals come through management services. As Wheeler puts it, 'A lot of my work is still done on the street.' He explains this, saying:

> Well, at the coffee shop, I meet people at the mall, you know, walking around and just connecting with people out there. It's like McDonald [past mentor] used to talk about his psychiatry when he was here. He said just greeting your patients on the street and then attending to them and listening to what they're saying and kind of making mental notes about it is supportive psychotherapy. I mean it is about connecting, it's about often valuing people.

For some of his time Wheeler is based in local and isolated communities such as Lutsel'Ke doing physical medicine and working around addictions and a lot of recovery follow-up, encouraging people to stay with whatever their part of recovery may be. His employer wants him to act as an addiction consultant to a variety of communities, not just Lutsel'Ke. The community contacts are also through people coming through town for meetings and conferences or when he is fortunate enough to travel to communities where he regularly gets referrals.

Bruce Stewart (B.S.):
> Does your medical background help you in any way here?

Ross Wheeler (R.W.):
> I was working in a family practice and the part that seemed to be more satisfying for me and my patients was not when I was looking in their ears and giving them a prescription and off they go. It was when they would be talking about their problems, and that's when I first started using stuff from my own life, talking about that, and people would

take notice of that and they would sometimes incorporate those things into their lives. But it seems to be that I would share my experience about something – people seem to take note of that. And then, when I got into recovery coming on 14 years ago now, I accelerated that process.

The advice in mental health work is not talk about your personal stuff. In my experience it's been quite the opposite, especially when we talk stories together. It's using that Hawaiian phrase of 'talking story' which makes a lot of sense to me. This means you just talk and talk and it's back and forth, and that's what I mean by 'talking story'. Talking story not just in an informal way, but I've been trained to bring in some cognitive aspects to that and I don't know exactly how it's woven in, 'cause I'm not sitting there thinking 'Gee, I should go here, here and here' as it's going on. I tend to be more free flowing than that. Perhaps it's sort of undisciplined in that kind of way as I don't always know the direction it is going in. But if it happens to go way over there, that's fine, let's go way over there, because that's where you're at, you know.

The practice that I'm involved in is primarily in the field of people dealing with addictions. Now with the addictions come dual problems, depression and other anxiety kind of disorders and things of that nature. Because I work at the psychiatric ward there are some purely psychiatric kinds of problems like schizophrenia. But the work that I'm really involved in is the work around addictions and what is largely involved with getting people to move from pre-contemplation into contemplation, into action, you know. Some of the work is about having to maintain, and then there's always the work of dealing with relapse. That's the learning of relapse. How do you get back on track? So I work in intervention at all those different levels.

Following on from this introduction, Wheeler discusses his journey into accepting the importance of spirituality in his life. In response to questions about how he sees spirituality, he had several points to make. The role of Alcoholics Anonymous (AA) has been of particular significance for him.

R.W.: Spirituality should mean more and more to me. I remember when I first got sober, within months of going to AA, I went to an Al-Anon roundup. They used to have these great roundups. Then there was the first book I found on spirituality and recovery, which described a whole bunch of different ideas about the necessity for spirituality. It was by Father Leo Booth and he talked about spirituality and recovery and this described a whole bunch of different ideas about the necessity for spirituality [Booth 1985]. Also the Big Book [Alcoholics Anonymous 1976] talks about grasping the thin reed of recovery. It's like sweet grass and the feather in a way. There's the wonderful visual image where you are hanging off the edge of the cliff. You're hanging off a little branch and what you don't see is the shelf below you, so you ask God for help and the answer is 'let go', 'cause he sees the ledge, but you don't. So the instinctive question – is there anybody else up there? The letting go, that whole 'step three' process. Turning it over and letting it go and believing in a power greater than ourselves in a society, but taking a decision to do that, making a decision to turn our will and our lives over to the care of God as we understood 'God'. Which is great.

At the AA, you all come. You can bring whatever God you want – we don't care. That guy, that guy and that guy, it doesn't matter. That whole sense of letting go, and I remember thinking, 'God, if I let go, who will I be? There will be no me in all of this. Anyway, how do I get all the money I want and all the recognition and all those things? It'll never come.' I've come to understand that of course it'll come, but it is harder to fall than to leave…somehow the letting go idea was very foreign to me, totally foreign to me as an alcoholic, you don't let go of anything, other than your job, families, stuff like that.

B.S.: AA makes a strong connection that if you don't get the spiritual part, you are at greater risk of relapse.

R.W.:   Oh yeah, for sure. AA's conception is that there is a spiritual illness, an obsession of mind and allergy of the body when we know it's not an allergy, but we know it's an obsession of mind. Of course today what we are getting is the neurobiology and the idea it's clearly a brain disease, not spiritual at all. Well, I would've bought into that at one point, but today I think, 'Okay that's fine, it's a brain disease', but with a spiritual component, because the hole is still in all of us. That's a fundamental belief. I believe that we all have a hole in our soul, sort of, a hole inside which probably sits in our belly somehow, in some sort of symbolic way, and we try to fill it with sex, drugs and rock 'n' roll and whatever else.

B.S.:   How do you define spirituality now?

R.W.:   To me it's about meaning, it's about connection, it's about completing the circle. It's often the missing piece for me and it seems for people I work with, it's their missing piece. The one they don't pay attention to when they're out of balance. Well they're out of balance because it's not there. It's like, does it reside in the hole? Remember Jung said that alcoholics were on a low-level spiritual quest. But at a low level, you miss the mark, there's always a yearning, a searching, and this is what is wonderful. So there is the spiritual thing, in order to fill the yearning, which I thought was thirst for alcohol, or thirst for women, or thirst for prestige, or power.

Power doesn't work for me. I tried power once and I was bad at it. Twenty years ago and it was bad. It reminds me of that phrase, you know, 'if what you want is not what you need, you'll never get enough of it'. So the spiritual quest is to try to fill the void, the hole. I think the hole in a lot of our patients is from the pain, and I think it's in all of us, maybe we always feel that pain and so I've tried a whole bunch of different ways to fill it and it doesn't work. It remains there. One of the things I've read which really quite impressed me was the only thing you can fill it with is love, and this whole question of love and what that means. Every now and again I catch a glimpse of it, I get it, I hear what you're saying. It can only be filled with love and only is filled when we reach our God. It is as though in our individual human life, the time that we spend here as spiritual beings on a physical journey, we are a drop of water vapor and what we do eventually is just rejoin the ocean. That's when we become part of the (w)hole. For a brief period of time, we're thrown up.

I see this in Hawaii when the waves come in and the wind blows the top off the waves, it's a beautiful sight. Sheer water goes up in the air and I think 'Oh, that's our life', but then it falls back down and the current goes out again – searching to get back there – not that you want to die, but you want to be in it. Near death, people talk about this overwhelming feeling of love. You can't put any other words to it. I've come close to it on a couple of occasions. It's like peace and that's where spirituality is, it's in there somewhere. Search for it maybe. So as to a definition, I don't have a strict definition. But I've read all kinds of definitions. They all make sense to me, you know, but to me it's about questioning, it's about who we are, where am I in my life, where am I in my world and how do I find a little peace? Where do I find the cookies?

B.S.:   Cookies!

R.W.:   And think of what those cookies did for us when we were kids, on a warm afternoon, having a nap. I just remember that I do it here, have a nap in the afternoon, the sun's coming through, it's hot and delicious…if you had cookies in bed. It's a very spiritual moment.

B.S.:   In what ways does spirituality help?

R.W.:   It's opened up more dialog with patients. This is not cognitive behavioral work. It's opened up often fruitful areas of discussion with people and some people just get right into it and they just want to, oh wow, it really gets

them going, you know! People will run with it. Others, I
don't know how they take it. They may think I'm a flake, I
don't know, and they're too polite to say anything. But
that's all right. I mean, I used to think I was flaky. You
know, I just don't have to think that way now.

B.S.:   How did you make this shift?

R.W.:   I don't know. I think it was the quest, asking the questions,
          searching for answers. Always feeling like, 'There's more to
          check out here.' I wish I had a culture. We started with this
          question earlier, I wished I had a culture and I sort of
          identified with the Indian culture, but what comes out of
          that is that I identify with the Indian culture, 'cause I
          identify myself as a human being. They have some
          wonderful rituals. The rituals of the sweat lodge, crawling
          on your face among the earth. You know 'James' calls it
          being in the mother womb…and the pain, the pain of life
          which is the heat and how together we endure and things
          happen in there. I go in there thinking that maybe
          something really important will happen. I'm always
          looking for that, always looking most every day, but then
          something happens.

*After exploring his personal understandings about the spiritual dimension, which
informs his approach to life and work, Wheeler was asked to explain how he applies
certain spiritual ideas and practices in his work.*

B.S.:   Can you tell us about some of the key concepts, symbols
          and rituals reflected in your professional and personal
          work?

R.W.:   I suppose the one that I've been exploring most and using
          most lately is the First Nations concept of the medicine
          wheel. If you don't want to look at it that way, one could
          say instead that life, human beings, families, communities,
          nations are organized and there are four rungs of activity.
          These are the mental, emotional, physical and spiritual. We
          must attend to them all and life is about being in balance
          with that. I don't see all of my training as primarily in the

physical realm. My work is much removed from that now, so that I'm working with people in all those realms, meeting physical needs and that might be drugs and medications. Then the whole question about their beliefs and…so there's an interesting question about the medicine wheel and balance.

Looking at balance, I found that, certainly, in dealing with the Dene people up here, that's been a much better place I think to go… They all understand physical medicine, but what really seems to connect people and what people really get hungry about is the much more spiritual realm. What I've been trying to do, and what I've been able to do to a certain extent, is help them with a whole series of names and people they can connect with to do this. These people can then meet in communities, meet here or there with those people who are doing this work. They're not psychiatrists or doctors or anything like that, I mean they're pipe carriers [a sacred pipe is given to a respected healer, by his elders, as recognition]. A First Nations doctor would be a pipe carrier. And some of them deal primarily with spiritual healing, but the ones I met were also using herbs, so they are working in all the realms and talking about their beliefs.

I use the concept of the medicine wheel with most people. I'll use it directly as a symbol with the First Nations people and I use smudge [a regular cleansing ceremony]. I've just been using smudge with sweet grass for prayer, offering and cleansing, and some people feel quite okay to bring sage. I like it myself, there's something about it, and it breaks me from being outside to being here [*points to his heart*]. 'Harold' has just given me a feather. He said, 'You can use it however you want', and I'm thinking I'll use it probably with smudging and I need to get some moose hide or something on here [*points to the shaft of the feather*] so you hold it without dropping it.

B.S.:   What does it mean, to be given a feather?

R.W.:   Well, that's a good question. I think for me and from what he was saying the feather is a symbol. The feather is the red road, the sweet grass road. The quill base of the feather and the road have many side trails and they go off in positive and negative directions. So you need to keep on the path. The feather can be used to fan the sweet grass 'cause you never blow on the sage, so you fan it and you can use it to almost wash people down or to smoke. In a First Nations' group, which is like a healing circle, they're always holding their feathers while talking. It's not interactive, people listen to whoever is holding the feather [*Wheeler lays the feather down*].

B.S.:   In laying down the feather is the direction of the shaft important?

R.W.:   The direction doesn't seem to be important but the side is – you never lay it down upside down. So that's what he told me. And what it means to me is that at least in my practice here in Yellowknife I'm gaining some sort of recognition that I'm sensitive to the First Nations issues. People will phone me and say, 'Look I got your name from somebody and they said you're a good person to talk to.' That to me is a consultation, that's the referral. Somebody say's you're a good person to talk to. Then we talk. That means an invitation to talk. I just think that's where the work seems to be taking me anyway.

At this point, Stewart asked Wheeler to explain how it is that a non-Aboriginal with Western medical training has received these gifts and requests from the Aboriginal communities. His response to this intriguing question indicates that sincerity meets with recognition across cultures, and that actions, such as going to the sweat lodge, speak louder than words.

R.W.:   Being Canadian, I remember when I was first up here, my two best drinking buddies would be going on and on about their cultures and their heritage, and I'm sitting there thinking 'I don't have any of that stuff'. So I tried a whole bunch of different things, you know. Hanging around with

native people 'cause that was who I met when I first got
here, and getting involved in the Aboriginal Inquiry [the
MacKenzie Valley Pipeline Inquiry of the mid-1970s,
headed by the then Justice Thomas Berger, where
Aboriginal peoples' views had importance in determining
whether or not there should be pipeline development in
the area]. It was an attempt to be acceptable, to be
welcomed, you know: to get out there and find out. But
also there was my own search around identity. I mean, I
knew I wasn't an Indian, but when I see movies like
Braveheart, I think it would be kind of neat to be Scottish. I
have a sense of not being rooted in anything or in any
place. I listen with great longing to people who talk about
their people coming from wherever. I listen to Dene people
talking about the land and some sort of mystical
connection they have with the land. It's not mystical, it's
just real. They talk about living in balance on the land in
harmony with what is going on there.

I remember when I first got to the sweat lodge I was
scared. I knew it was hot and I thought I would get
claustrophobic and part of it was, 'What if I have to run out
'cause it's too hot?' I would embarrass myself. When you
hear men talking about how it's really hot and sweaty and
they stuck it out, a bit machismo, smoke going on, you
don't want to run when it gets hot and sweaty. I remember
being very afraid, and I'm always afraid within the first ten
minutes in a sweat lodge. 'Alex' says, 'Pray, pray, pray, just
pray.' I used to use a third step prayer from AA and I got
down to just using one phrase of it, and I would say it over
and over and over and the sweat lodge would cool down.
Of course it didn't change temperature, but I sure did. I
think one of the things about Dene people is that if you're
willing to walk with them on their walk they will talk to
you about their walks.

I was talking about a friend of mine who's got a son
who appears to have attention deficit disorder at school
and the mother wants him to have [the medication] Ritalin.

She's a native woman. She knows that's not the answer, but she's at her wits' end over how to deal with this kid. The startling thing about the kid is when Dad sits with him, he's nine years old, on his knee, on the front of the ski-doo and they're heading for the bush – six hours on the ski-doo, the kid never moves. That's not attention deficit. The kid knows where he's going. He gets out there and both parents describe how in the bush he's a totally different kid. There are all kinds of interesting psychodynamic reasons for all that, but what really strikes me is that he's on the land. There's something there. Something real for that kid holds him and allows him to take energy and control himself and focus. I mean he's the one who listens to the animals. He hears the animals before his parents do.

B.S.: 'Hears the animals'? What do you mean by that?

R.W.: Well, when they'll be out and they're maybe hunting or something he'll know that the animals are near because he hears them or he calls it hearing, something like that. So, he's a different kid in the bush. To me the answer for him is not Ritalin, it's 'Go live in the bush'. His parents can do that, there are reasons they can't or won't or whatever, but you think the kid could be happy in the bush. You know, for a time maybe.

When I was in Deline two summers ago 'William' wanted to talk and his wife wanted to talk and all these people wanted to talk – where can we go? Sitting in 'William's' smokehouse in his backyard was beautiful. The teepee smelled of smoked fish and spruce, it just seemed so perfect for a place to talk, it was private but it was right there. You could hear the lake beside and you're sitting on a stump and you think, 'Man, this couldn't get much better than this.' Listening to all those guys telling their stories, sharing back and forth. That's where it always felt good to me.

Wheeler next talks about his own and others' perceptions of spirituality in the Christian and secular world.

R.W.:   Talking about spiritual practices, I'm now in a centering prayer group with 'Ellen' over at the Catholic church. I'm not a Catholic, but I go there Monday nights. It's a movement within the Catholic Church, very interesting, about use of prayer where you try to practice the presence of God. It's from their liturgy and Christ figure. But it's a really neat kind of deal, 'cause you do at least a 20 minute meditation in the middle of this.

I was at a recent retreat, talking about ritual and symbolism and how important that was to people, and it wasn't known it was so important until I got older and it was taken away. I remember going Christmas and New Year's Eve to the Catholic church. They had some of the traditional carols, but they were played with guitar and it was like rock 'n' roll Christmas carols. That's not right! Then I went over to the Anglican church. I was doing Anglican prayers that I hadn't done in 45 years. They were rolling off my tongue, I didn't even have to open up a prayer book and that felt, 'Wow! This feels really, really good.' So I know there's something about that repetition, about the certainty and I would feel it now. There's a symbol there – I look at the First Nations people and the whole ritual of doing things, not that that is the whole thing, but it's a base to start from.

B.S.:   Is there something about rituals that seems reassuring and perhaps makes us feel part of something larger?

R.W.:   Well I think so. I mean the Catholic Church hasn't survived for 2000 years because it was based on a bad idea... The whole thing of ritualizing. I remember I've done that at home and in treatment and other places where you just burn secrets that poison us. In fact even the Big Book talks about that, which is quite remarkable when you think it's a book written by a drug addict and stockbroker. He stumbled onto something. He had no idea what he had stumbled on except that it was big, and of course he tapped into this deep vein of spirituality that runs through all cultures, whether it has all different kinds of expressions to it. I think that that is the river in which I try to bathe and what continues to be the best.

And it's interesting talking with white people, I think there's a sense with white patients that I deal with that the whole question of spirituality is a real missing link for them because it's all been tangled up with the church and religion. The church — a lot of people have fallen away from church or have had bad experiences at church. So when you talk about spirituality they say, 'I've got no time for that', but I then try to tease that out and I ask, 'What about meaning, how do you connect, what do you connect with and believe?'

B.S.: From what you are saying, people moved away from the church, at least some European people, but now as a result there's a need to replace it with something.

R.W.: Yes, I think people need to have something that makes sense and if you don't have at least some spiritual questing, then I think people get out of balance and the healing can't be complete until you essentially complete the circle. I mean there's circles in all kinds of things, you know — four seasons. You talk about grieving, letting go of things, or changes that happen — you have to pass through all the seasons in order to have those kinds of changes made. I mean, from my own experience I want to change things, but they don't change quickly, I need to be patient.

B.S.: That looking means some hopefulness, that there's something there?

R.W.: Yes, just to discover more. In some respects I've made fun of it in AA meetings, you know, being an alcoholic, my addiction is about 'more' of anything, you know, but it's also more of this. I want everything this program promises me. How to handle situations intuitively, how to handle situations previously unmanageable, not worry about financial security, and service to our fellow man.

B.S.: Do you see any limitations or barriers in utilizing spirituality in helping others?

R.W.: None; there's only so many cognitive behavioral tricks you can pull, but spirituality is infinite. Look for the meaning here, look for the meaning there and it's a thirst, a constant searching. It's like that idea, I'm sure it's not a new idea, that it's a thirst only God can fulfill: that to join up with whatever it is we rejoin after death is when we become on the path.

B.S.: Are there any dangers that we might distort the spiritual message to suit our own ends, or perhaps misunderstand the message?

It is worth noting, in his response to this and subsequent questions, that Wheeler talks about the place of the mentor to help with discernment and supervision when working in this area. The interview concludes with a second look at the journey taken by Wheeler and how his understanding of the spiritual symbols and rituals of First Nation people has been an important part of this journey.

R.W.: I think that's entirely possible. There are false prophets everywhere... I think that the way I would keep myself in check would be to constantly talk about it and share with other people, to see where my motives were, and always checking on how my motives were doing. To me that is part of one of the things they warned us about in AA. The whole idea of humanness and greed is that all those things can carry the most well-meaning person away. I look at my own thing around it and think, well am I confusing being a character with having character?

B.S.: How can you be clear that your actions have spiritual integrity and you are not simply fooling other people or yourself?

R.W.: You can pray for guidance. Realizing that probably my role here is to be of service to others and I'm not even sure what it is, but it seems to be taking me in this direction which is why we're having this conversation. It's not to sit and look at sore ears. I've moved away from that quite a while ago. The only way I know, and it's really hard, is talking to people and being as open as I can and really looking at my motives and trying to get honest feedback from people. Am I over the edge here, too crazy? It has been difficult, I mean I don't know... One of the things I'm not too sure I like about the way we do mental health or the way Western medicine does mental health is we don't think there's any necessity for the therapist to have a therapist... It's a constant renewing thing and so yeah, it's great to be analyzed, but you need to continue to be analyzed.

B.S.: How do you understand mental health healing and its relationship to spirituality? Do you think it is understood differently by Aboriginal and European people?

R.W.: Well, in some respects, and I think of what I've been taught and courses I go to, mental health healing reminds me of physical healing. You have a broken leg therefore we put a pin in your femur and put a cast on your leg, send you off to a physiotherapist and give you some drugs and come back and see me in six weeks. You're done. It's a very nice technical service, you know, flawless in the way it's presented. If people get functioning and get to feel okay with their lives and move on from there, that's great. That's probably all it is about. You need to be comfortable in your own skin.

And then again, one can look at those holy questions if you choose to. If you feel pretty good with your life and all you need to do is to talk it out, get a little consultation on how to deal with this problem and then get on with it, that's all you need. It just strikes me that there's more to it, because we're human beings – there's more to us as human beings than just, 'How do I deal with this?' Lots of people would be happy with that and that's good. But I think there's a lot of people who aren't happy with that, it's incomplete, it doesn't get them where they want to go. I mean when I first sobered up, I didn't even know where I wanted to go. I had no idea of where it was I could go. The questions weren't even questions. The look of spirituality and the searching for spirituality has been all about questions, lots and lots of questions. Some people don't even want to ask them and there's nothing wrong with that. So the conversations I had with those people tended to be a lot shorter, much more focused on drug side effects. And sometimes that can be satisfying work, but again it's like putting a nice rod down the leg, I mean it's there, it's done, there's not a lot to it.

When I get to look at some of the broader issues the question of balance for me is more exciting. To talk and to work in that area – I think it opens up for people the same kind of things as it opened up for me. Lots of questions, lots of seeking for answers. With Aboriginal people, it's so much part of their culture, it is their culture. It's getting back to the basics, like where am I in my life, where am I in my world? Those questions are very central to their healing.

Life is not a series of mechanical behaviors such that once you get to mechanical behaviors, life is okay. Are you suicidal today? No, I'm not today. Calling that a day is a bit unsatisfactory because a person is still not connected, so I think people end up just repeating, repeating, and repeating. If it just stays at that upper level, then the more spiritual questions connecting with culture and meaning in your life and family are ignored. The questions get deeper as time goes on, so I think the healing focus makes people more balanced. I can learn that, deeper and wider. It's like you get greedy for it. This is rich stuff. This is food. Sometimes I think we feel that consumer items treat the soul, but they don't. They end up being thin gruel and I know that, I can sense it, I can feel this other.

B.S.:   So we're hungry and starved, perhaps spiritually, and some people have lost it, other people haven't had it.

R.W.:   I think, I didn't even know I was hungry. I knew I was thirsty for cognac, thirsty for whiskey, but I didn't know I was hungry. I think the looking is what suits me best. What spoke in the wheel am I going to generally perceive now? The center is always the same. It always leads to the center. The center is God, our power, or whatever.

B.S.:   Does the fact that you say you don't know what is at the center bother you? Do you need to know that?

R.W.:   No! The fun is in looking, continuing to look. I think I was always looking, I just didn't know it. I was looking at the 'Red Road' recovery tapes. They talk about taking a bottle of whiskey, and your spirit goes into the bottle and you spend the remainder of your time looking in bottle after bottle after bottle for your spirit.

B.S.:   You mean the liquid comes out, the spirit goes into the bottle.

R.W.:   Yes. Spirit is come until spirit is come. Spirit against the spirit. I mean for 5–600 years alcohol in our culture was called 'spirits'. The enervating principle, 'aqua viva', that was the original name for scotch or something like that – the spirit of life. I mean the popular Norwegian vodka you serve is like life water. There's something in there that elevates, it does all kinds of stuff, who knows, but there's something about that experience. I didn't know it was a spiritual need... I just knew it was a hunger, I was hungry.

B.S.:   Discovering you were spiritually hungry helped?

R.W.:   Oh yes. Now I look everywhere, just checking it out. I look at Hawaiian spirituality, I like their use of water and plants, and I'm growing some plants here. It's their secret. They use it like First Nations people use sweet grass, but they don't burn it, they bless with it, bathe themselves in it. First Nations offer tobacco to the land, to 'Mother Earth'.

Giving tobacco to the land is offering a sacred message. If you take a sacred medicine given by the creator and misuse it, it will bite back, it'll give you lung cancer, emphysema, high blood pressure and all those kinds of things. Maybe it's the same with alcohol. Alcohol is fine until you overuse it. Power is fine. So any of those gifts, any of those tools that we have are great in balance. I mean, don't overuse them. But when we overuse them, they bite... The power of addictions has been around for five million years. Very strong, very deeply rooted. The simple cognitive tricks are playing way up on the top floor of the building but if the problems are in the basement, it might not connect, you know. You got to get down in the basement.

With that practical image, Wheeler's interview ended. His account of recovery from addiction and professional development has provided a fresh and revealing description of searching for healing and the spiritual realm. The colloquial and down to earth coverage of his ways of working also shows how someone trained in technical and conventional Western medicine can with sensitivity operate from a spiritual platform to the benefit of people whose cultural and spiritual understandings are not secular but sacred.

Acknowledgements

We are grateful to Gail Charlebois for transcribing this audiotape.

References

For the reader who wishes to pursue the literature on Alcoholics Anonymous, we offer the following resources:

Alcoholics Anonymous (1976) The Big Book (3rd edn). New York: AA World Services.

Booth, L. (1985) *Spirituality and Recovery: Walking on Water.* Florida: Health Communications.

Bristow-Braitman, A. (1995) 'Addiction Recovery, 12 Step Programs and Cognitive-Behavioral Psychology.' *Journal of counseling & Development 73,* 414–418.

Chapter Nine

Heroes' Journeys
Children's Expression of Spirituality through Play Therapy

Judith Morris

I am not a mechanism, an assembly of various sections.
And it is not because the mechanism is working wrongly,
that I am ill.
I am ill because of wounds to the soul, to the deep emotional
self
and the wounds to the soul take a long, long time, only time
can help
and patience, and a certain difficult repentance,
long, difficult repentance, realisation of life's mistake, and
the freeing oneself
from the endless repetition of the mistake
which mankind at large has chosen to sanctify. (D.H. Lawrence 1977
p.620)

The role of spirituality as an integral and essential part of human development is gaining prominence in many of the helping professions (Canda
1988; Chandler, Holden and Kolander 1992; Northcut 2000; Stanard,
Sandhu and Painter 2000). This has led to a growing literature which
examines the function of religion and spirituality in development, and
their relationship to the therapeutic process (for example, Goldberg 1996;
Kahn 1993; Straussner and Spiegel 1996; Ulanov 1996; Worthington

1989; Zinnbauer and Pargament 2000). There is, however, no generally agreed definition of spirituality and often the term is used interchangeably with religion or religiosity (Ganje-Fling and McCarthy 1996; Stanard *et al.* 2000). A useful distinction between spirituality and religion is made by Stanard and her colleagues. They define religion as an 'adherence to the beliefs and practices of an organised church or religious institution'. Spirituality is defined as 'the transcendent relationship between the person and a Higher Being, a quality that goes beyond a specific religious affiliation' (Stanard *et al.* 2000, p.205). It is from this perspective that children's expressions of spirituality will be examined.

The authenticity of children's spiritual experiences has been a matter of contention (Hoffman 1998; Hunt 1995; Wilber 2000). Armstrong (1984) suggests several reasons for this. Children are less able to articulate their experiences, and because they are emotionally immature they are less likely to integrate these experiences with the rest of their personality development. In addition, children may repress memories of these experiences, as Wickes comments:

> Experiences of timeless realities may come to the very young child... As the child grows older, problems of the outer world press upon him [*sic*]. His ego must grow to meet the demands of greater consciousness and numinous experience may appear to be forgotten by the ego, but it is remembered by the Self – that sage who from the beginning lives in the psyche of the child and speaks the defining word in times of peril. (Wickes 1966, p.ix)

Moreover, Armstrong argues that the genuineness of children's experiences is discounted because there are 'no clear maps for making sense out of transpersonal childhood experiences' (Armstrong 1984, p.225).

In general, Western psychological models of human development, such as those proposed by Erikson (1963) and Maslow (1971), are incremental and stage-specific. The child is conceived of as undifferentiated, an empty vessel or tabula rasa, and development is the result of acquired experiences in life that are integrated in a linear progression from one stage to the next, with issues of spirituality seen as belonging predominantly to later phases in life. Armstrong (1984) suggests that the richness and variety of children's transpersonal experiences can only be explained if the child is seen as a being greater than the developing individuality defined by traditional developmental psychologies. He examines explanations of child development from other perspectives, such as theosophy and other metaphysical and Eastern theories, which clearly acknowledge a spiritual dimension within the child. These theories are based on underlying assumptions that the child comes into life with an innate knowledge, either from previous lifetimes or an independent spiritual existence.

In Western contemporary psychologies, two theorists who make reference to childhood manifestations of spirituality, Jung (1930) and Wilber (1979), also postulate inborn knowledge, which is contained in deep and complex structures in the unconscious. This emerges into consciousness as a result of the actualizing process through the individual's life. Neither Wilber nor Jung elaborate these ideas substantially in relation to childhood (Armstrong 1984). Because Jung's theories also provide an in-depth analysis of the meaning of symbols and the process of therapy, it is proposed to use his concepts as a framework for examining children's expression of spirituality and its function in their healing processes.

Jung was one of the earliest Western psychologists to recognize the relevance of spirituality and religious practice to the needs and workings of the human psyche. He asserted that all human problems are spiritual: 'A psychoneurosis must be understood, ultimately, as the suffering of a soul which has not discovered its meaning...the cause of the suffering is spiritual stagnation, or psychic sterility' (Jung 1978, p.252). Unlike Freud, who had a negative attitude towards religion and spirituality and saw them essentially as products of illusory wish fulfillment (Freud 1930/1961), Jung viewed religion and spirituality as realities that are fundamental to human experience and psychic evolution.

> Religions are psychotherapeutic systems in the truest sense of the word, and on the grandest scale. They express the whole range of the psychic problem in mighty images; they are the avowal and recognition of the soul, and at the same time the revelation of the soul's nature. (Jung 1978, p.336)

Furthermore, Jung emphasized the natural healing powers of the psyche, which he believed could be set in motion both by cultural religious rituals and by therapeutic or spiritual experiences. He claimed that this is because of the basic structures he discovered in the psyche that he termed 'arche-types', such as the shadow, animus/anima, the 'Wise Old Man' and the 'Great Mother', and, ultimately, the 'Self'. These unconscious components of the psyche are revealed through the symbol-making experiences of dreams, fantasies and sometimes visions. At times when an individual seems to have reached a psychological impasse, often caught between the claims of apparently irreconcilable opposites such as love and fear, active and passive, good and evil, the emergence of a meaningful image from the unconscious can be the instrument of psychic change. Jung named this process the transcendent function, which mediates between the pair of warring opposites and unites them through a reconciling symbol. This is experienced consciously as a change in attitude that enables the individual to change their behavior in a natural and stable way (Bradway 1985).

The processes of individuation, which is the gradual realization of the Self, can be aided in adult therapy by the use of 'active imagination', where the individual pays attention to the archetypal symbols emerging from the unconscious, interacts with them and integrates them into consciousness (Hannah 1981). For children, symbolic play provides an analogous process of individuation: 'Through its dual functions of bridging between ego-consciousness and the unconscious and making possible creative imagination, it reveals…ultimately an expression of the self' (Stein, in Stewart, 1981 pp.35–36).

Individuation takes place over the lifetime, and as such the process is never complete, so much as remaining an ideal. Jung differentiated two phases of development. The first half of life is focused on the adaptation of the psyche to outer reality, with the individual becoming established in personal relationships, the world of work and, for most people, family life. The second half of life is characterized by preoccupations with philosophical or spiritual questions, such as values, creative endeavors, and the search for life's meaning, culminating in the preparation for and acceptance of death (Mattoon 1981). Although Jung saw this second phase exclusively as pertaining to the process of individuation, the developmental school of post-Jungians argue that individuation is a life-long activity and, in all its essential features, can be observed in children (Samuels 1985).

Certain areas of experience are particularly conducive to the individuation process (Mattoon 1981). In personal relationships, many unconscious facets of oneself are encountered in a projected form, and part of the individuation process can be achieved by withdrawing these projections from others and integrating these qualities into the consciousness of the individual's personality. The religious quest can be another arena for the individuation process because the Self is both the pattern for individuation and the image of God. Some of the central experiences of individuation, such as the hero's journey, the metaphor of death and rebirth or the image of the divine child, are paradigms of religious experience. The ultimate integration of the personality can be described as wholeness, the result of individuation, or as union with God, the goal of the religious quest. Finally, therapy constitutes an opportunity to work through a special relationship, that of client–therapist, in order to integrate parts of the personality, seeking to bring consciousness and the unconscious into a harmonious relation, a process which is necessary for the attainment of wholeness (Mattoon 1981).

Jung's research did not specifically examine childhood, although he did mention that in children's drawings and dreams he found 'Self-symbols' like those he had discovered in material brought by adults in therapy (Sidoli and Davies 1988). This was subsequently confirmed by other analytic psychologists, including Fordham (1969), who saw evidence of psychic wholeness in children's artwork. Kalff (1980, p.65) also observed in children's therapy through sandplay 'how close the child's psyche is to spiritual and healing forces'. Examples of children's expression of spirituality are presented in this chapter, where the case material of three children – Jason, Daniel and Kathy – demonstrate children's use of symbols and metaphors through the media of artwork, floor games and sandplay.

The search for gold: Jason's work through art and computer programming

Jason's parents separated when he was three years old, and he was left in his father's care. Already he was emotionally disturbed. He suffered severe separation anxiety and was so aggressive towards other children that he had been excluded from several day-care centers and nurseries. Subsequently, his schooling was punctuated with a series of expulsions, first from a special unit and then from several residential schools for maladjusted children. By the age of 13, he was locked up in secure accommodation. He had knowingly vandalized a policeman's house, causing devastating damage. More seriously, he had killed all the pets. This incident was the latest in a series of assaults of escalating violence.

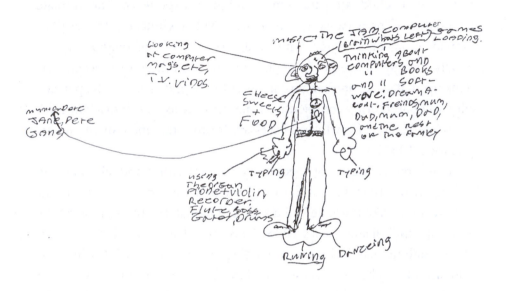

Figure 9.1 Jason's self-portrait, illustrating his use of his body, dreams and thoughts to express his feelings

Jason's first artwork reveals the issue of a tug-of-love between his parents, re-enacted through an ongoing custody battle. In the initial assessment of his attachments (Morris 1996), Jason was asked to draw pictures of himself and his family tree (Figures 9.1 and 9.2). In these pictures, he showed his tendency to be over-adaptive with a poor sense of self and an inability to form discriminating relationships with his attachment figures. Additionally, a diffuse sense of belonging was related to his poor understanding of his family structure. In a subsequent session, Jason was shown a

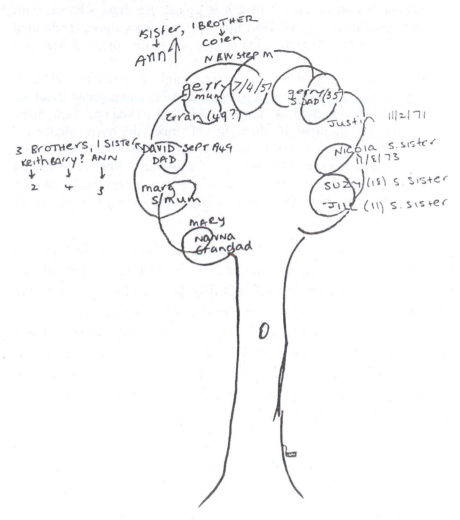

Figure 9.2 Jason's family tree, including all members, but without indication of their relationship to each other. Note the tiny computer attached to its trunk.

genogram of his family (Figure 9.3), depicting his exclusion from both his mother's and his father's households. Jason responded to this by modifying his original drawing of the family tree and creating a new picture (Figure 9.4) with the following story about a computer's journey:

> There is a power supply coming to the tree. Then one day there is an explosion and the computer leaves the tree. Jason gave a kind of nervous laugh under his breath. 'It's funny because the computer leaves footprints

behind. It doesn't know where it is going.' He drew a house, with question marks in the windows and a question mark above. He decided to call the house 'Dixons Ltd', the shop where the computer had been bought. 'I'll just show you the back of the house.' He then drew bars on the windows. He gave another nervous laugh. 'One day there'll be an explosion here.' He drew the barred window out on the ground, and the computer went back to the family tree. He then picked up a thick, black felt-tip pen. He drew the shouting policeman, the heart inscribed 'I love?', the social worker with a swastika on his chest. He then blotted out all the family tree except his mother and step-father. When I commented that he had covered over everyone's names except his mum and step-father, he wrote 'DAD' in very large letters along one side of his drawing.

Jason seems to have identified with the computer in his story: the explosive departure from the family tree; the computer's question about its origins, and its move to a place behind bars (like Jason's placement in secure accommodation); the yelling policeman (related to Jason's recent vandalism); his broken heart; and the indication of his preferred attachment to his mother. My comment elicited Jason's addition of his father's name to the picture, showing the sense of the torn loyalty caused by the tug-of-love he was caught in between his parents. Some weeks later, he commented, 'I am tired of being piggy in the middle.'

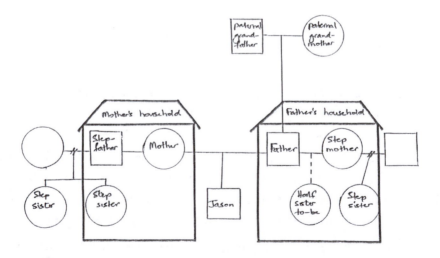

Figure 9.3 Jason's family tree as genogram, drawn by the author

Figure 9.4 Jason's family tree, drawn after seeing the author's genogram

Soon after this, Jason created his first computer game. 'Bertie the Bug' depicts a delinquent on a raid, trying to escape trouble, but he finds his way impeded by moving obstacles. The aim of the game is to reach the safety of home. However, in the writing of the computer program, there is no route home. The game reflects a profound sense of aloneness and mirrors the genogram drawn by myself, showing that Jason belonged to neither of his parents' households. Jason, like Bertie, had no home to go to.

Jason soon embarked on an ambitious project that took many weeks to complete. His next computer program, 'In Search of Gold', emulated the commercial product, with a tape of the computer program accompanied by a booklet and map, and everything fitting into a specially decorated box. The journey starts, like all classic heroes' journeys, with a descent to the underworld. This is followed by various encounters with archetypal figures, who are asked for help. At the beginning of the game, these figures are often obstructive, reflecting Jason's experience of rejection and his inability to make relationships in the real world. At each destination, the player is given options about what action to take. Several feminine figures are unhelpful: the old woman with false teeth, who cannot speak clearly; a girl skipping and a woman hanging out her washing, both of whom give wrong directions. At another stage, when the player is trapped in a room, all means of help are blocked. The various options are: 'help', 'dig' and 'read the map'. The responses are, respectively: 'You have no one to help you'; 'You dig up sand, you get nowhere'; and, 'Sorry, you dropped your map as you entered the hut.'

Gradually the choices begin to include options which, if not actively helpful, are at least not obstructive. For instance, when the player bargains with an old man for a safe passage across the fast, white, flowing river, the options are: a compass, whereupon the old man magically disappears; a knife, and the player is stabbed; very little food, which is 'taken jealously and as an offence', but the player escapes; and gold bars or a map to 'pass in peace'. At the sewer, the guardian angel saves the player and returns him or her 'fully back to health'. By the end of the game, when the final destination of the 'misty house' is revealed, the map shows the pathway forward. The message is, 'Go carefully. You will be OK.'

As the sessions continued with Jason, work was also undertaken with the various significant adults in his life (Morris 1996). In particular, Jason was helped to repair the relationship with his father. He learned to state his needs more clearly so that his father could respond appropriately and he was made aware of his father's stalwart consistency demonstrated by his regular visits and telephone calls. Jason was also helped to let go of the idealized fairy godmother image of his mother, by facing the reality of her repeated broken promises while continuing to enjoy her extravagant gifts of a computer and an organ.

Jason's work shows how changes in his internal world, represented by symbols and metaphors, are parallel to changes in his outer reality, with reparative work undertaken in relation to both of his parents. Three different heroes' journeys are presented. In the first journey, depicted through artwork, Jason identifies with the computer, and projects elements of his life story and unresolved issues onto the computer. Similarly, 'Bertie the Bug' represents aspects of Jason, his delinquency and his lack of a safe haven. In contrast, the third journey is an example of active imagination, a technique which is not defined by the medium used but rather by

> the relationship between the ego and the unconscious. The unconscious can be expressed in an infinite number of ways, including poetry, stories, direct dialogues, verbal description of images, clay, painting, dance, photographs, movies, music and collage. Doing these things does not in itself constitute active imagination. The ego must react to what has been expressed, draw conclusions, and put them to work in life before the process can be said to be complete. (Dallett 1984, p.28)

Jason interacts with the archetypal figures he encounters: the old man, the skipping girl, the old woman and the guardian angel. The aim of the journey is to search for gold, a symbol of the Self from alchemy. The final destination is the house, another symbol of the Self, its misty nature suggesting something insubstantial.

Each of the journeys had an emotional impact that was felt by both the child and myself as therapist. However, with the third journey, the experience of accompanying the hero in his search for gold had an added numinosity. The emotional and yet intangible quality of energy that was released through the changing nature of the archetypal encounters, and the sense of homecoming at the final destination, epitomizes the process of the transcendent function. It illustrates the interplay between the ego and the active unconscious as the hero confronts and converses with various counterpositions presented by the unconscious through different archetypal symbols. In addition, the emotionality of the experience of reaching the misty house, as the resolution of the epic struggle to search for gold, demonstrates an encounter with the Self and the sense of connection with a power beyond the psyche – 'something beyond our conscious awareness of being, something that feels bigger and as if it knows more' (Ulanov 1996, p.7). This was my first shared spiritual experience with a child in therapy.

For Jason, the survival of his heroes never seems to be in doubt. Rather, their struggles are more a matter of what help will be available on the journey. This contrasts with the case material that follows, where the very existence of Daniel's hero, the 'little prince', seems to be in question. As with Jason, Daniel's work shows the difference between projective techniques, such as are demonstrated in his painting which simply reveals his feelings, and the deeper healing that comes from active imagination, which Daniel undertakes by means of a floor game.

Daniel's floor game: the survival of the little prince

Daniel, aged ten, had lived in residential care for several years, coming from a household with domestic violence and a complex history of neglect and sexual abuse. For the first year in care, Daniel made sporadic progress, with no discernible pattern to the alternating periods of apparent stability and sudden reversion to disturbed, bizarre behavior. At the time Daniel started therapy, he was unable to make and sustain relationships, either with his caregivers or with his peer group. He was unable to play or occupy himself constructively. His learning at school was inconsistent. He was unable to read or to master simple mathematical concepts yet had a rich store of general knowledge about nature and science, and outstanding construction skills and artistic ability.

In therapy, Daniel[1] used a variety of media, including painting and art materials, floor games and sandplay. His capacity to use imagery and symbols is exemplified in the following account of one of his sessions, which took place at a time of particular adversity. Considerable changes in staffing and children had occurred in the residential unit where he lived. Also, Daniel was not coping with the transfer from a special class to mainstream education. Because of his deteriorating behavior, a decision had been made to apply for a therapeutic residential school, though he had not yet been told of this.

Daniel arrived at this session in an apparently desultory mood. He complained about being bored, stating that there was nothing of interest in the playroom. He couldn't focus on any activity. He repeatedly toured

---

1   Further case material from Daniel's therapy has been examined (Morris, in press) through his use of narcissus as a metaphor. Daniel's therapy has been analyzed in the context of the quality of his day-to-day care and decision making about treatment and placement options, using a framework of attachment theory.

the room, half-heartedly picking up objects from the shelves, fingering them, and putting them back making derogatory remarks. He made several forays to the easel and paints before he eventually settled.

The painting started with black. At first his involvement seemed cautious, perhaps reluctant. Gradually there was a growing sense of intensity in his concentration and effort – more black paint, though it was not evident to me what he was depicting. Careful strokes with a deftness of movement that was typical of Daniel, and fascinating to watch. Purposeful, dextrous fingers that could work quickly and creatively, accompanied by total absorption with the task in hand. I waited quietly and patiently to see what would be revealed.

Suddenly, Daniel lost patience. He seemed frustrated with what he had done. Broad, fast strokes swept across the page, destroying what he had been making. He continued energetically until the brush ran out of paint. He indicated that he had finished, that he didn't want to try again. He walked away from the easel commenting that he had wasted the paper. He then added under his breath, barely audibly, 'like the waste of my life'.

Daniel's concentration again seemed fragmented. He toured the playroom again, repeating his earlier complaints. He eventually stopped at the shelves of toys, amongst which there was an array of fighting men and two castles, one large and the other small. He picked up a little ball and threw it at the fighting men, knocking them down. He seemed to derive a certain amount of pleasure from watching them fall. He then took down the two castles, and set them out on the floor. The large castle was defended by larger and more numerous fighting men. The small castle was placed directly opposite, undefended. From the small castle, a prince on horseback set forth, brandishing a sword, and accompanied by two small fighting men. Their task was to overthrow the large castle, which seemed unassailable. The battle that ensued was long and difficult. Both of the prince's companions were killed. The little prince, against all odds, eventually won. He started to enter the large castle, cautious and alone. Suddenly a new adversary, a flying dragon, appeared from nowhere. It swooped down and devoured the prince.

The dragon was hollow, and Daniel forced the prince inside, pressing him down as far as he could. He then tried to retrieve the prince, but found that it was impossible to get him out. He spent a considerable time trying to rescue him. There was somehow a hopelessness, a lack of energy about his attempts, which were unsuccessful. He eventually handed the dragon to me. He indicated that I should try, but then wouldn't allow me to pursue the task. Daniel's focus became diffuse. The remainder of the session was occupied with playing a board game, though there was no evident enthusiasm or satisfaction for the game. Moments before the end of the session, Daniel picked up the dragon. With apparent ease, he rescued the little prince. Both the dragon and the prince were dropped to the floor and Daniel departed, seemingly nonchalant and at ease with himself.

The following week, Daniel's caregivers reported that he had returned to the unit relaxed and settled. His behavior at school improved markedly. Furthermore, the shift in Daniel's emotional state was reflected in his approach to the next therapy session. He discovered that I owned several cats and that I was looking for a new home for one of them. This became the focus for his work. On arrival at the playroom, he immediately engaged with the art materials, including two large cardboard boxes. He started to make a cage for transporting the cat to its new home. His activities occupied the whole session. They were purposeful and continually punctuated by comments about what he was doing and why. He expressed concern about the cat's feelings. This was reflected in the great care and thoughtfulness he took in furnishing the cage in order to meet the cat's needs for comfort, safety and a way to see where its journey was going.

Daniel had expressed his feelings of despair in several ways: his desultory attitude of dissatisfaction with the playroom and its contents; the destruction of his painting in black; his comment about his wasted life; and the questionable survival of the little prince in his take-over bid for the large castle. Through the metaphor of the hero's journey, Daniel portrayed his own struggle to survive with limited emotional resources. The prince's entry into the belly of the dragon depicts a death and rebirth, offering the possibility of emergence of the Self. The last minute rescue from the devouring monster seems to represent a mustering of Daniel's energy to face the adversity of his outside world.

Daniel's floor game is another example of the technique of active imagination. With both sandplay and floor games, the child is presented with shelves of miniature objects. These can be used to create scenes – on a mat for floor games (Wells 1911/1976) and for sandplay, in a shallow tray painted blue on the bottom and sides to represent water and sky and partially filled with sand (Bradway and McCoard 1997; Kalff 1980; Mitchell and Friedman 1994; Stewart 1984). In the choice of objects, archetypal images emerge from the unconscious, creating an opportunity for inner and outer reality to come together. As tangible, concrete objects in the floor game or sandplay, these images can be explored and used experimentally until ready for integration into the ego (Gordon 1984). There is a resultant activation of regenerative and healing energy through the 'transcendent' function. This process was evident in Daniel's floor game, where the prince's eventual victory heralds Daniel's renewed energy for coping and adapting to the situation in the residential unit and at school. Additionally, in the next therapy session, he unconsciously anticipates the proposed move of placement through his identification with the cat. Similarly, in the following case material, Kathy's use of sandplay also releases energy for transformative changes in both her inner world and her outer reality.

Kathy's sandplay of the nativity scene: the rebirth of the Self and finding forgiveness

Kathy, aged nine, is in foster care. She has thrived in many aspects of her development, and her placement has been stable for several years. Recently, however, she has disclosed memories of sexual abuse that date back to babyhood. As she gradually reveals her perceptions, it becomes apparent how confused she is, for instance about differentiating her experiences of sexuality and abuse from those of sensuality and nurture.

Kathy began writing frequent letters to her birth mother, who had sexually abused her but whom she still loves and idealizes. Her letters started by demanding an explanation for what her mother did, but they always finished with Kathy retracting her allegations and assuring her mother of her undying love. This loving attitude towards her birth mother contrasts with her recently changed relationship to her foster mother. Since the disclosure of abuse, Kathy continually provokes her foster mother's rejection, to the extent that the placement is teetering on the edge of disruption. Daily caregiving experiences that were once a source of pleasure to both Kathy and her foster mother are now the scene of escalating battles and the (unintended) re-enactment of abuse. For instance, Kathy jerks her head deliberately during hair brushing to ensure that she is hurt by her foster mother.

During her therapy sessions, Kathy increasingly engaged in sandplay. At first, her scenes in the sand tray are chaotic and uncontained. The stories associated with the scenes are incoherent, anarchic and full of conflict. It was difficult to interpret what Kathy was communicating, and so no attempt was made to give her insight into her disruptive behavior. Nevertheless, it seemed that her use of numerous symbols representing good and evil reflected her polariszation of good and bad between her birth mother and foster mother, respectively. An explanation was given to her social worker and foster parents about the mirroring between Kathy's inner world and her outer reality. This provided some meaning to her recent behavioral difficulties in the foster home. Furthermore, affirmation of the foster mother's experience of being a 'witch mother' paradoxically gave her reassurance in the face of Kathy's unrelenting attacks. It was evident that somehow Kathy needed to integrate good and bad, and thus allow herself to experience both qualities in both of her mother figures. Yet the pathway for this healing step was unclear.

Then suddenly Kathy's sandplay changed. During the session itself, the shift was subtle. Kathy started as usual, collecting numerous objects from the shelves and lining them up alongside the sand tray. Most of the objects were the same as she had chosen in previous weeks. She began creating her scene in the sand, returning from time to time to the shelves for more and more objects, occasionally picking new ones and leaving most of the old ones discarded outside the sand tray.

The miniature figures of Joseph, Mary and baby Jesus caught her attention and were added to the sand tray. The objects already placed in the tray were rearranged so that they encircled the nativity scene. Mary was placed lying down on a bed and the baby put inside the hollow figurine, with only his head emerging. It was clearly the scene of the baby's birth. More people were added, and it seemed that they were coming to admire the new baby. It felt like a scene of jubilation. Kathy took a china bell from the shelves, and shook it so that it rang, a small tinkling sound, as she called like a town crier, 'Jesus is born. Jesus is born.' More and more people arrived and crowded around the birth scene. The mood changes. It feels threatening, and there is a sense of foreboding. Dinosaurs and dragons have started to arrive. They approach the baby's birth place, pushing between the other admirers. Suddenly the sandplay is abandoned. It is not clear whether the baby will be safe or not.

For several weeks, the birth scene is re-created. Again, the bell is rung: 'Jesus is born. Jesus is born.' The crowds of people arrive to celebrate the baby's birth. Each time, there is a sense of reverence and wonderment as the story of the sandplay unfolds. Each time, there is a build up of tension, as I wonder whether the dinosaurs and dragons will arrive. And each time, they do.

In a further development of the story, the baby is plucked from the safety of its mother and carried away by one of the dinosaurs. There is a sense of horror and timelessness as I watch the monster retreat to the opposite end of the sand tray, with the baby held in its open jaws. It is unclear whether the baby needs rescuing. If it did, there is no one nearby. Each session the sandplay is re-created, and each time the same questions arise. Will the baby survive? Will Kathy abandon the sandplay and leave the baby to its unresolved fate?

Eventually the day of reckoning arrives. The nativity scene and the whole story of the baby's precarious survival is re-told. The baby is removed from its mother's care and again is held in the dinosaur's mouth. Then Kathy returns to the shelves of miniatures and takes down a completely new object – a swan, a special symbol of protection because it is the only bird that carries its young. From the various swans available on the shelves, Kathy chooses one that is transparent and hollow, made of glass. This swan is also a container that can open, having a top and bottom half. The baby is taken from the dinosaur's mouth and is placed within the swan. The baby is returned to the birth scene. Safe, at last!

Through these weeks, Kathy's letters to her mother had been changing, as she dared to hang onto her accusations of sexual abuse instead of retracting them. She expresses anger towards her birth mother alongside her continuing statements of love. At the same time, she returns to a more comfortable relationship with her foster mother, accepting her nurturing and yet also at times still provoking rejection. She expresses fear that if her mother acknowledges responsibility for the sexual abuse, there might be legal action and a resultant imprisonment. Kathy makes a tape for the 'government' as a plea against her mother's possible criminal conviction for the abuse, asking them to forgive her mother for what she has done. She asks to join the local church and to be baptized, although neither her birth nor her foster family have a religious background.

In her sandplay of the nativity scene and the precarious survival of the divine child, Kathy brings together various archetypal images of the feminine. Mary, the swan and the dinosaur each represent different qualities of the anima: the life-giving and nurturing; the protective and the devouring, potentially destructive aspects of mothering. As Kathy integrates the good–bad split in her internal world, she is able to make subsequent changes in her relationships with both of her mothers, now experiencing each of them as both good and bad. Her rage and repeated attacks on her foster mother have destroyed neither their relationship nor the placement. Kathy has a new-found trust, and a belief that her anger towards her birth mother and her demand that she take responsibility for her abuse need not destroy her birth mother.

Ganje-Fling and McCarthy (1996) outline various obstacles that impede the re-awakening of spiritual development in survivors of sexual abuse: mistrust, despair, anger, conflicts about responsibility for the abuse. It seems that Kathy has been able to negotiate these obstacles, and thus reach a stage of forgiveness. This is represented in the sandplay by the birth of the divine child (symbol of Self) and the jubilant admirers circling the birth scene in a symbol of wholeness. Kathy's work through her sandplay demonstrates the process of therapy:

> The aim [of therapy] is to provide a maternal space or psychological womb…in this safe 'space' healing of the inner psychological wound can occur, the Self can be constellated and the inner child re-discovered, with all of its potentiality for creativity and renewal. (Weinrib 1983, p.28)

Sharing Kathy's enactment of the nativity scene in her sandplay was profoundly moving. The ringing bell, the repeating cry, 'Jesus is born. Jesus is born', and the new-found safety of the baby rescued by the swan had the special quality of numinosity that typifies a spiritual experience. The retrieved memories of her sexual abuse resulted in Kathy being embroiled in the conflict of the seemingly irreconcilable opposites of good and evil in her birth mother. She re-enacts this in her relationship with her foster mother, in the initial sand trays of anarchic turmoil and eventually in the sandplay scene with the birth of the divine child and the monster's threat to its survival.

Through the transcendent function there is a bringing together of opposites of good and evil with the emergence of the reconciling symbol of the swan and a resultant change in Kathy's outer world, in the quality of her relationships with both her birth mother and her foster mother. In addition, her request to be baptized demonstrates the Jungian view that the religious quest can be an arena of experience that is crucial to the individuation process. This is because the Self, represented in Kathy's therapy by the divine child and its salvation, is both the pattern for individuation and the image of God.

Confrontation with the God-image and the parallel exploration of the meaning of religion can also be seen in Axline's classic account of her therapeutic work with Dibs (Axline 1964) when it is interpreted from a Jungian prespective. In Dibs' construction of a miniature village (Axline 1964, pp.95–101) the church emerges as a reconciling symbol, with its appearance in duplicate signifying a new insight coming into consciousness (Bradway and McCoard 1997). The metaphor of church-believers enables Dibs to recognize the contrast between the loving relationship with Jake the gardener and his grandmother and his parents' inability to meet his emotional needs. The arrival of springtime growth in his village represents the release of energy from the transcendent function that is later reflected in Dibs' changed relationships to his parents.

Dibs' therapy culminates in a visit to the church viewed from the window of the playroom, whose chiming bell is a continual connection to the real world outside the sessions (Axline 1964, pp.185–187). Dibs' encounter with God and the enormity of 'God's house' make him feel vulnerable but afterwards he comments that he was filled with 'brightness and beauty'. His visit causes him to ponder the nature of God and he again uses the symbol of the church and church-believers to examine his understanding of the different qualities of his relationships with his various caregivers.

Axline's play therapy with Dibs is non-directive or child-centered, based on existential and humanist psychologies. These focus on personal growth and healing rather than pathology, with an underlying philosophy that the child has an innate capacity to strive towards growth and maturity and an abiding belief that the child is able to be constructively self-directing (Axline 1947). Through her account of Dibs' therapy, Axline (1964) demonstrates the use of the therapeutic relationship to give a child the courage to delve deeply into their inner world and to create the opportunity for self-exploration and self-discovery.

As with the children discussed here, Dibs used the therapeutic process to find images and a metaphor that express the unresolved issues in his internal world, helping him to integrate aspects of his personality, while at the same time enabling him to change his life outside the sessions. Through the transcendent function, unconscious material from the inner world is brought into a more harmonious relationship with the realities of his outer, conscious world. Furthermore, for each child, the moment of transformation is imbued with a numinous atmosphere. When the revelation of the unconscious occurs and is made conscious through the emergence of a self-image, it is felt by the child and the therapist as awe-inspiring and yet mysterious, a spiritual experience which releases energy for healing.

Summary

The hero's journey seen in Jason's computer game and Daniel's floor game, the metaphor of death and rebirth in Daniel's floor game and Kathy's sandplay, and the God-image of the divine child in Kathy's sandplay (and in Dibs' church visit and miniature village) are all paradigms for religious experience. As Mattoon (1981, p.188) comments, 'the ultimate integration of the personality can be described as wholeness, the result of individuation, or as union with God, the goal of the religious quest'. Jung saw the attainment of a religious attitude, or what has been defined as spirituality in this chapter, as essential to the individuation process.

However, while Jung stated that each person has an inner image of God, he was not making a claim about the existence of a God per se (Mattoon 1981; Ulanov 1996). Ryce-Menuhin (1992) comments on this paradox for non-church-believers who, by working through their active imagination, can find themselves in touch with the God-image:

> ...the 'awake dream' of sandplay creation often contains a rich and varied working through of a patient's spiritual religious dilemma. Many objects representing gods and goddesses are available together with shrines, retreats, churches, temples, cathedrals and chapels... Many agnostics and atheists have discovered through sandplay the unconscious release of integrative archetypal material which consciously enables them to contact the God-image within their own psyche. (Ryce-Menuhin 1992, p.104)

Kathy, similarly, finds herself looking at the God-image in her work through active imagination and seeking answers to religious issues. She asks to join her local church and to be baptized. Her question raises the issue of how to include spiritual and religious dimensions in our work with clients.

Goldberg (1996) suggests that a concern with a client's religious beliefs does not have a proper place in the therapeutic endeavor. On the other hand, she considers it legitimate to explore metaphysical content, the 'poetic, descriptive and evocative imagery and language' which is related to religious experience but doesn't demand the unquestioning acceptance of a religious belief system by either the client or the therapist. She thus creates the same distinction as Stanard and her colleagues (2000) between religion and spirituality. Goldberg suggests that this material provides a pathway to the 'functional' content, where religion/spirituality is examined in terms of the function it serves in creating the matrix of meaning in an individual's life.

Goldberg defines this rather narrowly in terms of self–object functions only, whereas others, such as Worthington (1989), see spirituality as per-forming a variety of functions: a means to relate to powerful and mysteri-ous elements beyond the individual's control and to understand what is unknown or unanswerable; a source of hope and reassurance, especially in the face of uncertainty or distress; a sense of purpose or calling that affirms an individual's efforts beyond immediate extrinsic rewards (for example, money or fame); and a sense of connection through identifying with other like-minded individuals. Khan (1993, p.29) also relates spirituality to the quest for meaningfulness in an individual's life, which he sees as essential because 'it is a cause of enormous grief in the soul to be subjected to situations that one does not understand, or to be unable to see the meaning of the whole life'.

The examples of children's therapeutic work outlined in this chapter illustrate the way a symbol or insight or new attitude arrives from the unconscious and exerts a numinous effect on the child and therapist. This leaves a sense of being touched by the beyond, a power that needs to be paid attention to and trusted. These children have expressed their spirituality through a myriad of evocative images: the negotiations for safe passage with the old man by the fast-flowing river in the search for gold; the undaunted prince who succeeds in capturing the castle only to be devoured by a dragon; and the swan's rescue of baby Jesus from the clutches of the dinosaur. The children's work illustrates the unconscious as a treasure-house of imagery, which can be accessed through children's play and the work of the active imagination in the service of the healing process of the transcendent function. Their work shows evidence of transformation, both in the children's internal worlds and in their life outside the sessions.

It has been said that spirituality is 'the courage to look within and trust. What is seen and what is trusted appear to be a deep sense of belonging, of wholeness, of connectedness, and of openness to the infinite' (Shafranske and Gorsuch 1984, p.233). For children who have already faced considerable adversity in their young lives, it is with a sense of humility and privilege that I have been witness to their expressions of spirituality as they risk entrusting themselves to a process that provides an opportunity for them to heal themselves. Each of the children discussed has embarked on a journey towards wholeness, a perilous journey where they will encounter struggle and suffering such as they have depicted in the heroes' journeys enacted during therapy sessions, a journey that will continue throughout their lives:

> The search…for this balance of the soul is a lifelong undertaking. It is the basic task and the ultimate goal of psychotherapy. For this center is also the place where the Divine filters through into the soul and reveals itself in the God-images, in the Self. It represents the moment of quiescence when the image of God can be perceived in the polished mirror of the soul. (Jacobi 1965, p.130)

References

Armstrong, T. (1984) 'Transpersonal Experience in Childhood.' *The Journal of Transpersonal Psychology 16*, 2, 207–230.

Axline, V. (1947) *Play Therapy: The Inner Dynamics of Childhood.* Boston: Houghton Mifflin.

Axline, V. (1964) *Dibs: In Search of Self.* Harmondsworth: Penguin.

Bradway, K. (1985) *Sandplay, Bridges and the Transcendental Function.* San Francisco: C.G. Jung Institute of San Francisco.

Bradway, K. and McCoard, B. (1997) *Sandplay – Silent Workshop of the Psyche.* London: Routledge.

Canda, E. (1988) 'Spirituality, Religious Diversity, and Social Work Practice.' *Social Casework 69*, 4, 238–247.

Chandler, C.K., Holden, J.M. and Kolander, C.A. (1992) 'Counseling for spiritual Wellness: Theory And Practice.' *Journal of Counseling & Development 71*, 168–175.

Dallett, J. (1984) 'Active Imagination in Practice.' In M. Stein (ed) Jungian Analysis. London: Shambhala.

Erikson, E.H. (1963) *Childhood and Society.* New York: Norton.

Fordham, M. (1969) *Children as Individuals.* London: Hodder and Stoughton.

Freud, S. (1930/1961) *Civilisation and its Discontents.* Edited and translated by J. Strachey. New York: Norton.

Ganje-Fling, M.A. and McCarthy, P. (1996) 'Impact of Childhood Sexual Abuse on Client Spiritual Development: Counseling Implications.' *Journal of Counseling and Development 74*, 253–258.

Goldberg, C. (1996) 'The Privileged Position of Religion in the Clinical Dialogue.' *Clinical Social Work Journal 24*, 2, 125–136.

Gordon, R. (1984) *Bridges: Metaphor for Psychic Processes.* London: Karnac.

Hannah, B. (1981) *Encounters with the Soul: Active Imagination.* Boston: Sigo Press.

Hoffman, E. (1998) 'Peak Experiences in Childhood: An Exploratory Study.' *Journal of Humanistic Psychology 38*, 1, 109–120.

Hunt, H.T. (1995) 'Some Developmental Issues in Transpersonal Experience.' *The Journal of Mind and behavior 16*, 2, 115–134.

Jacobi, J. (1965) *The Way of Individuation.* New York: Penguin.

Jung, C.G. (1930) 'The Stages of Life.' In R.F.C. Hull (ed) *The Collected Works of C.G. Jung.* Vol 8. New York: Pantheon.

Jung, C.G. (1978) *Psychological Reflections.* Princeton: Bollingen.

Kalff, D.M. (1980) *Sandplay: A Psychotherapeutic Approach to the Psyche.* Boston: Sligo Press.

Khan, P.V.I. (1993) *Counseling and Therapy: The Spiritual Dimension.* London: Souvenir Press.

Lawrence, D.H. (1977) 'Healing.' In V. de Sola Pinto and F.W. Roberts (eds) *The Complete Poems.* Harmondsworth: Penguin.

Maslow, A.H. (1971) *The Farther Reaches of Human Nature.* New York: Putman.

Mattoon, M.A. (1981) *Jungian Psychology in Perspective.* New York: The Free Press.

Mitchell, R.R. and Friedman, H.S. (1994) *Sandplay: Past, Present and Future.* London: Routledge.

Morris, J. (1996) *A Social Work Assessment of Children's Attachments.* Unpublished Master's thesis, Manchester University.

Morris, J. (in press) *The Emotional Tie that Binds: Weaving the Healing Tapestry for an Attachment Disordered Child.* Paper presented at the National Conference of the New Zealand Association of Psychotherapists, Wellington, New Zealand, February 2001.

Northcut, T.B. (2000) 'Constructing a place for religion and spirituality in psychodynamic practice'. *Clinical Social Work Journal 28*, 2, 155–169.

Ryce-Menuhin, J. (1992) *Jungian Sandplay: The Wonderful Therapy.* London: Routledge.

Samuels, A. (1985) *Jung and the Post-Jungians.* London: Routledge and Kegan Paul.

Shafranske, E.P. and Gorsuch, R.L. (1984) 'Factors Associated with the Perception of Spirituality in Psychotherapy.' *The Journal of Transpersonal Psychology 16*, 2, 231–241.

Sidoli, M. and Davies, M. (1988) *Jungian Child Psychotherapy.* London: Karnac.

Stanard, R.P., Sandhu, D.S. and Painter, L.C. (2000) 'Assessment of Spirituality in Counseling.' *Journal of Counseling & Development 78*, 204–209.

Stein, M. (ed) (1984) *Jungian Analysis.* London: Shambhala.

Stewart, L.H. (1981) 'Play and Sandplay' in K. Bradway, K.A. Signell, G.H. Spare, C.T. Stewart, L.H. Stewart and C. Thompson (eds) *Sandplay Studies: Origins, Theory and Practice.* San Francisco: C.G. Jung Institute.

Stewart, L.H. (1984) 'Sandplay and Jungian Analysis.' In M. Stein (ed) *Jungian Analysis.* London: Shambhala.

Straussner, S.L.A. and Spiegel, B.R. (1996) 'An Analysis of 12-Step Programs for Substance Abusers from a Developmental Perspective.' *Clinical Social Work Journal 24*, 3, 299–309.

Ulanov, A.B. (1996) *The Functioning Transcendent: A Study in Analytical Psychology.* Wilmette, IL: Chiron.

Weinrib, E. (1983) *Images of the Self.* Boston: Sigo Press.

Wells, H.G. (1911/1976) *Floor Games.* New York: Arno Press.

Wickes, F.G. (1966) *The Inner World of Childhood.* New York: Mentor.

Wilber, K. (1979) 'A Developmental View of Consciousness.' *Journal of Transpersonal Psychology 11*, 1, 1–22.

Wilber, K. (2000) *Is There a Childhood Spirituality?* (http://www.ecampus)

Worthington, E.L. (1989) 'Religious Faith across the Lifespan: Implications for Counseling and Research.' *The Counseling Psychologist 17*, 555–612.

Zinnbauer, B.J. and Pargament, K.I. (2000) 'Working with the Sacred: Four Approaches to Religious and Spiritual Issues in Counseling.' *Journal of Counseling & Development 78*, 162–171.

Chapter Ten

Spirituality and People with Disabilities

Patrick Favaro

Introduction

People who choose professions or lifestyles in which they support others are often moved to do so by life experiences, belief systems, dissatisfaction with other paths, or by some unexplainable force within themselves. They are somehow drawn to the poor, the disadvantaged, and the needy. People stay in these professions or lifestyles because of the meaning that they discover in them. Such choice is a manifestation of our spirituality. Whether we are part of a religious practice or not, we are all spiritual beings. Our spirituality pushes us to make choices in our lives. In his book *The Holy Longing*, Ronald Rolheiser describes spirituality:

> Spirituality is about what we do with the fire inside of us, about how we channel our eros. And how we do channel it, the disciplines and habits we choose to live by, will either lead to a greater integration within our bodies, minds, and souls, and into a greater integration or disintegration in the way we are related to God, others, and the cosmic world. (Rolheiser 1999, p.11)

I am a member of L'Arche, a community where people with developmental disabilities, and their assistants, live, work, and pray together. We form local communities that are linked together in an international federation. We are men and women from many intellectual capacities, social origins, religions and cultures.

In the following chapter I will share my personal experience of spirituality and how this has led me into community. I will share an account of the spirituality of L'Arche, the need for members of our community to have a sense of belonging and communion, our need to participate in authentic and 'known' relationships, how we use ritual and celebration as an expression of our relationships, and how we hope that our life together has an impact on the broader society.

The spirituality of L'Arche

L'Arche was born in 1964 when one man was moved to change his life. Jean Vanier, who was a naval officer and academic, met and befriended Father Thomas Philippe, a Roman Catholic priest. Father Thomas was chaplain of an institution for people with disabilities in a tiny village in the north of France. Through his relationship with Father Thomas, Jean found himself inspired to radically change his path, move to this tiny village, buy a little run-down house, and welcome two men with disabilities, Raphael Simi and Philippe Seux, to live with him. These four men became the founders of L'Arche. In his book *An Ark for the Poor*, Jean Vanier writes:

> I was deeply impressed by the men who had become Fr. Thomas's friends. He had sensed their spiritual openness and their place in God's heart. Each one had so much life, had suffered so profoundly and thirsted so deeply for friendship. Within each gesture and each word was the question: 'Will you come back?', 'Do you love me?' Their cry of pain and their thirst for love touched me deeply. (Vanier 1995, p.15)

The founding story of L'Arche is the first insight into the overall spirituality of L'Arche. Jean entered into relationships with people whose rejection and marginalization by society had resulted in their deep seated loneliness and pain. Central to L'Arche is the invitation to respond to another's pain and suffering, and to be faithful in our relationships. As we are faithful with one another we grow in our sense of belonging and communion. As we grow in this sense of belonging and communion, we are more able to realize the gift of our life, and to share with others from the source of that gift.

As other people heard about and witnessed Jean's experiences, they were drawn to this life in community with people with disabilities. They recognized the gifts of people with disabilities, and wanted to create a place of belonging for them where they could grow. They began to see the capacity of people with disabilities to relate at a profoundly spiritual level. Spirituality is central to our life together in L'Arche. We seek to be aware of the fire inside us and how it is revealed in the simple daily acts we engage in with one another. We look for the meaning and purpose in each of our lives and encourage one another to become more fully the person we are each meant to be.

While the founders of L'Arche were all of Roman Catholic tradition, as others came they were moved to recognize their spiritual call beyond one particular tradition. Quickly L'Arche spread to India and Canada and we found ourselves called to see our common humanity beyond our religious and cultural boundaries. People with disabilities lead us to see that these boundaries are somewhat artificial, and that really we are called to embrace our part in the universal family.

The gifts of people with disabilities

When I first came to L'Arche, it was for one year to experience an intentional community where people were choosing to live and work together. This was to be prior to my moving on to a career path. I was introduced to L'Arche and sensed that this could be a place for me to spend a short period of time. Like most assistants, I arrived thinking that I was going to 'serve the poor' for a year. The day I arrived at the house in which I would live, I learned that there was another new member coming to visit from a large institution about 200 kilometers away. Alfred was coming to visit in order to have interviews at a potential workplace in preparation for a later move to the community. When we went off to meet him at the bus station, I met a man with his eyes closed, withdrawn, and quiet. He could hardly look at us and was basically wordless. Little did I know that Alfred was to become one of the most influential teachers of my life.

A few months later, Alfred made the move to our community. As time went on and we both settled into our new community life, Alfred and I began to discover each other. Alfred had lived for 40 years in a system where his basic need for respect was not met. He had food and shelter. There were other people around him, but probably he had no idea that he had something to contribute to them. As we lived our life together with the others in our home, Alfred began slowly to see that we were growing to love him. He began to trust us. His eyes opened more and we discovered that he had a voice! Every day we paid attention to the daily needs of one another, and every day Alfred's heart was more and more revealed.

One year in community led to another. In my third year, I made the decision to leave to become a student. The night at the dinner table when I told people I would leave, Alfred was sitting beside me. He was voiceless again. Without words, he reached over and covered my hand with his. In his silent gesture Alfred communicated with me on a profound level. This gesture led me to a deeper search over the coming months and a re-evaluation of my decision. I was moved to stay and to enter further into relationship with Alfred and the others in the community. Alfred had invited me into a deeper experience of belonging.

Rosie is another member of our community who has taught me about belonging and relationships with others. She is someone who, over time, has grown into a mature, caring woman. Recently we were all at an anniversary celebration of a sister community. Together we were about 200 people at a catered dinner. As our table was served, I could tell that the servers were used to something different than they were encountering that night. During the first courses, they were very discreet as they served and had little interaction with us. By the third course, Rosie turned to the woman who brought her plate and said, 'You're the best cooker!' Later Rosie looked up at the same woman, swooped the whole room with her hand, and exclaimed, 'This is my family!' Her face beamed with happiness.

People with disabilities have a capacity of the heart that is contagious. When they feel secure, they are able to teach others about authentic relationship through their simple everyday gestures. They invite us into the way of the heart, where our being with one another is much more important than what we're doing together. They invite us into knowing that we belong. They invite us into greater authenticity and fuller integration.

The gifts of our relationships with one another in community

All of us need a sense of community in our lives. We need to know that we are connected with others. The bonds that Alfred, Rosie, and I have are supported and sustained as we belong to a broader community. Supporting people with disabilities in their daily lives can sometimes be a challenge. Living in community with other people can be a challenge! In daily life we sometimes face impossible situations. We need to know that we are bonded together with others on a similar path. We support and are supported.

When we meet a person with a disability, it is common for us to experience first the need that the person has. Perhaps she cannot speak or comprehend a verbal way of communicating. Perhaps he cannot take care of his basic needs such as eating, bathing and dressing. Perhaps she lashes out in offensive ways because she has experienced long periods of institutional confinement, and has felt deep rejection. As a person walking with people with disabilities, I have sometimes felt completely inadequate in responding to their needs. I have experienced how the anguish of another can evoke my own pain and anguish. I have experienced the same routines over and over again as monotonous and draining.

One of the people in our community seemed to return to infancy when he came to live with us. Even though he was a fully grown adult, he reverted to crying like an infant for hours on end. A psychiatrist helped us to see that it may have been the first time in his life that he felt safe and able to express his deep wounds from birth. With time his crying turned to screaming. I lived with him for several years during these passages. Some days were excruciating for me. His anguish caused my anguish to erupt. I had to seek help beyond our home and beyond the community in order to cope and to support him in the way he needed. Through years of loving and carefully thought-out responses, he grew and so did the rest of us.

Like many others in L'Arche, Henri Nouwen was invited into relationship with unexpected teachers. Henri describes his personal experience of relating to a man named Adam. Henri was a brilliant spiritual leader who left his world of academia to live in a community of L'Arche. When he arrived he was asked to support Adam on a daily basis. Adam did not care about Henri's thoughts or writings. He could not read them! At times

Henri did not comprehend why the community asked him to support Adam.

> At first I had to keep asking myself and others, 'Why have you asked me to do this? Why did I say yes? What am I doing here? Who is this stranger who is demanding such a big chunk of my time each day? Why should I, the least capable of all the people in the house, be asked to take care of Adam and not of someone whose needs are a bit less?' The answer was always the same: 'So you can get to know Adam.' (Nouwen 1997, p.43)

With support and encouragement at every step, Henri gradually saw the gift of Adam and the gift of their relationship. 'Gradually, very gradually, things started to change, and because I was more confident and relaxed, my mind and heart were opening for a real meeting with this man who had joined me on life's journey' (Nouwen 1997, p.46).

Living in community is a challenge! We come to community with all our different experiences, personalities, biases and expectations. When we are all together we can sometimes rub each other the wrong way. Dialog and time are often critical elements to building community.

A few years ago the community named a new leader for the home in which I lived. This person and I grated on each other's nerves almost daily. It was terrible. We had to speak about what we did not like or appreciate about the other's actions. It was a big stretch for us to live together. This went on for several years. It could only go on because we believed that we were called to learn from each other. As time went on the conflicts lessened to the point where we began to appreciate each other. The community then invited this person to lead another home. It was difficult for me to see him go!

We need to feel a sense of belonging with the people we 'are serving', and with the others 'who are serving'. People with disabilities can show us a way to belonging. We are invited to apply this learning in other areas of our lives. People with disabilities accept us the way we are. We are invited to accept them and others in the same way.

As we continue on such a path, we are led to discover the deeper meaning of our being together. We can gain a sense of calling or purpose to our living together. As I am faithful to the everyday life of supporting a person with a disability, I am invited to see beyond his disability into the gift of his life. As I am faithful to living community with people who are different than I, I am invited to learn from our differences, our idiosyncrasies, and the tensions that come between us in our daily life.

As we live and work together we become 'known'. Quickly others see my gifts as well as my biases and idiosyncrasies. Being known is an essential element of building community and living a spiritual life.

Dianne is a friend of mine who sometimes comes to our community for worship. She has a particularly beautiful singing voice. Karen is a long-term member of the community who notices people. She happens to be hard of hearing. Recently, at community worship, Karen had not seen Dianne enter the room and take a seat behind her. When the time came for us to sing, Karen was startled. She turned around, looked at Dianne with her usual welcoming smile, and said, 'Oh, it's you!' Karen heard Dianne's voice, knew her, and turned to welcome her.

People with disabilities often call us to be faithful to simple daily routines. But through this faithfulness they call us to a much deeper reality. They call us into relationships of the heart where we both know the other and are known by them. They welcome us at a profoundly spiritual level, and invite us to respond to them and to others with the same sense of welcome. In his book *Becoming Human*, Jean Vanier describes how authentic relationships lead us to greater wholeness and inner unity:

> When we are in communion with another, we become open and vulnerable to them. We reveal our needs and our weaknesses to each other. Power and cleverness call forth admiration but also a certain separation, a sense of distance; we are reminded of who we are not, of what we cannot do. On the other hand, sharing weaknesses and needs calls us together into 'oneness'. We welcome those who love us into our heart. In this communion, we discover the deepest part of our being: the need to be loved and to have someone who trusts and appreciates us and who cares least of all about our capacity to work or to be clever and interesting. When we discover we are loved in this way, the masks or barriers behind which we hide are dropped; new life flows. We no longer have to prove our worth; we are free to be ourselves. We find a new wholeness, a new inner unity. (Vanier 1998, pp.89–90)

Our actions transform the world

People are made for community. We are made to be in relationship with one another. But sometimes we can carry on our lives without touching an essential invitation to enter into authentic relationships with others, to learn from them, and to offer the essential gift of our own life. As we experience authentic relationships, our relationships can become a witness for others around us.

Celebrations are important for us in L'Arche. In our ordinary daily life we seize opportunities to be together. Throughout the year we celebrate feasts and moments of significance for members of the community. We find ways to worship together to touch into the spirit that we believe has brought us together. Our evening meal is a central gathering point for our community life. In each of our homes we spend time together during the meal. We use this time as an opportunity to invite people who want to meet us and discover more about our community life. We also welcome people we particularly want to support. The meal becomes a moment when we can strengthen others and ourselves be strengthened as a community. This strengthening happens as we spend time with one another, listening to and sharing what is important in our daily lives.

In L'Arche, birthdays are important. We often invite friends from outside the community to celebrate with us. Birthdays are moments when we specifically mark the gift a person has been for the people he lives with. We have a special meal followed by the sharing of gifts. We ask the person being honored to tell the story of how he came to the community. Everyone around the table then has the opportunity to speak to the gift of this person's life for us. We end by asking the person where he finds meaning in himself.

Someone who once was invited to Bernice's birthday came to speak with me years after the celebration. Bernice was a woman who never spoke with words. She needed a lot of help with her personal care. She was also an independent sort who preferred to pace around the house rather than to sit with people. Even so, the people who lived with Bernice knew her intimately. At her birthday, as the celebration progressed, the guest was amazed at the presence of Bernice with the others, how they helped to tell her story, and how they spoke lovingly of her gift to them. The guest was inspired by the intimacy that was among them.

A sacred ritual for us in L'Arche is expressed in the washing of the feet. This is sacrament that expresses our desire to be instruments of service, learning and inspiration for one another. A few years ago a person from our local government authority for people with disabilities came to meet us at our community worship. He came during the time we would celebrate this ritual. I was nervous as I realized that he did not know us well, and that sometimes newcomers to our community can be uncomfortable with the washing of the feet.

As the evening progressed I noticed that he was seated in one of the small circles where a member of our community who has a profound physical and developmental disability was also sitting. Without assistance she can do nothing. Seated beside her was a person who often assisted her. We were invited to observe silence and to wash the feet of the person beside us. This gesture would continue around the circle until we had all washed another's feet, and had our feet washed. It happened that a second person needed to help the person with a disability wash the feet of her assistant. This occurred spontaneously and without much fuss.

After the worship our visitor approached me and said that he had never seen or experienced anything like this. He said that for many years he had worked in circles where people talked about full equality and the integration of people with disabilities. Assisting the person to wash the feet of her assistant was, for us, a part of normal living that often goes unnoticed. For him, it was an unspoken lived example of authentic equality and integration.

All of these celebrations help us to continue to understand more about the invitation to relationship and how we are called to relate to the world around us. We can learn the importance of community from people with disabilities and the others with whom we live. As we are rooted in the spiritual dimension of our shared life, it has an effect on all our relationships.

One Sunday afternoon this past summer, I was in a large city in Europe sitting at a bus stop with a friend waiting to go to a museum. As we sat there, I noticed a man standing at a crossroad nearby. Each time the light beside him turned red, he approached the stopped cars and asked the drivers for money. We watched as drivers of about 20 cars refused or ignored him. He persisted. Finally one driver reached out and gave him some change. As we got on the bus to drive away, my friend told me that a number of years earlier he had volunteered with the Salvation Army. They would go out through the night to help people on the street. He stopped volunteering when he realized that their circumstances would not change and this reality 'brought him down'. Many of us are only able to muster the effort to help others if we feel that changing another's circumstances is possible. Sometimes our efforts may result in very slow and insignificant change. If we are unable to see a significant impact from our efforts, we need the concrete support of others around us to encourage us to keep going.

I'm not sure I would have noticed the man approaching the drivers of the stopped cars had I not had the experience of living with the people of my community. Even with this experience, it is often difficult for me to face the poverty in another. If approached by the poor man at the crossroad, it would be easier for me to leave the window rolled shut than to lower it and speak with him. It is difficult for me to stand in front of poverty that I cannot change. But with the real support of a genuine community, I begin to see that I can be an instrument of transformation for another, and that I myself can be transformed. While I may not be able to eradicate the poverty, our simple presence with one another can be mutually transforming.

Summary

I believe that L'Arche and other communities like it were created by a spirit bigger than all of us with a purpose bigger than all of us. I believe that the world is transformed through the actions of all people struggling to improve the lives of people who are poor.

Mahatma Gandhi captured this sentiment powerfully when he observed that in order to reach real peace in the world, we must first look to children and keep working against war until peace and love, for which everyone the world-over longs, can be achieved (Mahatma Gandhi 1931, in Prabhu and Rao 1946).

In our world we sometimes witness and experience the suffering that is caused by physical and emotional poverty. Often people are crying out for authentic and intimate relationship. Often our fears prevent us from entering into relationship. People who are poor can lead us to see that weakness and vulnerability can bring us into greater union with others. When we are in relationship with someone who is poor, or when we share our own poverty, our relationship becomes an important witness to the world. We can participate in a much broader transformation from a sense of isolation in the world to a sense of communion and belonging.

References

Nouwen, H.J.M. (1997) *Adam: God's Beloved*. New York: Orbis Books.

Prabhu, R.K. and Rao, U.R. (1946) *The Mind of Gandhi*. India: Navajivan.

Rolheiser, R. (1999) *The Holy Longing: The Search for a Christian Spirituality*. New York: Doubleday.

Vanier, J. (1995) *An Ark for the Poor: The Story of L'Arche*. Toronto: Novalis.

Vanier, J. (1998) *Becoming Human*. Toronto: House of Anansi.

Chapter Eleven

End of Life Planning with the Aged
A Procedural Checklist or Ritual?

Randolph Herman

Ageing is no accident. It is necessary to the human condition, intended by the soul. Ageing is build into our physiology; yet, to our puzzlement, human life extends long beyond fertility and outlasts muscular usefulness and sensory acuteness. For this reason we need imaginative ideas that can grace ageing and speak to it with the intelligence it deserves. (James Hillman 1999 p.xiii)

With the advent of the burgeoning ageing population, there is an opportunity for social workers to be in the position of leadership to address the inherent ethical and spiritual concerns of advanced planning in health care. Planning for the last stages of life requires creative and sensitive support, education, and direction. But leadership requires much more than rhetoric; it requires soul searching on the part of the professional. Many social workers today are part of the 'sandwich generation' and are involved in advanced planning with their own parents and family and simultaneously with their clients (Myers 1989). Yet, ironically, many of them have neither participated in advanced planning nor completed their own health care directives (Herman 1999).

Professional education must include a self-evaluation of the social worker's own spirituality and how that may assist or hinder the process of working with the frail elderly in the last stages of their lives. As the theologian Thomas Merton stated, 'Souls are like athletes that need opponents worthy of them if they are to be tried and extended and pushed to the full use of their powers' (cited in Loeb 1999, p.14).

End of life planning

This chapter teases out some major issues in end of life planning for elderly facing death. It argues for ritualiszing the process. Advanced planning is the process of meeting with the aged client, their family and other health care providers over a period of time to educate, to assess for competency, and to review and complete a health care directive. The advanced health care directive, or living will, refers to the legal document that specifies how health care is to be carried out when the patient is unable to make his or her desires known or is no longer cognitively able to make decisions (Branco, Teno and Mor 1995; Galambos 1989; Glick and Hays 1991; Stone 1994). This document articulates the extent of medical intervention the client wants, if any, and who should act on their behalf as their health care proxy. Too often this legal process is handled as a procedural checklist, without consideration of the spiritual implications inherent in discussing the end of life.

Facing the death of the body requires more than rational planning formatted in a legal directive. The completion of an advance health care directive, as part of end of life planning, should include a dialog that focuses on self-determination. Although seemingly paradoxical, the process of 'handing over' or surrendering may in fact provide the client and the client's family with the direction needed amidst the pain and fear of the impending loss. Social caring must consider the spiritual dimension as part of end of life planning.

If done with the spiritual component in mind, end of life planning can be more than just a routine procedure, provided it embodies the best characteristics of a ritual. Fulghum (1995) defines a ritual as a behavior or a set of activities regularly repeated because it serves a profound purpose. It usually implies that symbolic meaning is attached to the behavior. Thus a ritual can maximize self-determination at a time when the elderly often feel the most powerless. Currently social workers, clients and their families are struggling to find meaning in living longer as well as facing longer deaths: 'This is their quandary, slow motion departure' (Blythe 1979, p.73). Society currently lacks the necessary rituals to help individuals consider the benefits versus the emotional, physical and financial costs of living longer and planning for their death.

Spiritual implications for social care workers

A parallel process occurs in the helping relationship that requires those in the position of social caring to consider what living longer means to them and how they wish to face their own death as they function as a professional with their dying clients. Jordon (1979) refers to this conundrum when he discusses the 'painful nearness' of worker to client, inherent in social caring. The spiritual implications of these questions have been minimally addressed in professional education and in social welfare agency policy. Due to the emphasis of keeping church and state separate, exploring the meaning and contribution of religion and spirituality has been a taboo subject. Religion has been considered outside the purview of the social services. Spirituality has been equated to religion and the differences not articulated. Hence, the implications of moving from a physical being to a non-being have been avoided in the context of the social caring relationship. The helper may be as unversed in the spiritual dialog as the client facing imminent decline and death. The increasing number of elderly worldwide speaks to the need to develop ways to grace ageing with the intelligence it deserves in facing these vexing concerns.

Demographics and ageing

Physiologists estimate the maximum human life span, an inherited species characteristic, to be around 120 years (Smith 1995). In fact by the year 2050 there will be close to 20 million people over the age of 85 in the USA (Longino 1994). What may be even more amazing is the prediction of over 5 million who will be over the age of 100 by the year 2080 (Dychtwald and Flower 1990). Not only is a large cohort ageing but a sub-set of that group will live longer than the individuals and their families have planned for and longer than community social services have planned in order to address their emotional, physical, financial and spiritual needs (Kim 1995;

Manton 1990). Although those years stretching into the new millennium seem far away, for those in the sandwich generation who have ageing parents and maturing children, the challenges are already present in their personal lives. In their professional lives, many social workers are now focusing on the problems facing the ageing population and their families. This can be an inherent bind for the social worker who must cope with the 'objective' demands of ageing clients and the 'subjective' experiences of their own ageing family members.

One of the most difficult problems is deciding what is old in our youth-based culture because ageing in and of itself is generally not problematic. But living to be 'old old', as defined by Bernice Neugarten, has many inevitable challenges that are played out in the cognitive, physical and spiritual dimensions (Neugarten and Hagestad 1976). Some common predictors of being defined as frail and elderly are being female, having a number of illnesses, being perceived by others as having many unmet needs, having a poor self-perception of health, and having a limited sense of control over one's life (Mui 1993). Being female also entails being the major caregiver to many older family members or friends (Hooyman 1997). Frailty of identity is perhaps one of the most significant factors in creating an awareness of age (Butler 1975). Once a person faces a serious physical loss or limitation, even if it is temporary, the reality of moving forward toward death is unavoidable and the concomitant series of losses give rise to existential questioning.

Existential questioning

Robert Butler (1975) poses the difficult question of 'Why survive?' when facing the gradual accumulation of losses in both relationships and physical and cognitive functioning that is coterminous with the last stage of the life cycle. Whether the ageing process is defined as something to be conquered by medical science and technical innovation or whether it is defined as the final part of the life cycle with its own inherent meaning, at some level each person addresses the questions of why survive and how to die (Idler and Kasl 1992). These questions have become exceedingly more complex with the advent of technology which can prolong life, thus adding quantity, but not necessarily quality. The cultural avoidance of death and the myth of a 'good death' create many barriers in addressing the topic.

Another complication of scientific medical advances is that the majority of the elderly become what Homsby (1998) refers to as the 'cyborg class'. They are no longer 'totally human' in that their remaining alive is dependent on medical devices and medicines. For example, the hip replacement, hearing aid, pacemaker, and synthetic insulin have enabled ageing populations to increase their longevity. But the question about quality of life has major ethical, economic and spiritual ramifications for clients, their families, social workers and other members of the health care team.

The Self-Determination Act of 1990

In the USA the federal government passed the Self-Determination Act of 1990 requiring all nursing homes and hospitals to discuss living wills with every new admission. Each state in turn has passed laws to deal with living wills or health care directives as part of the entire process of advanced planning. In the state of Minnesota the Health Care Directive Act of 1998, Minnesota Statutes Chapter 145C, provides general guidelines for preparing an advanced health care directive. As part of the implementation of that legislation, a form was developed by the University of Minnesota Department of Continuing Education (Stum 1998) to assist in completing directives. This document was formulated to include specific questions about physical, spiritual and religious wishes.

The timing of the Self-Determination Act is not an accident. It represents the groundswell of the 'baby boomer' generation now confronting the implications of dying in their parents' generation, in their own generation and for their children (Cohen 1995; Steinberg 1997; Weick and Pope 1988). The frail elderly and the disenfranchised poor are potentially more vulnerable to neglect and abuse as they are the groups least considered. Giddens (1991) talks about the process of 'disembedding' to describe the reality of people becoming progressively distanced from family and friends as they become more involved with professionals, due to illness or longevity. The 'old old' often find themselves involved with social workers because they have outlived family and or outlived their financial assets (Rosen 1995). For the first time in their lives, the 'old old' become clients, asked to address their dying process by working on their living will or advanced health care directive with a total stranger.

However, most social work practitioners are unprepared to address those spiritual dilemmas which surface in assisting clients and their families in making advanced directives. Although the procedure for creating advanced directives is not just for the elderly or terminally ill, it often takes old age and/or a shift in health status for people to formally make their wishes known (Butler 1975). In many hospitals, nursing homes and home health service agencies, the advanced planning process has been reduced to a procedure, a series of forced choice questions, administered to meet federal, state and agency guidelines. In fact, negotiating a health care directive requires a variety of professional skills to deal with the emotional, spiritual and physical concerns as well as an ability to develop a relationship with people in different stages of grieving. But high caseloads and organizational time pressures create barriers to forming the 'traditional caring relationship'. Brief interventions with a frail elderly client not only work against a meaningful exchange, but also make valid, informed consent questionable and hinder true client self-determination.

Advanced planning: toxic or tension-relieving?

Coleman (1988) argues that advanced planning should become a ritual. He argues that preparing advanced health care directives is an essential part of social work practice. In the face of rapidly changing technological innovations, social workers and their clients must assess the dilemma of life sustaining procedures and life support considerations. Social workers involved with clients, family and other health care professionals are central to the discussion of the difficult subject of the 'quality versus quantity' life experience. Coleman suggests that advanced planning as a ritual offers all involved a process for dealing with this complex issue and its ramifications. Advance health care planning creates an opportunity to consider the spiritual facets of living, ageing, and dying. Engaging in a spiritual dialog offers a way to address the challenges of diversity and the various beliefs and cultural practices about health and wellness as well as illness and death.

Yet, ironically, few social workers have had any specific education or training in this process (Derezotes 1995). Paradoxically, in the face of the ageing demographics, schools of social work in the USA have decreased their coursework in gerontology over the past two decades and rarely offer courses that specialize in spirituality (Brody 1970; Greene, Barusch and Connelly 1989; Greene *et al.* 1992). Those working with the 'old old' are mostly undergraduate social workers who are often very young and frequently work without supervision in nursing homes and hospitals (Lubben, Damron-Rodriquez and Beck 1992). These social workers deal with painful and complex end of life decision making. Too often their learning has been 'by doing' without the time to reflect and to critically review the many challenging issues that arise. Currently the Council on Social Work Education (CSWE) is attempting to redress the failure of educational programs to adequately address ageing in undergraduate and graduate social work education through their SAGE project, but curricula changes are a deliberate and slow process (NASW 1998).

In a dialog about social work, Foucault (in Chambon, Irving and Epstein 1999) describes the impact the playwright Samuel Beckett had on his thinking. Beckett's work underlined his 'deep distrust of rational efforts to shape, explain and dispel the chaos of human affairs' (p.28). To some degree, the health care directive and the advanced planning process is indeed an example of the legal and professional worlds colluding to produce a simplified procedure to 'handle' the complex interweaving of ageing, dying and modern technology. Foucault felt that the unfolding of truth is most difficult amidst the many layers or subjective realities that mask power relationships in society.

> One may then suppose in our civilization a whole technology of truth that scientific practice has step-by-step discredited, covered up, and driven out. The truth here does not belong to the order of that which is, but rather of that which happens, it is an event. Truth is not given by the mediation of instruments such as those found in modern laboratories; it is rather produced directly, inscribed by the body and the soul of a single person. Far from being regulated by rigorous rules of method, 'truth' as the outcome of an ordeal is provoked by rituals. (p.44)

Foucault felt that one of the most propitious places for truth to unfold was in the human struggle that occurred during terminal illness. This came to pass for Foucault, when he himself died with complications from AIDS. The struggle in preparing the health care directive can enable a client to face the truth that his or her life is ending and thus can be viewed as a ritual with transformative power. Considering what lies beyond death is potentially transforming and can open the door to deeply spiritual insights.

But 'transformative knowledge is disturbing by nature. It disturbs commonly acceptable ways of doing and disturbs the person implementing it' (Chambon *et al.* 1999, p.53). Therefore, there are reasons for the health care directive being limited to a rational procedure and avoiding the spiritual because the depth of truth at the point of dying may be as terrifying as it is enlightening. The confusion that exists in practice is not just the result of agency policies and their attempt to fulfill the law. The ambiguity reflects the tension around spirituality in the caring relationship, especially among the professionals who assist in end of life planning. It is this tension that embodies the potential creative power in end of life planning, as well as the fearful aspects.

For example, the health care directive, if done as a procedure that is static and non-reformative, in essence becomes a toxic habit. The advanced planning process becomes a missed opportunity to dialog about dying with all concerned parties (family, professionals and the client) and lessens the client's potential to maximize control over their destiny. To move beyond the procedural, those affected must discuss that which is unknown (how long till death?), uncomfortable (will there be pain?) and unforeseen (taking ultimate responsibility for living/dying). Currently the health care directive, if limited to a procedure, is a cognitive way to minimize discussion, a cerebral way to deal with a noble death by treating the process as a checklist. This process avoids the spiritual by concentrating on the physical in a rational manner, and provides a false assurance of control. For the untutored, the procedural process is efficient and non-threatening to all the involved parties. This raises the question of how to encourage the new and not-so-new social workers to expand the process to include a more 'soulful' dialog.

Preparing for that 'soulful' dialog

To 'train souls' requires an educational setting that allows free discourse for students to openly discuss their understanding of the spiritual. Most public universities are unable to provide this sort of forum due to the separation of church and state required by federal financing and many private colleges and universities have moved away from their religious and spiritual base (Branco 1998). Education should include not only the factual components and tenets of the world's religions but there should be an opportunity for students to explore their own spiritual/religious development. If spirituality is defined as that which moves people toward higher states of connectiveness, consciousness, and meaning, then it should be part and parcel of life-long learning required of professional caregivers (Derezotes 1995). Once in practice, supervision and/or peer support could encourage the professional social worker's continued development and refinement of their own spirituality as well as increasing their knowledge about the religious and spiritual diversity within their client's community.

Inherent in the spiritual journey is the ongoing social work commitment to self-determination and social justice. Self-determination has been a cornerstone of the profession and is a primary value for advocating for clients who are not being heard. The elderly are a growing population who face major issues in self-determining their last phase of life (Erikson 1986). Cumulative loss, both physical and emotional, combined with ageist beliefs and policies, create many barriers for the successful implementation of advanced health care directives.

Three of the most difficult issues for social workers and other health care providers considering the ethical implications for self-determination in advanced health care planning are: increasing diversity and decreasing homogeneity, conflicting professional viewpoints, and the dilemmas of assessing competency.

Increasing diversity and decreasing homogeneity

Due to increasing diversity and decreasing homogeneity among clients and staff, the homogeneous nature of health care facilities is rapidly changing. Within the nursing homes, wards are designated for certain maladies, specializing in areas such as dementia and mental illness. It is in these specialized wards that social workers seem to experience the most complicated situations in ensuring client self-determination as part of end of life planning. The advanced planning process becomes much more complicated if the patient has major cognitive dysfunction, has little or no ability to provide clear informed consent, has no local family support, is unknown to the social worker and presents a challenge in cultural, religious and ethnic differences (Capitman, Hernandez-Galllegos and Yee 1992).

Conflicting professional viewpoints

Maximizing the principle of self-determination and judging its priority among conflicting principles and values can heighten differences within the profession of social work, between other health care professions, and between specialized wards in the nursing home. Research demonstrates that there is more of a consensus on the medical team and among the social workers on the right of the client to self-determine maximum medical intervention (full code), if the client is cognitively alert, able to hear, able to give informed consent, and is not deemed medically futile (Herman 1999). Once the client becomes cognitively dysfunctional due to dementia or mental illness as well as frail in health, a staff consensus tends to migrate toward no medical heroics and allows the patient to die with minimal medical intervention. The social worker working in this environment must deal with the ethical dilemma of a client's right to complete medical treatment and the denial of treatment because of the doctor and staff bias against clients who display cognitive dysfunction.

Assessing competency

An increasingly more powerful dilemma is social worker anxiety over making the judgement of a client's competency (Dickson 1997). There are at least two sources of this anxiety. Social workers may question whether their professional education and training has provided them with sufficient knowledge and skill to assess client competency to complete a health care directive. Second, social workers worry about the liability they and the nursing home assume in client competency determinations (Herman 1999).

To date there are no known successful suits filed on behalf of someone 'wronged' by not fulfilling their living will or honoring their directions in a health care directive. But in the litigious society of the USA, the question of legal risk is indeed a pressing reality for social workers and for their host agencies (Miles and August 1990). Since social workers are often called in at a crisis point, their role as the client advocate takes on even more meaning, if even after death, failure to honor the client's wishes can be seen as professional negligence.

Co-determination...

Even though there are many clients with the ability to provide informed consent, despite questionable competency, the social worker is involved in dialog that links them to the client and their family. In this context the social worker is often asked for their professional opinion, which takes on a form of co-determination (Herman 1999). Co-determination is a mid-point between sole client self-determination and client incompetence, a legal determination that permits others to determine their fate. The danger inherent in co-determination is the current lack of clear guidelines to guard the social worker against inadvertently taking control of the situation. For example, working with a profoundly deaf client with mild dementia raises critical questions about the power of professionals in assessing competency for the frail elderly. What level of client competency is required to take part in end of life planning is part of a larger discourse in society and requires more research.

Foucault (in Chambon *et al.* 1999) describes social work as evolving into a profession that provides surveillance and control over people's lives. In a potentially ironic twist, the social work profession's commitment to client self-determination in advanced planning may in fact be a subtle form of societal control over the frail elderly. If the consensus 'do not resuscitate or intubate (DNR/DNI)' is favorable for responding to acute medical crisis for the frail elderly, the social worker may be an unwitting party to a fundamentally conservative cost containment and ageist agenda. In assisting the client to what seems to be a consensus about choosing quality of life over quantity, the social worker may be helping the clients to an 'early out', thus eliminating the high costs of the last year of life (Krugman 1997). One social worker in the author's (1999) research commented on her surprise at how biased she was in favor of the DNR/DNI for all elderly until she found herself adamantly objecting to it and wanting full medical treatment when her beloved grandfather was dying. She said this 'epiphany' gave her an insight into clients, families and doctors who wanted maximum life-sustaining interventions, even when the clients were seen to be cognitively dysfunctional or medically futile.

...And power relations

What society sees as most valued, in relation to the rights of a frail elderly person, becomes a major issue of concern. Medical and scientific technology is available to extend the life of the frail elderly, albeit at expense, without regard to quality of life. The ability of family and medical staff to override the advanced health care directive provides opportunities for the client's wishes, whatever they may be, to be ignored.

Added to this dilemma is social work's relatively lower status in the professional hierarchy in a medical team. Their youth, lower educational level (mostly Bachelor of Social Work in nursing homes), low salaries, and diverse expectations from administration combine to make the social worker less able to act as an equal member of the team. Even the social workers themselves report that they tend to defer to the doctors and nurses in contested cases. For example, one social worker said, 'I like to have the doctor have more involvement in that discussion, because that is whom clients and family rely on. They see the doctor as all knowing, so I think the doctor needs to take a more prominent role' (Herman 1999).

Social workers' ambivalence about their relative power in the medical team is further complicated by the way the advanced health care directives are developed. On the one hand, creating a ritual offers social workers opportunities for enhancing the spiritual aspects of end of life planning. On the other hand, a ritual has a marked tendency to reify the stratification of the existing professional hierarchy. In the nursing home this would support the doctor at the top with control over the flow of information and final decision-making power. Paradoxically, by ritualising end of life planning, the client's ability to self-determine could be further limited as well as the social worker's ability to advocate on their behalf.

There are indications that even medical staff have expressed anxiety around the issue of competency and making decisions for others around end of life planning (Johnston and Pfeifer 1998; Rutecki *et al.* 1997). The nursing home is turning to another profession, their lawyers, to establish policies to protect all concerned in making decisions in those 'gray area' scenarios (Herman 1999, p.127). The debate comes full circle because the issue of legal decision making and state involvement in people's lives is about control, whether it is on behalf of the individual, their family, the social worker or other members of the health care team. This raises the difficult question of how realistic is self-determination when the client is frail and elderly and what are the ethical and legal implications for the social worker if co-determination is a reality in practice.

Co-determination requires a clear opinion from the professional social worker and/or other members of the health care team. During the last stages of life clients and concerned family members turn to professionals to assist them through the complex maze of medical and spiritual decision making. Criteria, which assist the social worker in providing the most ethical response, are incomplete and need to be developed. If the social worker tells the client what to do, this violates the principle of self-determination. But part of the discourse of advanced health care planning has to do with assigning power to someone else in the form of a health care proxy. It is somewhat of a paradox that advanced planning is about ensuring some modicum of control over the last phase of a client's life, and yet the major questions, inherent in the process, are about giving up control.

Discussion

In spiritual terms, this giving over of control to remain in control can be considered to be the act of surrendering. To surrender is an act of empowerment at the deepest level. 'When people bear responsibility, live as they would like to live, combat the temptation to inner despair or keep chaos from invading the center, this is the stuff of spirituality' (Simmons 1998, p.73). But accomplishing this is not easy and may be seen not only as a retreat to privatization but as a move to interiority, which is a conscious choice to withdraw into self. Moody (1986) argues that this is an unsatisfactory way to resolve questions about the meaning of life and of old age. Although some may be able to take this spiritual journey alone, 'not everyone can develop this depth without the support of others' (p.81). This raises a challenging question: considering all the current complexities of ageing and dying, can social work as a controlling and a caring profession serve as an intentional community of meaning to assist clients in considering the full implications of surrendering to the transcendence from the physical to the spiritual?

This dilemma resurrects the question of how ageing is to be defined. If it is a time to fight the ravages of time and remain as young as possible for as long as possible, then the goal is control. If ageing is nothing more than dying (Nuland 1994), it is about cumulative loss and eventual giving over to an inevitable physiological process. But it can also be defined as a time in which the idea of control is challenged and all parties involved must reconsider what can and cannot be controlled. Control of bodily movement and time are major values in contemporary society, often confounded by the ageist belief systems that militate against understanding the last phase of the life cycle. Loss of control creates a period of liminality during which new ways of meaning can occur, as part of the existential clarification of the place of death in life. 'When we reach the choice point when movement (both physical and social) is no longer an option, we learn to transcend the limitations of time–space–movement to higher levels of consciousness' (Newman 1994, p.57). The health care directive does not deal with these weighty and controversial topics. But in preparing the health care document, both the religious and spiritual realm are unavoidably invoked.

The spiritual dimension must be distinguished from the religious (Cascio 1998), but both are part of the health care directive. The religious questions pertain to selecting a minister, giving details about funerals and clarifying burial requests. These issues are more easily sorted out than those emerging from the spiritual questions. The procedural aspect of advanced planning pertains to these questions and is more easily quantifiable. The spiritual questions ask about meaning of life and of death, the value one gives to the body in relation to cremation or burial and to the sanctity of the internal organs in relation to organ donation/transplants. These questions are more part of the ritual in end of life planning and require some degree of trust in order to establish a relationship between the social worker and the client. Both religious and spiritual questions can be related as well, demonstrating that a religious tradition or principle may coincide with a person's spiritual beliefs.

Finally, the social worker faces the difficult task of assisting the client in naming a health care proxy who will carry out their wishes once they are no longer able to communicate with medical staff and family. The social worker is in the invidious position of advocating for the implementation of the client's health care directive, often confronting family and/or members of the medical team with differing opinions. Knowing about a client's spiritual concerns does not in and of itself provide a strategy for social workers with relatives who may totally disagree with ageing clients who are dying. The ritual must include ways in which the social worker can continue to negotiate on the client's behalf so that the advanced health care directive remains a viable tool for advocacy.

End of life planning for the elderly presents a leadership and educational challenge for social work. The process of completing health care directives requires much more research and dialog as the ageing population expands and the ability to keep people alive improves. Educational and practice communities must continue to find ways to incorporate spirituality in the ritual of end of life planning (Meske 1994). The caring professions face a major challenge to develop spiritually within themselves as well as to provide skilled service to others because 'people who work with the oldest old and treat them with dignity do so, at least in part, because they recognize their spiritual struggles and are willing to share in them' (Simmons 1998, p.73). Ageing and dying have a most humbling effect on how a profession cares. 'When you stand in the river, the beginning and the end are always with you' (anonymous Hmong saying).

References

Blythe, R. (1979) *The View in Winter: Reflections on Old Age.* New York: Penguin.

Branco, B.J. (1998) *The Dying of the Light: The Disengagement of Colleges and Universities from their Christian Church.* Grand Rapids, MI: W.B. Eerdmans.

Branco, K., Teno, J. and Mar, V. (1995) 'Advanced Care Planning Among Nursing Home Residents Prior to Patient Self-Determination Act.' *Journal of Health and Social Policy 20*, 1, 37–52.

Brody, E. (1970) 'Serving the Aged: Educational Needs as Viewed by Practice.' *Social Work 15*, 42–51.

Butler, R. (1975) *Why Survive? Being Old in America.* New York: Harper and Row.

Capitman, J., Hernandez-Gallegos, W. and Yee, D. (1992) 'Diversity Assessments.' *Generations 15*, 73–76.

Cascio, T. (1998) 'Incorporating Spirituality into Social Work Practice: A Review of What to Do.' *Families in Society: The Journal of Contemporary Human Services 79*, 5, 523–531.

Chambon, A., Irving, A. and Epstein, L. (1999) *Reading Foucault for Social Work.* New York: Columbia University Press.

Cohen, G. (1995) 'Intergenerationalism: A New "Ism" with Positive Mental Health and Social Policy Potential.' *The American Journal of Psychiatry 3*, 1–5.

Coleman, N. (1988) 'Planning for Incapacity: Two Perspectives on Safeguards. Advance Directives Preserve Autonomy Despite Incapacity.' *Health and Social Work 13*, 1, 71–72.

Derezotes, D. (1995) 'Spirituality and Religiosity: Neglected Factors in Social Work Practice.' *Arete 20*, 1, 3–15.

Dickson, D. (1997) 'Law, Ethics, and Social Work with the Elderly: Self-Determination.' *Journal of Law and Social Work 7*, 2, 105–126.

Dychtwald, K. and Flower, J. (1990) *Age Wave: The Challenges and Opportunities of an Ageing America.* New York: Bantam Books.

Erikson, E. (1986) *Vital Involvement in Old Age.* New York: Norton.

Fulghum, R. (1995) *From Beginning to End: The Ritual of Our Lives.* New York: Ballantine Books.

Galambos, C. (1989) 'Living Wills: A Choice for the Elderly.' *Social Work 34*, 2, 182–185.

Giddens, A. (1991) *Modernity and Self Identity.* California: Stanford University Press.

Glick, H. and Hays, S. (1991) 'Innovation and Reinvention in State Policymaking: Theory and the Evolution of Living Will Laws.' *Journal of Politics 53*, 3, 835–850.

Greene, R., Barusch, A. and Connelly, R. (1989) *Social Work and Gerontology: An Update.* Washington, DC: Final Report to the Administration on Ageing and the Association for Gerontology in Higher Education.

Greene, R., Gueres, R., Vourlekis, B., Gelfand, D. and Lewis, J. (1992) 'Current Realities: Practice and Education Needs of Social Workers in Nursing Homes.' *Journal of Gerontological Social Work 18*, 3/4, 39–54.

Herman, W.R. (1999) *Social Work Practice and Advanced Planning: A Ritual or Procedure? Ed.D dissertation, University of St. Thomas.*

Hillman, J. (1999) *The Forces and Character of the Lasting Life.* New York: Random House.

Homsby, A. (1998) 'Surfing the Net for Community: A Durkheimian Analysis of Electronic Gatherings'. In P. Kivisto (ed) *Illuminating Social Life: Classical and Contemporary Theory Revisited.* London: Pine Forge.

Hooyman, N. (1997) 'Is Ageing More Problematic for Women Than Men?' In A. Scharlach and L. Kaye (eds) *Controversial Issues in Ageing.* Boston: Allyn & Bacon.

Idler, E. and Kasl, S. (1992) 'Religion, Disability, Depression, and the Timing of Death.' *American Journal of Sociology 97*, 4, 1052–1079.

Johnston, S. and Pfeifer, M. (1998) 'Patient and Physician Roles in End-of-Life Decision Making: End-of-Life Study Group.' *Journal of Internal Medicine 13*, 1, 43–45.

Jordon, W. (1979) *Helping in Social Work.* London: Routledge and Kegan Paul.

Kim, P. (1995) 'A Service Model for the Ageing and the Aged: An International Perspective'. In P. Kim (ed) *Services to the Ageing and Aged: Public Policies and Program.* New York: Garland.

Krugman, P. (1997) 'Does Getting Old Cost Society Too Much?' *New York Times Magazine*, 6 March, 58–60.

Loeb, P. (1999) *Soul of a Citizen: Living with Conviction in a Cynical Time.* New York: St. Martin's Press.

Longino, C. (1994) 'A Population Profile of Very Old Men and Women in the United States.' In R. Enright (ed) *Perspectives in Social Gerontology.* Boston: Allyn & Bacon.

Lubben, J., Damron-Rodriquez, J. and Beck, A. (1992) 'A National Survey of Ageing Curriculum in Schools of Social Work.' *Journal of Gerontolgical Social Work 18*, 3/4,157–171.

Manton, K. (1990) 'Mortality and Morbidity.' In R. Binstock and L. George (eds) *Handbook of Ageing and the Social Sciences* (3rd edn). San Diego: Academic Press.

Meske, C. (1994) 'Rituals and Family Strengths in Later Life Families: A Three-Generation Comparison.' *North Dakota Journal of Human Services 1*, 1, 30–36.

Miles, S. and August, A. (1990) 'Courts, Gender and "the Right to Die."' *Law, Medicine and Health Care 18*, 1/2, 85–95.

Moody, H. (1986) 'The Meaning of Life and the Meaning of Old Age.' In T. Coles and S. Gadow (eds) *What Does it Mean to Grow Old?* Durham: Duke University Press.

Mui, A. (1993) 'Self-reported depressive symptoms among Black and Hispanic frail elders: a sociocultural perspective'. *Journal of Applied Gerontology 12*, 2, 170–187.

Myers, J. (1989) *Adult Children and Ageing Parents.* Virginia: American Association for Counseling and Development.

National Association of Social Workers (April 1998) 'End-of-life Education Urged in Practice Guide.' *NASW News 43*, 4.

Neugarten, B. and Hagestad, G. (1976) 'Age and the Life Course.' In R.H. Binstock and E. Shanas (eds) *Handbook of Ageing and the Social Sciences.* New York: Van Norstrand Reinhold.

Newman, M. (1994) *Health as Expanding Consciousness* (2nd Edn). New York: National League for Nursing Press.

Nuland, S. (1994) *How We Die.* New York: Knopf.

Rosen, A. (1995) 'The 1995 White House Conference on Ageing: Implications for Social Work.' *NASW Social Work Practice Update.* Washington DC: NASW Press.

Rutecki, G., Cugino, A., Jarjoura, D., Kilner, J. and Whittier, F. (1997) 'Nephrologists' Subjective Attitudes toward End-of-Life Issues and the Conduct of Terminal Care.' *Clinical Nephrology 48*, 3, 173–180.

Simmons, H. (1998) 'Spirituality and Community in the Last Stages of Life.' *Journal of Gerontological Social Work 29*, 2/3, 73–91.

Smith, D. (1995) 'Why Do We Live So Long?' *Journal of Death and Dying 31*, 2, 143–150.

Steinburg, M., Cartwright, C., MacDonald, S. and Williams, G. (1997) 'Self-Determination in Terminal Care: A Comparison of GP and Community Members' Responses.' *Medical Journal of Australia 166*, 3, 131–135.

Stone, J. (1994) 'Advance Directives, Autonomy and Unintended Death.' *Bioethics 8*, 3, 223–246.

Stum, M. (1998) *Minnesota Health Care Directive: A Suggested Form.* Minnesota: University of Minnesota Extension Services.

Weick, A. and Pope, L. (1988) 'Knowing What's Best: A New Look at Self-Determination.' *Social Casework 69*, 10–16.

The Contributors

Romeo Beatch is a psychologist with theology training, currently in private practice after several years managing and developing a community-based counseling service. He is working on the development of an alternative treatment program for Dene men within the Canadian correctional system.

Jim Consedine is a Catholic priest and ecumenical prison chaplain. He is also the national co-ordinator of the Restorative Justice Network in New Zealand and an international speaker on issues relating to restorative justice. He is the author of three books on spirituality and restorative themes and lives in a Catholic Worker community in Aotearoa New Zealand.

Mary Eastham is a facilitator for Creative Journeys, an organization for special needs adults. A former director of the Pastoral Centre in Palmerston North, Mary is also a tertiary chaplain for the Catholic diocese of Palmerston North, Aotearoa New Zealand. She holds a PhD in religious Studies and a Master's in Theology.

Patrick Favaro is a member of L'Arche, an international federation of communities where people with developmental disabilities and their assistants share life together. He served as Community Leader of L'Arche in Calgary, Canada, for eleven years and is currently Regional Co-ordinator for L'Arche in Western Canada.

Randolph Herman is assitant professor of social work at the University of St Thomas and the College of St Catherine, Minnesota. He has worked in many settings including a military hospital with Vietnam returnees, child welfare and adoption, rural community mental health, with the severely mentally ill and with anger management and grief support groups. He presented a paper at the Second International Conference on Spirituality and Social Work.

Judith Morris is a social work consultant in childcare and a therapist. Trained in Britain, she specialized in working therapeutically with children and their caregivers after her involvement in the early stages of implementing direct techniques with children in British social services departments. She has a particular interest in the application of attachment theory to this work.

Ksenija Napan is a senior lecturer in the School of Community Studies at UNITEC, Auckland. Her interest is in the continuous improvement of teaching and learning processes by shaping them to fit students' cultural, social, spiritual and learning needs. She has presented at many conferences and published widely in the field of social care and spirituality.

Mary Nash is a senior lecturer in social work at the School of Sociology, Social Policy and Social Work at Massey University, Aotearoa New Zealand. She is a former editor of the *Social Work Review* and is author of books and journal articles in the field of social care.

Bruce Stewart is a senior mental health worker at the Jan Sterling Centre, Yellowknife, Canada. He has extensive clinical, managerial and research experience with First Nations and Europeans.

Ross Wheeler is a Canadian medical doctor with extensive cross-cultural and international medical, therapeutic and program development experience in psychiatry, addictions and mental health. He is involved in 12 Step program, and works on integrating professional and personal experience to help addiction recovery.

Mary Woods is a mathematician, researcher, community worker, adult educator and facilitator. She leads workshops on volunteer management and is author of *Volunteers: A Guide for Volunteers and their Organisations*. Mary was a member of the three-person team who devised and delivered 'Women at the Well', a program to train Catholic women as volunteer community workers.

Subject index

Author index